To Kitty —
Beloved of God

Psalms for Life

A DEVOTIONAL OF ENCOURAGEMENT FOR THE WEARY

Kathy Foor

Ps 42: 1-2

Blessings!

KATHY FOOR

WESTBOW
PRESS
A DIVISION OF THOMAS NELSON
& ZONDERVAN

Scripture taken from the Holy Bible, NEW INTERNATIONAL VERSION®. Copyright © 1973, 1978, 1984 by Biblica, Inc. All rights reserved worldwide. Used by permission. NEW INTERNATIONAL VERSION® and NIV® are registered trademarks of Biblica, Inc. Use of either trademark for the offering of goods or services requires the prior written consent of Biblica US, Inc.

WestBow Press books may be ordered through booksellers or by contacting:

WestBow Press
A Division of Thomas Nelson & Zondervan
1663 Liberty Drive
Bloomington, IN 47403
www.westbowpress.com
1 (866) 928-1240

ISBN: 978-1-4908-7803-4 (sc)
ISBN: 978-1-4908-7805-8 (hc)
ISBN: 978-1-4908-7804-1 (e)

Print information available on the last page.

WestBow Press rev. date: 5/29/2015

Dedicated to my beloved husband, who has encouraged
and inspired me to be all that God has intended me to be.

I am not a professional writer. I have written this manuscript in obedience to God and with much trepidation. The project originated when I was a young mother with three preschoolers. I was weary, empty really, with no time or energy for seeking God. A dear friend suggested that if I had no time for Bible study, perhaps I could at least read a few verses in Psalms each day.

Wearily, I began to do just that. I confessed to the Lord that I needed him and longed to be in his Word but lacked energy and time. I asked him to please teach me from his Word and give me wisdom for my day. It may not surprise you (but it did me) that he did just that! As I have been in the habit of keeping a journal since High School, I wrote down the little nuggets of wisdom the Holy Spirit gave me each day.

Several years later, I was teaching an adult Sunday school class and decided to use the lessons I had learned in Psalms as the content for that class. I read each Psalm and sorted them by a number of topics which I might use for the class. Each week I gave the class Psalms to read based on a particular topic.

Many years and several relocations later, I used that same Bible study again to teach a women's group at my church. I sensed God wanted me to take this writing further, but didn't quite know how or when I would find the time. I asked the Lord for wisdom and instructions and had the thought to write a daily devotional which I could share with a few friends. This would help me to be accountable, give me feedback about my writing, and move me forward in the process of writing the lessons God has shared with me over the years.

Now, after several years of writing daily devotionals for my friends, it is time to take the next step. I have prepared a devotional through Psalms which offers nuggets of truth that gave life to my weary soul and restored me to wholeness and health from depression, weariness, and hopelessness. I hope it will encourage you in your journey with the Savior and bring you life in his name.

The Path of Life

> You make known to me the path of life; you will fill me with
> joy in your presence, with eternal pleasures at your right hand.
> (Psalm 16:11)

The psalmist has found the path of life and joy in God's presence. He has found eternal pleasures at God's right hand. How can I find what the psalmist found? How can I know this joy? How can I find the path of life of which the psalmist speaks? Where can I find his presence? If I want what the psalmist found, then I need to seek. I need to ask God to show me. I need to ask the Holy Spirit to help me. I know I cannot find what the psalmist found on my own. I have tried and failed. *Father, I am encouraged by this verse today. I find hope in knowing that you promise in your Word to make the path of life known to me. You promise to fill me with joy in your presence. Oh God, I long to know you more. I need the life you promise in these words. I am so weary and filled with sorrow. Will you help me seek? Will you help me find this kind of joy? Amen*

Food for Thought

> Taste and see that the Lord is good; blessed is the one who takes
> refuge in him. Fear the Lord, you his holy people, for those who
> fear him lack nothing. The lions may grow weak and hungry, but
> those who seek the Lord lack no good thing. (Psalm 34:8-10)

Psalm thirty-four is a good way to begin a new year. I, like many people making resolutions for the coming year, have made a goal to lose weight. I remember this being a goal last year too, but I didn't succeed. Failure is a poor motivator! Besides making this a goal, I have to consider why I failed and what I can do differently this year to succeed. A lot of people have suggestions for how to lose weight, and many of them are good, but for me, the battle of losing weight (or any other bad habit) always begins in my heart and mind. My thoughts and attitudes about this issue will dictate whether I succeed. The Lord reminded me that my thoughts are a key to the solution. There are a number of lies that can sabotage my weight loss. *This is too hard! I can't do it! I'll just have this today and start again tomorrow. I don't have time to exercise.* I could go on and on with the lies and excuses that get in my way. However, God reminds me to take every thought captive unto Christ. In Christ, I can do all things. Nothing is impossible with God. Next, I have to shift my focus. The more I focus on food, the more I tend to eat. Go figure! Instead, I need to refocus on the Lord. Why? Because when I am overeating, it isn't usually because I am hungry for food. Often it is a spiritual hunger that is not being satisfied. When my spirit is empty, I often go to food instead of to God. However, food will never satisfy my craving for God. If I begin to practice the words in this Psalm, "taste and see that the Lord is good," the Lord will satisfy my spiritual hunger, and I will not need to go to food. I have to trust God to lead me moment by moment through the battle. Whatever your goal this year, let's ask the Lord to help us know the victory that is ours through Christ, and let us seek him with all our hearts.

The Glory of the Lord

> May the glory of the Lord endure forever; may the Lord rejoice in his works—he who looks at the earth, and it trembles, who touches the mountains, and they smoke. I will sing to the Lord all my life; I will sing praise to my God as long as I live. May my meditation be pleasing to him, as I rejoice in the Lord. (Psalm 104:31-34)

What is the glory of the Lord exactly? I think it is difficult for us to really comprehend the glory of God completely, but if we were to put an image to it, I think the image would be Moses standing before the burning bush. That day Moses saw the glory of God. When Moses went to Mt. Sinai to receive the Ten Commandments, he came back looking different because he had experienced the glory of God. Only when we get to heaven will we fully comprehend the glory of the Lord, but for now we have a small glimpse. We see the glory of the Lord with our eyes in the mighty things he does like the earth he created, the great volcanic eruptions, the mighty earthquakes that shake the earth, or the devastating winds of a hurricane. Yet God's glory is more than any of those. We can experience the glory of God when we sense the nearness of his presence during a time of worship or that wondrous time when we surrender our lives to him as he makes himself known to us. For this we sing. For this we praise him. For this we rejoice. Let our meditation be pleasing to the Lord today as we consider his glory, and let's praise him because his glory will indeed last forever!

Finding Delight in God's Commands

> Praise the Lord. Blessed are those who fear the Lord, who find great delight in his commands. Their children will be mighty in the land; the generation of the upright will be blessed...Even in darkness light dawns for the upright, for those who are gracious and compassionate and righteous. (Psalm 112:1-2, 4)

What a wonderful promise! I hope you will take time to read all of Psalm 112 today. It contains great encouragement. The promise in these verses is for the one who fears (honors, respects, or stands in awe of) the Lord. The more you get to know God, the easier that is. This promise is for the one who finds great delight in God's commands. *Great delight*—that is like the feeling you get when you open an awesome Christmas present or when you watch your child play in his first recital. It is not drudgery or hard work! It brings great joy. The Bible says God's commands are not burdensome. Not only that, but they are a delight to those who follow them. Do you know someone who finds God's commands burdensome? It is usually a person who believes in God but hasn't surrendered to his lordship. Since the heart is not fully surrendered to God, following his commands is impossible. This person still wants to have his feet in both worlds, and sadly, doesn't know what he is missing by trying to hold on to his old life rather than letting God make him a new creation. The promise in these verses is for the upright, gracious, compassionate, and righteous person. Take heart if you fall short in these areas! It is only through Christ that we can be any of those things, and the more we give our lives over to him, the more those qualities will shine forth. So, you say, my children aren't mighty in the land. Well, friend, perhaps time will tell that. Many of God's promises come later. For now, we walk by faith. We believe the promise and pray for him to accomplish everything he would desire to do in the lives of our children, and who knows what he might do with them one day!

A Proud Heart

My heart is not proud, Lord, my eyes are not haughty; I do not concern myself with great matters or things too wonderful for me. But I have calmed and quieted myself, I am like a weaned child with its mother; like a weaned child I am content. Israel, put your hope in the Lord both now and forevermore. (Psalm 131)

Is there anyone who really considers himself or herself proud? Do we recognize haughtiness in ourselves? Americans tend to be very proud people. When faced with an argument, are you always right in your own eyes. Then you may struggle with pride. When you listen to the ideas of others, are you convinced your ideas are better? Do you see clearly the faults of those around you but overlook your own? Then pride may be a problem for you. Do you prefer to be the one to give help rather than receive it? Then pride may be a problem for you. How do you face the problem of pride and come to the place where you can honestly say your heart is not proud? It is simple really. We need to stop the bad habit of comparing ourselves with other people and begin to measure ourselves against God's standard— Christ. Friends, we do not do this in order to beat ourselves up and feel like a worthless worm! Satan is a skillful accuser. We do not need to join him. When we come to Christ, it is easy to see that he is all things we are not. If we have love, it is because he gave it to us. If we are talented, it is for his glory. If we are in a place of leadership, it is to serve like he did, not to boss people around or to have control. Pride is dealt with as we still and quiet our souls and come before a holy God. There we can see ourselves as we are, as he sees us. We can recognize our great need and receive help from him. We can accomplish great things, but in doing so, we will know that it is his work in us, and we will freely give the glory where it is due. Let humility become a way of life.

A Moment with God

May my cry come before you, Lord; give me understanding according to your word. May my supplication come before you; deliver me according to your promise. (Psalm 119:169-170)

How is your prayer life? I love the intimate and dynamic prayers found in Psalms. I have learned to pray by simply praying the Word of God. The psalmist is honest with God. He speaks to God as though he is right there. He always seems to be longing for more of God. He always prays according to God's will and God's Word. He doesn't rush off his list and then move on. The psalmist always seems to linger, just loving to be in God's presence. I am inspired as I read Psalms to seek a deeper walk with the Lord and to pray according to his Word and his will. The intimacy that we see in Psalms is the kind of intimacy the Lord desires to have with us if only we will choose to seek him. Prayer is not a thing we do to grow in our Christian walk, friends. It is the very essence of our relationship with God. If you are married, you know that there are times that you communicate on a very intimate level, and there are other times that you just stay on the surface talking about things that don't matter very much. At times you feel closer to each other than at other times. You really have to work in a marriage to stay closely connected. It takes time, energy and thoughtfulness. The same is true about our relationship with God. To find the intimacy with God that he longs for us to have doesn't happen by accident. It happens because we deliberately make the time and effort to draw close to him. There is never a moment wasted, though, when we spend it with God. Every moment we come to him in this kind of intimate prayer, we will find him faithful. He will draw us close and help us to know him better.

He Knows My Name

> The Lord is exalted over all the nations, his glory is above the heavens. Who is like the Lord our God, the One who sits enthroned on high, who stoops down to look on the heavens and the earth? (Psalm 113:4-6)

I love the mental picture I get in my head as I read these verses! There is God in all his glory looking down from his heavenly throne watching all of us down here on earth. Like someone holding a snow globe that has just been shaken, he can see all of the little people inside. God is able to hold the entire universe in his hands! And yet, in all his wondrous glory, he cares for you! He knows you by name. He sees your heart and knows your thoughts. Wow! God is infinitesimally big and at the same time he sees and recognizes the infinitesimally small. I am amazed by that! Consider the delicate snowflake with all of its beauty or the largest solar system. Our God is responsible for them both. What a mighty God we serve! There is none like him.

A Steadfast Heart

> My heart, O God, is steadfast, my heart is steadfast; I will sing and make music. Awake, my soul! Awake, harp and lyre! I will awaken the dawn. I will praise you, Lord, among the nations; I will sing of you among the peoples. For great is your love, reaching to the heavens; your faithfulness reaches to the skies. Be exalted, O God, above the heavens; let your glory be over all the earth. (Psalm 57:7-11)

To be steadfast is to be firmly established, firm in purpose, or unwavering[1]. The twelfth chapter of Hebrews tells us that we ought to have our eyes firmly fixed on Jesus, the author and finisher of our faith. It also tells us that Jesus endured the cross because he was fixed on the joy before Him. What joy? That the Father would be reunited in fellowship with his people once lost in sin. The psalmist says his heart is steadfast. When is there a need to be steadfast? When there is trouble, we need to be steadfast. When we have a commitment to keep which is not easy to keep, we need to be steadfast. When we are facing something difficult, we need to be steadfast. We must not give up on the things God has given us to do. How do we remain steadfast? The key is in the rest of these verses. Praise God. Sing. Tell others what God is doing in our lives. Let God's love, which is greater than we can imagine, strengthen and encourage us. Let us not be weary in doing what is right but be steadfast as we fix our eyes on the Savior.

He Guides the Humble

> Good and upright is the Lord; therefore he instructs sinners in his ways. He guides the humble in what is right and teaches them his way. All the ways of the Lord are loving and faithful toward those who keep the demands of his covenant. For the sake of your name, Lord, forgive my iniquity, though it is great. Who,

then, are those who fear the Lord? He will instruct them in the ways they should choose. (Psalm 25:8-12)

There is almost another foot of snow on my porch as I look out this morning. That makes a total of about three feet this past week! It reminds me of a winter many years ago when my husband and I were living in our first home. I was teaching then. God had stirred within my heart a sense that a change was about to take place in our lives. I did not know what, but that winter we had twenty-four snow days! It was unheard of! The city schools hardly ever closed for snow. The drifts in the rural areas were seven to eight feet high! Driving down the road was like going through a tunnel. It was amazing! Even more amazing was that each snow day I felt urged to clean house and organize all of our things. I sorted, labeled, cleaned, organized, and had a great time doing it! Just for your information, this is not something I normally do well or often! In March, my husband got a job transfer to Wisconsin and we needed to be moved to Milwaukee by June! If God had not urged me to be doing all that organizing, or had not granted me all those snow days in which to do it, life would have been more than crazy! Now, I am not so self-centered as to think that my whole community had to suffer snow days so that I could get my household together, but God sure did make those snow days a blessing in my life as I listened to his direction. The verses above remind us that God wants to be active in our lives, leading, guiding, and instructing us in his way, if we will choose to listen and obey.

The Lord is My Strength

Praise be to the Lord, for he has heard my cry for mercy. The Lord is my strength and my shield; my heart trusts in him, and he helps me. My heart leaps for joy, and with my song I praise him. (Psalm 28:6-7)

I awoke during the night, and began to play back a conversation I had yesterday with my sister about my mom. I couldn't get back to sleep because I started worrying about what to do and say in the situation. I was rehearsing what I might say to encourage my sister, and trying to figure out what I needed to do. My heart was in anguish, and I knew I could not afford to lose any more sleep. I also knew two things about my fretting. It was not going to change the situation, and it did not reflect a trust in God. Oh, how easy it is to take up our own burdens and try to figure out on our own what to do in difficult situations! I finally prayed and asked the Lord to grant me peace so I could sleep. I am thankful this morning that the Lord did indeed hear my cry for mercy and gave me sleep. He also reminded me that he is in control of this situation. He will give me words as I need them, and more importantly, he will grant me peace as I trust him. There are two times verses like those are a special blessing: when you need them because you are in a difficult situation, and later when the difficulty is passed. Then our hearts can leap for joy and we can give thanks to the One who is ever faithful to be our strength in time of need. When we do not have strength on our own, he is faithful not simply to *give* us strength but to *be* our strength.

The Blessing of Walking with God

Blessed are all who fear the Lord, who walk in obedience to him.
You will eat the fruit of your labor; blessings and prosperity will
be yours. (Psalm 128:1-2)

Do you ever wonder what it means to walk in his ways? How is that different from walking in your ways? Is there a difference? The Bible tells us that God's ways are not our ways, but have you discovered the difference? We can live life loving God and trying with all our hearts to serve him, but never discover how to walk in his ways. Yes, it means we keep his commands, but there is much more than that. It is not so much following God's rules as it is following God. With our human minds, we cannot figure out the ways of God. The only way to discover his way is to seek him with all our hearts and to obey his leading. We must surrender our will to his and allow his Spirit to direct our steps. It begins as we allow God to be a part of our everyday lives. As we go through today, let us invite God to join us and not just finish our Bible reading and put it on the shelf for the day. Whatever your job, as you do it today, ask God for his wisdom, so you can do your job his way. Invite the Lord to lead your steps today, and be mindful of how he leads. You cannot learn all this in a day. Very similar to a young toddler learning to walk, there is much wobbling and toddling before actual walking begins to take place.

God blesses those who learn to walk in his ways. Are you already walking in his ways? Draw closer. With God, there is always more to learn. Just like our earthly parents enjoy when we spend time with them, our heavenly Father enjoys when we seek him with yearning hearts.

God Is Our Refuge

> God is our refuge and strength, an ever-present help in trouble. Therefore we will not fear, though the earth give way and the mountains fall into the heart of the sea, though its waters roar and foam and the mountains quake with their surging. (Psalm 46:1-2)

When you find yourself in trouble, what do you do? Do you find your refuge in God? I remember hearing Corrie ten Boom[2] speak about being imprisoned by the Nazis during World War II. Her Christian family was hiding Jews in a secret hiding place in their home until they were discovered and put into a prison camp. Even in the midst of such unspeakable sorrow, Corrie learned to find her hiding place in God. Only he can give peace when there is a storm raging about you. He is faithful and is able to keep you safe in the palm of his hand when life brings deep sorrow and trouble. I don't know why he sometimes allows us to go through such difficult times, but I do know that he is with us and will strengthen us through the difficulty. Perhaps those hard times are there to help us learn how faithful God is. Perhaps it is only in the difficult times that we seek him earnestly and find ourselves under the shelter of his wings. When we finally grasp the greatness of God in a difficult time, it is not a lesson we soon forget. There is deep and abiding joy in his presence that the troubles of this life cannot penetrate. May you find rest in his presence today.

Examine My Heart

> Hear me, Lord, my plea is just; listen to my cry. Hear my prayer—it does not rise from deceitful lips. Let my vindication come from you; may your eyes see what is right. Though you probe my heart, though you examine me at night and test me, you will find that I have planned no evil; my mouth has not transgressed. (Psalm 17:1-3)

How are you doing with your New Year's resolutions? If you are like most of the world, you have already broken at least one resolution, if not more. We mean well, don't we? We think about what we really need to do to be healthier or more in-tune with God. We want to do what is right, but it is so easy to revert to old ways! You have to wonder how the psalmist can say these words to God. He is asking God to test him, because he is sure that he is without blame. How can this be? I wonder if the psalmist is filled with pride and like the Pharisees only *thinks* he is without blame. Perhaps he is simply referring to this particular situation. Maybe he has been wronged and is trusting God to vindicate him rather than trying to clear himself. That is hard to do. When we feel someone has wronged us, we want to declare our rights and tell everyone we meet, so we can get them on our side. We want to vindicate ourselves. When we have been wronged, it is difficult to let it in God's hands and wait on him to make it right, but it is so wonderful to see God move on our behalf when we do! He rewards those who trust him. As for our resolutions, what do we do when the goals we set seem too difficult to achieve? I think it is the same thing the psalmist has done here. Ask God to examine our hearts. Ask him if our goals are the right goals. Ask him to enable us to meet our goals so that he is glorified in us. Ask him to accomplish in us what he wants, and help us lay aside our own desires. We can forgive ourselves for failures and move forward one step at a time. Today is a new day. Let us rejoice and be glad in it!

God Is My Joy and Delight

Send me your light and your faithful care, let them lead me; let them bring me to your holy mountain, to the place where you dwell. Then I will go to the altar of God, to God, my joy and my delight. I will praise you with the lyre. O God, my God. (Psalm 43:3-4)

I was correcting my students' reading papers one day and realized that they had missed a key idea in one of the stories they had read. Not only that, but they had also misunderstood an essential Bible truth. The question was, "Where is God's temple now?" The answers ranged anywhere from Gaza to all over the world. Needless to say, I had some follow up work to do! We are very fortunate as New Testament saints. In Old Testament times God was only truly known by a few. Moses met with God on Mt. Sinai. When the Israelites traveled through the desert after being set free from captivity in Egypt, God was with them in the pillar of smoke. We do not have to go anywhere to find God, because he is with us, Emmanuel. Christ not only purchased salvation for us on the cross, he made the way for us to meet with God right here and now. Hallelujah! Even so, there are many people who are pretty confused about who God is. Some are looking inward for God because they believe they are God. Even today, these words can be a wonderful prayer. *God, send forth your light and your truth, let them guide us to your holy mountain, to your holy place.* May God guide us to where he is—his very holy presence—where we can know him and love him and worship him, for in his presence is the fullness of joy! We do not need to come to a physical altar, but when we pray we must know that we come before the very altar of God in his heavenly dwelling! As we meet with him, he restores our souls. He is our joy and our delight, and we can do no less than to praise him with all of our hearts.

Rejoice in the Rubble

> Truly my soul finds rest in God; my salvation comes from him.
> Truly he is my rock and my salvation; he is my fortress, I will
> never be shaken. (Psalm 62:1-2)

Following a devastating earthquake in Haiti recently, I heard a news report on the radio about groups of people who were gathered together singing praises to God. You might wonder how this could be. When these dear people had lost everything, how could they praise God? The truth is in the verses above. They may have lost all of their worldly goods, but God saved *them*. Their lives were spared. He is their salvation, not just for eternity, but for this tragic moment in time. Even in devastation, our souls can find rest in the Lord, because he is our peace. Even without a home, he is our fortress. Even in such tragedy, there can be a blessing. These precious children of God were praising him amidst the rubble, and the world was watching. Their neighbors were watching. Wouldn't it be amazing to see whole communities come to Christ as their eyes are opened to see that he is their salvation. He can help them to start again, both physically and spiritually. We can learn from this too. Whatever the "rubble" may be in our lives, we can find rest for our souls in Christ alone. We can experience him as our fortress and we can truly say, "I will never be shaken."

God Satisfies My Needs

> Let them give thanks to the Lord for his unfailing love and his
> wonderful deeds for mankind, for he satisfies the thirsty and fills
> the hungry with good things. (Psalm 107:8-9)

So often these past two weeks I have discovered that there are many Psalms that have verses about food or being hungry. I am sure they have always been there, but I love how God brings me to the very word that I need for encouragement and help in my daily struggles. At the risk of bringing up the subject of those New Year's goals again, I must share with you how faithful God is in helping me in my time of need. God, who knows my heart, reminds me that it is not will power that will help me find victory but his power. I know that self-control is a fruit of the Spirit, and maybe one I am lacking the most! However, I also know that I cannot muster it up. I have seen so often that the harder I try in my own strength, the farther behind I get. When I find success through my own effort, the result is boasting and pride I must confess. There is no greater way to find humility than to have met failure upon failure in my own effort. How does one turn it around? Look at the verse above. He fills the hungry with good things. As I reflect on these verses, I realize that God is to be trusted with my hunger. He provides for those he loves. Doesn't it bless you through and through to know that the living God cherishes you? The reminder that I am cherished by the Lord fills my longing heart with joy! It is good to be reminded that the love God has for me is not connected in any way to how much I weigh! He loves me because I am his. Even so, he cares about my struggle and longs to help me with it. As I learn yet again to trust him to help me, I will be satisfied not in what I eat, but in Christ alone!

He Cares for Me

> Cast your cares on the Lord and he will sustain you; he will
> never let the righteous be shaken. (Psalm 55:22)

In these troubling times, it can be easy to worry and bear a load of care. Even believers are not immune to the cares of this world, but God tells us in his Word that if we cast our cares on him, he will sustain us. He will help us to keep going. He will carry our burden. I know that is true in my head, but sometimes I have trouble accepting this truth in my heart. Sometimes I carry my cares on my own, and when they weigh me down I want others to see my great burden and feel sorry for me. I sometimes have a great deal of difficulty surrendering my cares to God, and I have discovered the reason is a matter of trust. If I hold on to my cares, perhaps I will think of a solution. Maybe I will receive extra attention from the people around me. If I cast my cares on him, it is like casting them into the sea. They are gone and I might not see them again. Isn't that the point? If I cast my cares on him, I give them up. I give them to him. I trust that he is going to provide a solution at some point, and I can be free of the burden. That is the part that holds me back. I will have to trust God and wait, and I am not good at waiting. There is great freedom when we cast our concerns over to God and take him at his word. There is peace, assurance, and hope that he knows a better way or has a better solution, and those who put their hope in him are never disappointed. Whatever your cares, give them to the Lord. He is faithful.

A New Heart

> Wash away all my iniquity and cleanse me from my sin. For I know my transgressions, and my sin is always before me. Against you, you only, have I sinned and done what is evil in your sight; so you are right in your verdict and justified when you judge. Surely I was sinful at birth, sinful from the time my mother conceived me. Yet you desired faithfulness even in the womb; you taught me wisdom in that secret place. (Psalm 51:2-6)

As we were driving through town on our errands yesterday, I took note of the changes that have occurred with the beautiful snow that had fallen several weeks ago. Once it covered everything in a beautiful blanket of white. As the temperatures have gotten warmer, the snow has melted almost completely away and what is left is dirty from all the traffic and chemicals put on the roadways. Isn't that a good picture also of our lives with Christ? We are cleansed from our sin, so that we are white as snow, but because of our sin nature it isn't long before what was once clean and white becomes covered with grime again. As believers, we must not pretend that we do not have a sin problem. I think that is the number one thing that unbelievers have against us. They think that we think we are without sin. Until we reach heaven and leave our sin nature behind, there will still be sin to conquer in our lives. Yes, those blaring sins may be dealt with, but do not neglect the sins of the heart. If we come before the Lord with an honest and humble heart, he will forgive our sins, and we can maintain that freshly fallen snow purity in our lives. If we pretend, even with ourselves, that we have no sin, then we will become stained. Be assured, the people around you have noticed your shortcomings, and the Lord is surely aware of them. Sometimes we are the only ones who refuse to look at and deal with our sin, but when we come before the Lord, he reveals our heart, and we can become new as we seek his forgiveness.

Transforming Love

> Within your temple, O God, we meditate on your unfailing love. Like your name, O God, your praise reaches to the ends of the earth; your right hand is filled with righteousness. Mount Zion rejoices, the villages of Judah are glad because of your judgments. Walk about Zion, go around her, count her towers, consider well her ramparts, view her citadels that you may tell of them to the next generation. For this God is our God for ever and ever; he will be our guide even to the end. (Psalm 48:9-14)

It is good to meditate on God's unfailing love. His love is deeper than the deepest ocean. His love is wider than the widest canyon and higher than the highest mountain. His love is unconditional. His love never fails. His love transforms our lives. His love is eternal. His love is personal. He knows each of us by name and calls us his own. We love only because he first loved us. Greater love has no one than this, to lay down his life for a friend. We must tell of his great love to the next generation. We must make sure our children and our children's children know that God loves them. We do well at teaching children the many stories the Bible tells, but unless we help them to understand that God loves them, we have failed to reach them for Christ. We must learn to love others as God loves us. Let the love of God be your encouragement today, for he is our God forever, and he will be our guide even to the end!

Faithfully Seeking

God looks down from heaven on all mankind to see if there are
any who understand, any who seek God. Everyone has turned
away, all have become corrupt; there is no one who does good,
not even one. (Psalm 53:2-3)

What does God see when he looks down on us from heaven? Does he find his
children faithfully seeking him, or are they busy doing other things? It is pretty
clear that we live in a country that no longer seeks him. All around us are people
who have turned away from God and are becoming more corrupt every day.
Listening to the news for five minutes will tell you that. There are murders,
robberies, and even school bus drivers who are drunk or out of control, but
what does God see when he looks down on your church or your family? Does
he find people who understand and are seeking him? Have you considered what
it means to seek God? It isn't like hide and seek where God is hiding and we
need to find him. It isn't like a giant cosmic puzzle that we have to put together.
God is looking for faithful followers who will seek his face throughout all of
life, those who will call upon his name not just in times of trouble but will be
looking to him all through life's journey. Those who seek him will talk to him
not merely once a day at bedtime while they are drifting off to sleep but all day
in all things seeking his will. He is so much more than just an invisible best
friend. He is our Lord and Savior, King of all kings! We must be seeking his
counsel in all of life, and be alert to his call to duty. We must look into his Word
with diligence, asking for guidance and encouragement so we can continue to
grow into the people he has designed us to be. We must make God's business
our business and not the other way around. Today, what will God see as he looks
down from heaven at you? Will he find you faithfully seeking him?

God Is with Me When Trouble Comes

Some trust in chariots and some in horses, but we trust in the
name of the Lord our God. (Psalm 20:7)

When Jesus came into the temple and took up the scroll and read from Isaiah,
"The Spirit of the Sovereign Lord is on me, because the Lord has anointed me

to proclaim good news to the poor…" (Isaiah 61:1-3), he was declaring that he was the Christ, the one chosen by God to fulfill this mission. As Christ followers, we have been ordained to carry out his mission here on earth. When we take to heart the calling of our Lord to preach good news to the poor, to bind up the broken-hearted, and to bring release for the prisoners, there is bound to be a battle. Satan does not want us to accept our mission. He wants us to believe someone else will do it, so we don't have to. We can stay in our comfort zone. However, when we realize that this is indeed our mission wherever we are, then Satan will confront us and put barriers in our way. I am thankful, though, that Christ did not leave us alone to do battle. When Satan confronts, we can call on the Lord and know that he not only hears but will give us victory in the situation. Hallelujah! Some trust in how much power they have or how much wealth they have or how many talents they have, but if we trust in the name of the Lord our God to help in time of trouble, he will answer us when we call and we will rise up and stand firm.

God Is a Promise Keeper

> Praise awaits you, our God, in Zion; to you our vows will be fulfilled. You who answer prayer, to you all people will come. When we were overwhelmed by sins, you forgave our transgressions. Blessed are those you choose and bring near to live in your courts! We are filled with the good things of your house, of your holy temple. (Psalm 65:1-4)

Have you ever made a promise to God? Did you keep your promise? The word *vow* brings to mind marriage vows. We promise God and our spouse a lot in those vows. I wonder if we take our vows too lightly. We promise to love, honor and cherish our spouse, and we often fall short, don't we? We are ok with the "for better" part, but when we encounter "for worse" we often forget our promise. Sometimes we make promises to God when the situation is really terrible, and we promise him anything if he will just fix it. When things get back to normal, we are often quick to forget our promises. God seems to understand humans, though. He knows how easily we fall, and he has made a way for forgiveness. I am so glad for that! I am also glad that God keeps his promises! Consider all the promises that God has given to those whom he has chosen as his own. We are certainly blessed, and we are indeed filled with good things as we abide with him. Consider God's promises for you today. Rejoice and be glad!

Paradise Awaits

Praise the Lord, all you servants of the Lord who minister by night in the house of the Lord. Lift up your hands in the sanctuary and praise the Lord. May the Lord bless you from Zion, he who is the Maker of heaven and earth. (Psalm 134)

I awoke this morning to blue skies and sunshine. What a welcome blessing and a relief from the dreary weather we have been having. As you go about your business today, pray for God's people in Haiti. We are encouraged to hear of those who are praising God even amid the devastation of a recent earthquake. May the Lord bless them with an outpouring of his love and may they be encouraged by those who are providing help and assistance. Take time today to praise and thank God for his many blessings. He has rescued us from the dominion of darkness and brought us into the kingdom of light. He has forgiven our sins and given us new life. He has blessed us with his Holy Spirit to empower us for the work he has given us to do. He has promised us eternity with him in paradise. What a wonderful God we serve!

Rescued

I called to the Lord, who is worthy of praise, and I have been saved from my enemies. The cords of death entangled me; the torrents of destruction overwhelmed me. The cords of the grave coiled around me; the snares of death confronted me. In my distress I called to the Lord; I cried to my God for help. From his temple he heard my voice; my cry came before him, into his ears. The earth trembled and quaked, and the foundations of the mountains shook; they trembled because he was angry. Smoke rose from his nostrils; consuming fire came from his mouth, burning coals blasted out of it. He parted the heavens and came down; dark clouds were under his feet. He mounted the cherubim and flew; he soared on the wings of the wind. He made darkness his covering, his canopy around him—the dark rain clouds of the sky. Out of the brightness of his presence the clouds advanced with hailstones and bolts of lightning. The Lord thundered from heaven; the voice of the Most High resounded. He shot his arrows and scattered the enemy, with great bolts of lightning and routed them. The valleys of the sea were exposed and the foundations of the earth laid bare at your rebuke, Lord, at the blast of breath from your nostrils. He reached down from on high and took hold of me; he drew me out of deep waters. He rescued me from my powerful enemy, from my foes, who were too strong for me. They confronted me in the day of my disaster, but the Lord was my support. He brought me out into a spacious place; he rescued me because he delighted in me. (Psalm 18:3-19)

At the depths of despair when I was being terrorized by demonic oppression, I cried out to the Lord and he answered me. He came to my rescue and brought me to a safe place because he delighted in me. Our God loves us so much! He will come to our rescue when the enemy pursues us. Hallelujah! What a mighty God we serve!

God Is My Cheerleader

Be pleased to save me, Lord, come quickly, Lord, to help me. May all who want to take my life be put to shame and confusion; may all who desire my ruin be turned back in disgrace. May those who say to me, "Aha! Aha!" be appalled at their own shame. But may all who seek you rejoice and be glad in you; may those who long for your salvation always say, "The Lord is great!" Yet I am poor and needy; may the Lord think of me. You are my help and my deliverer, O my God, do not delay. (Psalm 40:13-19)

We all have people in our lives who want us to succeed and who are cheering us on as we run the race with Christ, but most of us from time to time also have people who just don't seem to like us. They look for our failures and are glad when we mess up. They are ready to say, "If that is what a Christian is, I don't want to be one!" Who do you listen to? If we are wise, we listen to neither. Sometimes our cheerleaders don't see our flaws and cannot help us grow beyond them. On the other hand, our accusers seek only our condemnation. God does not condemn his children. If we are wise, we take the remarks of others and press them through the sieve of God's Word. Let God, who knows us inside and out, be the One to cheer us on and the One who gently points us away from our failures and on to victory. If we are wise, we spend time with those who will encourage us, but we must remember that often we do not present the full picture of who we are to even our closest friends. When others put us down, we can become defensive and want to fight back or become discouraged. We must realize that Satan makes sure that believers have plenty of accusers, so that we will lose heart and focus and become impotent in our testimony. Even so, when we understand the truth that we are poor and needy, then we become a vessel that Christ can truly use. We are emptied of ourselves, so he can fill us with himself. Oh, how we need him to complete the work he has begun in us! Rejoice and be glad! He who began a good work in you will finish it! God is a wonderful cheerleader!

The Agony of Defeat

> Shouts of joy and victory resound in the tents of the righteous: "The Lord's right hand has done mighty things! The Lord's right hand is lifted high; the Lord's right hand has done mighty things!" I will not die by live, and will proclaim what the Lord has done. The Lord has chastened me severely, but he has not given me over to death. Open for me the gates of the righteous; I will enter and give thanks to the Lord. This is the gate of the Lord through which the righteous may enter. I will give thanks, for you answered me; you have become my salvation. (Psalm 118:15-21)

Have you ever been so defeated that you thought you might not make it? Defeat brings discouragement that burdens you down. It is exhausting! If you are an athlete, defeat comes right along with winning. I recently told that to a student who is learning to play basketball. It is only fun for him if he is winning. I kindly explained that great athletes don't just win well, they lose well too. Imagine that! When you teach a child a lesson, God often brings it back around to apply to your own life! We will have many battles in this life, won't we? I doubt we will win them all or even most of them. I am so grateful that in my spiritual battles, God's mighty right hand is ready to help me, ready to bring me victory. The Israelites suffered many devastating defeats, but always it was because they disobeyed God. They went the wrong direction. They forgot whom they were serving. In every case, where they were walking with the Lord, he gave them victory over their enemies, even those who could have whipped them with their hands tied behind their backs! Whatever your battles today, as you trust in the Lord, he will lead you to victory! You may suffer some defeats along the way. Everyone does, but even in your defeat you can learn God's lessons and be all the better for it. Give thanks today for the victory that is yours in Christ Jesus, and may defeat only lead you closer to Him.

God Isn't Hiding

> I remain confident of this: I will see the goodness of the Lord in the land of the living. Wait for the Lord; be strong and take heart and wait for the Lord. (Psalm 27:13-14)

They say some people have a "pie in the sky" view of life. It doesn't matter what is happening here on earth, because heaven will be wonderful. They focus on heaven to keep themselves from giving up when it gets tough down here. Although I agree that we ought to keep an eternal perspective, and we do know that heaven is going to be a wonderful place, I think the psalmist has it right. He is confident that he is going to see the goodness of God right here on this side of heaven. It is true that any suffering we go through in this life will not compare to the glory we will experience in God's presence when we meet him face to face. However, I don't think we have to wait until we get to heaven to see the goodness of God. Those who seek him will find him. He isn't hiding. He desires our love and devotion. He longs to help us in time of need. He celebrates with us in time of victory. When there is a struggle or we are going through a difficult time, the psalmist tells us to wait for the Lord. He tells us to be strong. He tells us to take heart. Why? Because the Lord is on our side, he will deliver us from trouble. Even in difficulty it is possible to see the goodness of God, if you are looking for it. In fact, I have been more blessed by seeing God's faithfulness in difficult times than when everything is going well. We need to be looking for God in our situation. Some people call them God sightings. God sightings are not just witnessing the blind receiving sight or the lame walking. We can see God at work every day in our midst if we have eyes to see and ears to hear. Are you looking for God? Have you seen him lately? Have you seen his faithfulness in action in your life or the life of someone close? Keep your eyes open—your spiritual eyes, that is—and you just might see the goodness of the Lord in the land of the living!

A Strong Tower

> Hear my cry, O God; listen to my prayer. From the ends of the earth I call to you, I call as my heart grows faint; lead me to the rock that is higher than I. For you have been my refuge, a strong tower against the foe. (Psalm 61:1-3)

"The name of the Lord is a fortified tower; the righteous run to it and are safe." (Proverbs 18:10) God is our refuge and strength. He is our refuge in time of need. The tower in the middle of the city was a place of safety for those who dwelt there when an enemy was about to attack. There is no greater protection from the storms of life than under the shelter of his wings, in the presence of the Almighty Lord of all creation. He is our safe place. Life's circumstances may be raging around us, but when we run to our Strong Tower, we are safe. Like a little child who is frightened by a thunderstorm runs to the arms of a loving parent for safety, so we can run to our heavenly Father. *Father, we love you, and we need you. You are the Mighty One, our Strong Tower. As we face the challenges of life here on this earth, we are grateful that you are with us. You surround us with your love and your protection. You keep us safe in the storm, Lord, and we rejoice in the knowledge that you hear our cries of distress. Oh Lord, lift up those who are facing difficult challenges in life today. Lift them up, and remind them of the depth of your love. May they see your strong arm of protection and be comforted. Amen*

The God Who Restores

> Sing to God, sing in praise of his name; extol him who rides on the clouds; rejoice before him—his name is the Lord. A father to the fatherless, a defender of widows, is God in his holy dwelling.

God sets the lonely in families, he leads out the prisoners with singing; but the rebellious live in a sun-scorched land. When you, God, went out before your people, when you marched through the wilderness, the earth shook, the heavens poured down rain, before God, the One of Sinai, before God, the God of Israel. You gave abundant showers, O God; you refreshed your weary inheritance. Your people settled in it, and from your bounty, God, you provided for the poor. (Psalm 68:4-10)

Following a recent earthquake in Haiti, we heard so much about the orphans. Fifteen days after the earthquake, there had been a young woman found alive in the rubble. It was such a blessing to see the outpouring of love from around the globe. I was amazed to see how much money, goods, and other resources came pouring in for Haiti's aid at a time when the world has been struggling so much with finances. People's generosity was a blessing to see. Many came to the aid of those little orphans who had nowhere to go. Many were brought to America to be adopted by loving families. God puts the lonely in families. God provides for the poor. I have heard some ask why God allowed this devastation of such a poor nation. Perhaps it was for the salvation of many. Sing praise to the God who restores!

Victory over Enemies

Rescue me from my enemies, Lord, for I hide myself in you. Teach me to do your will, for you are my God; may your good Spirit lead me on level ground. For your name's sake, Lord, preserve my life; in your righteousness, bring me out of trouble. In your unfailing love, silence my enemies; shelter me from all my foes, for I am your servant. (Psalm 143:9-12)

Unlike David, most of us do not have enemies with skin on, though some of us may have people in our lives who don't like us very much. They may be unkind to us, but few of us are being pursued by a physical enemy. However, I have experienced many enemies in my life that would love to bring about my destruction. They surely do everything they can to keep me from the Lord. Some of my enemies have been Pride, Self-Pity, Arrogance, Depression, Despair, Chaos, Strife, Rejection, Greed, and Grief. These enemies taunted me for years, lying to me about who I am. They played tapes in my mind that kept me believing lies rather than God's Word. Self-Pity kept me so focused on myself and my problems that I could not see God. Depression kept me useless for years. Strife brought Chaos and made my household absent of peace. Yes, these enemies were so much stronger than I was until I cried out to the Lord. One by one he shed the light of his truth on those lies and exposed them to my heart. Moment by moment he showed me how to be victorious by speaking his Word and refusing to allow those lies to control me. He took me, a broken and useless vessel, and in his unfailing love, he lifted me up, set my feet on solid ground and taught me how to walk with Grace, Mercy, Forgiveness, and Peace. He sheltered me from all of my foes, because I am his.

The Way to Victory

> Give us aid against the enemy, for human help is worthless. With God we will gain the victory, and he will trample down our enemies. (Psalm 60:11-12)

I spent a lot of years being afraid of the devil, and not really wanting to deal with the spiritual reality of demons and evil. I believed if I didn't think about it, it wasn't real and would go away. I know that is not terribly logical. Evil is either real or it isn't, and God's Word tells us that Satan is real and controls one third of the angels who were kicked out of heaven because of their rebellion against God. Ignorance of the truth is no protection against it, though. I was afraid of the devil because as a kid my dad would talk a lot about the forces of evil and the reality of their power. He wasn't afraid. He understood that in Christ he had authority over the powers of darkness, but I didn't. He tried to explain it to me, but I somehow never understood and became very afraid. I just wanted to live my life for God and forget all that stuff. There is one problem: Satan doesn't leave us alone just because we want him to! As we grow in Christ and seek to obey his call in our lives, we become a threat to the devil, and he will see that we are challenged. He will tempt us and try to get us off the track, out of focus, useless and powerless, and unless we understand the truth about him, the power that he has, and the ways that he works in the world, we will be vulnerable against his attacks. Praise God, who did not leave me alone in my ignorance, but when

Satan had gained victory over me and had greatly oppressed my life, making me useless and powerless in the kingdom of God, God intervened. He took me to the sixth chapter of Ephesians and taught me about the protection that he has given me, how to use and understand the armor of God, the way to victory, and how to live in that victory.

Call out to God

As for me, I call to God, and the Lord saves me. (Psalm 55:16)

Have you ever experienced a time when you were in such distress that you found yourself calling out to God all day long, asking him to bring an end to the struggle? Do you know someone who is in that place right now? The most wonderful news is that he hears your voice. He hears your call, and he will sustain you. While in the midst of struggle, he will keep you afloat, so you don't sink. Have you been kidnapped by discouraging thoughts or anxiety that you cannot seem to control? He will pay the ransom for your freedom. In fact, he already has! Let him help. Let him bear the burden you carry. Whatever the burden, give it to him. Relationship struggles, family issues, personal battles, problems at your job—whatever the problem, cast your cares on the Lord because he cares for you. Not in a place of trouble today? Someone you know is. Take a few moments and lift them up before the Lord. Stand in the gap for them. Be their advocate in prayer, and then perhaps encourage them with a word of hope. We are children of hope, aren't we? We are not alone in our struggles. Our God cares. *Thank you, Father, for caring for your children. Bless those who are struggling today with a word of hope. Strengthen them and let them see how deeply you love them, Lord. Amen*

The Microwave Parable

My people, hear my teaching; listen to the words of my mouth. I will open my mouth with a parable; I will utter hidden things, things from of old—things we have heard and known, things our ancestors have told us. We will not hide them from their descendants; we will tell the next generation the praiseworthy deeds of the Lord, his power, and the wonders he has done. (Psalm 78:1-4)

God still teaches in parables. One morning as I finished breakfast I heard the small voice of the Lord, "You need to clean your microwave cart today." I argued, but his voice was persistent. I gave in and got busy. My microwave was on a cart with drawers, shelves and a cupboard, so it took several hours to get the job done. "Move the cart to a new place," I heard. Why would I want to do that? Again his voice persisted, and I obeyed. I was sure this was going to be a lesson of some sort, but no instruction came. For the next few weeks, every time I went to put something into the microwave, I went to the old place! I had to stop and think about the fact that the microwave was in a new place. After a couple of weeks of this, the Lord said to me, "This is what it is like to learn to walk in my ways. When you are not thinking, you will find yourself going back to the old places. My ways are not your ways. You will have to learn to walk a new way, and it will feel strange for awhile, like finding a new path to your microwave." I got it! I understood what the Lord had been trying to teach me about learning to walk in his ways. It is a lesson I have never forgotten. Whenever God is doing a new thing in me, I find this parable a good reminder. Learning to walk in his ways takes time and a good deal of concentration until it becomes natural to us. What is God teaching you these days?

God Inhabits Praise

> I will exalt you, my God the King; I will praise your name for ever and ever. Every day I will praise you and extol your name for ever and ever. Great is the Lord and most worthy of praise; his greatness no one can fathom. (Psalm 145:1-3)

How great is our God! How often do we praise him? The psalmist sets a clear example. Every day is a day to praise him. Forever and ever we praise him. It is so easy to settle for so much less. We often come to God in a rush, asking for our many requests, and pouring our hearts out to him with every concern. God loves when we come to him with our needs, but how much more do you think God enjoys when we take time to praise him? How often do we simply come to God to bring him praise? I have been a part of many prayer meetings in many different places and have observed that for most of us it is much easier to bring God our list than to tell him how awesome he is. Here is a challenge for us: For the next few days, let's do as the psalmist did. Praise God every day. Let your prayers be filled with praise. In fact, just for today, don't ask God for anything. Just give him praise. The Bible tells us that he inhabits the praises of his people. When we praise him, we are able to sense his presence more clearly, and we can enjoy just being with him. *Lord, we praise you. With all of our hearts we praise you. You are so worthy of all our praise. You are a great King, our Mighty Savior, and we love you.*

God's Love

> The Lord is gracious and compassionate, slow to anger and rich in love. The Lord is good to all; he has compassion on all he has made. (Psalm 145:8-9)

Isn't God good? He is full of grace. His compassions never fail. His mercies are new every morning. He is slow to become angry with his people. We see in his Word that God does get angry, and he will judge those who refuse him in the end. When we see the full picture of who God is, though, we know that all he does is a reflection of his love for his people and his goodness. Even when he chastises those who disobey him, it is always for the purpose of drawing them back to himself once again. I remember what a difference it made in my own life when I came to understand how deeply he loves me. I had a lot of trouble believing that God could love me because I felt so unlovable. I wasn't bad. In fact, I was a goody two shoes. I tried so hard to be good, so people would love me. I am a perfectionist. I knew every flaw and every wrong I had ever done, and I just felt unlovable. I could understand and accept God's love for the world and for others but just couldn't accept his love for *me*. In compassion he reached into my life and poured down love on me until I could finally see and accept how much he loves me. It changed me forever! It has helped me to love others better too. Isn't it amazing that God who created everything went out of his way to love one lost soul and help her to understand the depth of that love?

A Strong Wall of Protection

> But I will sing of your strength, in the morning I will sing of your love; for you are my fortress, my refuge in times of trouble. You

are my strength, I sing praise to you; you, God, are my fortress, my God on whom I can rely. (Psalm 59:16-17)

We are again having a bunch of snow this morning, and it takes me back a few years to when my kids were little. They used to love building snow forts in the yard. This is the kind of snow that is so good for that. My son would work all day to build these igloo-like forts and then hide out in them for hours on end. It was all fun! The word fortress also brings to mind the heavy thick walls of a castle protected from outside invasion. It has a moat around it to add further protection. A fortress is a strong wall of protection. Spiritually speaking, it is such wonderful news that God is a fortress in times of trouble. Satan never stops trying to render God's people helpless, but God is our protection against the trouble the enemy sends into our lives. We can even sing in the midst of trouble because our loving God is our strength. He is our shield. He is our protector and sustainer. *O God, I sing praise to you this morning, because you are my strength and my fortress in the storm. You are my protector from the enemy's onslaught. My loving God, I sing praise to you and bless your holy name.*

Keeping Records of God's Grace

My heart is stirred by a noble theme as I recite my verses for the king; my tongue is the pen of a skillful writer. You are the most excellent of men and your lips have been anointed with grace, since God has blessed you forever. (Psalm 45:1-2)

When I was a sophomore in high school, my English teacher gave us a small composition book and required that we keep a daily journal. What we wrote in it was entirely up to us, though sometimes he would ask us to respond to a particular statement or question. I am so thankful for that assignment, because I have kept a journal ever since. Though not always daily, my journals have gone from just jotting down thoughts to keeping a record of prayers and thoughts to the Lord. I also write down those precious thoughts he gives to me and occasionally a verse or a song. Over the years, I am utterly amazed at all that God has done in me to transform my heart, mind and soul. I can return in a moment to days long past when I was tormented with many struggles and then praise God again for how he redeemed me from every one. It is an amazing record of my personal journey with the Lord. Periodically, I take down my journals and read what is in them. I am always encouraged by what God has done and all that he has taught me over the years. It is so easy to forget the goodness of the Lord when we hit a rough road, but to have a written record of his faithfulness is a testimony of his love and grace in my life. I encourage others who have never kept a prayer journal to give it a try. God has used the written word to bless his people in the past, and he continues to do so.

Whom Shall I Fear?

But I trust in you, Lord; I say, "You are my God." (Psalm 31:14)

Can you think of a situation where you got a chance to see if you trust God or not? Sometimes we take for granted that we do. Rather, in our mind, we are sure without a doubt that we trust God, but what happens when we are tested? I have grown up with many fears: fear of failure, fear of insects, fear of getting up in front of people, fear of high places, and the list could probably go on! It was not until I was a Christian many years that God showed me in his Word that fear was not from him. Rather, the opposite of fear is faith or trust in God. Whenever I let fear control my actions, I was demonstrating a lack of trust in him. Even though I thought I trusted God and wanted to trust him, the truth was that fear was controlling my life. One by one God has addressed those fears in my life, and helped me to learn to trust him. I can trust him, not because of my ability to trust, but because he is faithful to his word. He always keeps his promises. He is with me and will care for me. When I am becoming fearful, I call out to him, and I speak Bible verses out loud. I remind myself that he is faithful and trustworthy. I confess my fear and ask him to deliver me from it. I tell him I want to trust him and ask him to help me overcome the fear that is paralyzing me. He is faithful and has delivered me from all my fears!

Whole-Hearted Pursuit

Teach me, Lord, the way of your decrees, that I may follow it to the end. Give me understanding, so that I may keep your law and obey it with all my heart. Direct me in the path of your commands,

for there I find delight. Turn my heart toward your statutes and
not toward selfish gain. Turn my eyes away from worthless things;
preserve my life according to your word. (Psalm 119:33-37)

Where is your heart? Do you keep God's law and obey him with all your
heart? Do you dare asking God to turn your heart toward him and his
statutes, or is your walk with God half-hearted at best? I have discovered
something over the years. When I have been half-hearted in my devotion
to the Lord, it was only because I didn't know what I didn't know. I didn't
know what I was missing. I didn't know the great blessing of serving him
whole-heartedly. I have always thought that I loved God with all my heart,
but it wasn't true. For a long time my heart was divided. I loved God, but I
wanted what I wanted. When I began to pursue God wholeheartedly, it was
because I discovered that he was pursuing me! He wanted me to know him
more, to love him more, and to experience more of the life he was waiting
to give me. When he helped me to lay down the things that stood between
my heart and his, it transformed my life! A new passion for the things of
God was ignited, and I began to pursue him with all my heart. He has never
disappointed me! What joy to serve such a magnificent Lord! If you are not
yet pursuing God with all your heart, you do not know what you are missing!
Let this day draw you closer to the lover of your soul. He is waiting for you.

Your Heart Revealed

My mouth will speak words of wisdom; the meditation of my
heart will give you understanding. (Psalm 49:3)

The Bible tells us that what comes out of your mouth reveals what is in your
heart. What do your words reveal about your heart? Do you ever stop and
listen yourself? Are your words critical and harsh or gentle and encouraging?
Are your words full of pain or full of joy? Are your words all about you or
are they mostly about others? What do talk about? Do you talk sometimes
just because you don't feel comfortable with quiet? Do you get to the point
when you talk or do you give every detail? What does your talk reveal about
your heart? Have you known people who are so angry that everything coming
out of their mouths has an edge to it? Have you known someone who is filled

with peace? Their words are quiet and tender. The psalmist tells us that when he speaks from his heart it gives understanding and demonstrates wisdom. Wow! It can be a powerful lesson if we let the Spirit of God reveal our hearts to us through our words. We also must consider our tone. Have you seen the impact of a word spoken with a biting, hurtful tone? It cuts like a knife into the heart of the listener. May your words reveal a heart that is fully devoted to God. May your words bless those to whom you speak and give hope to those who hear them. Even more, may God fill your heart with grace, peace, and joy until it overflows from your lips to all with whom you speak.

Pure in Heart

> Surely God is good to Israel, to those who are pure in heart.
> (Psalm 73:1)

The psalmist is wrestling in his heart over the apparent lack of struggles in the lives of the arrogant. He admits to almost losing his foothold because he has been envying the wicked ones who seem to have it made, while he has kept his heart pure for nothing. He begins this Psalm reminding himself that the Lord is good to the pure in heart. Sometimes it seems the rich and famous have everything they want, while God's people often get by with so little. We can easily fall into this kind of thinking and lose heart. The truth is that while the rich and famous may have everything they think they want, many of them are empty of true happiness. They seek to fill the void in their heart with glamour, wealth, and fame but still come up empty. When we focus on what the wealthy have and become jealous because of what we lack, we lose sight of our true treasure. All that money can buy will soon be left behind, and all that we will have is the life we have lived before the Lord. Those who put their trust in him will find that he is all they need. God is surely good to those who are pure in heart! The fifth chapter of Matthew tells us, "Blessed are the pure in heart for they shall see God." When we read these words, do we not hope that it is we who are pure of heart? How can we be pure of heart? Psalm 51 tells us to ask the Lord to cleanse our heart and purify us from all our sin. Yes, this is the key to a pure heart. There is no one on earth who is pure of heart unless the Lord has cleansed him of his sin. A pure heart comes only from God. To keep a pure heart, we must allow God to continue his work within us day-to-day. *Oh Lord, thank you for your goodness and your promise to bless the pure in heart. Thank you that the only way for us to have a pure heart is through the cleansing atonement of the blood of Christ. Father, as we seek you this day, may our hearts be pure and holy. Thank you for your mercy and your grace. Amen*

In Times of Sorrow

The Lord is close to the brokenhearted and saves those who are crushed in spirit. (Psalm 34:18)

Most of us have at one time or other had a broken heart. There are many experiences that can leave us brokenhearted. In my times of sorrow, when my heart has been so broken that I couldn't imagine it ever healing, God was near to me. He comforted me and reminded me of his precious truth. He encouraged me with his love and offered me hope and promise. His Word tells us that his ministry is to bind up the brokenhearted. He has called us to do the same. How can we encourage those who are brokenhearted? We must love them as God does. We must be near to them and help them know they are not alone in their struggle. We can speak words of hope to them and offer them small gifts of kindness. God is gentle with the brokenhearted. He takes the broken pieces and restores them to wholeness, however long it takes. God never rushes the brokenhearted to "get over it" or "move on." Are you brokenhearted this day? Look to the Lord who can heal your wounds? Trust in his unfailing love and be encouraged by the knowledge that he is there to save. Do you know anyone who is brokenhearted? Pray for them. Offer them kindness and grace. Pray for those who are brokenhearted that they might be encouraged and renewed by the light of his love. *Oh Father, we know you are close to the brokenhearted. Draw them near today and lift them up. Let their broken hearts be made new, and allow them to see how you can bring good from this sorrow. Nothing is too difficult for you. Amen*

God's Unfailing Love

May your unfailing love be with us, Lord, even as we put our hope in you. (Psalm 33:22)

When we consider matters of the heart, ultimately we will come to the topic of love. We are only able to love because he first loved us. We have confused many other things with true love and if we want to understand what true love really is, we must look to the author of love, our gracious King, whose love never fails. Love is not just a warm feeling we get in our hearts when we are near a certain person. Love often brings with it a whole bunch of emotions, but what is it? 1 Corinthians chapter 13 tells us that love is patient and kind. To know true love, we look to God who demonstrates the love of Creator. He loves that which he has created. He loves me because I am his. This is like the love of a parent for a child, but infinitely more; for which of us as parents has loved our children unconditionally and without error? We love our children deeply and want the best for them, but our love for them often fails when our sinfulness gets in the way. God loves us perfectly. His love never fails. My heart can rejoice every day because I am loved perfectly by the One who calls me his. He knows my name. He knows every flaw I have, yet he loves me and accepts me as his treasure! Only he knows what he had in mind when he created me. His love draws me to himself where he can shape me into that wonderful design. What wondrous love is this! There is no greater love.

The Voice of Love

> He remembered us in our low estate His love endures forever, and freed us from our enemies. His love endures forever. He gives food to every creature. His love endures forever. Give thanks to the God of heaven. His love endures forever. (Psalm 136:23-26)

I wonder how many stories there might be of how God has demonstrated his love to his children. Probably, there are as many stories as there are people. Isn't it amazing that God, who knows us, knows exactly what we each need? He doesn't love us all the same. His love reaches into each of our hearts in so very many personal ways. Have you ever experienced a moment with God when you came to really understand how much he loves you? The moment we knew we were forgiven for our sin, we may have been overwhelmed by his love. In a quiet, lonely moment when we sought encouragement from his Word, we may have caught a glimpse of his tender love. In a moment of triumph, God may have allowed us to see his strong arms leading us to victory, and we knew at that moment the height and breadth and depth of his love for us. Imagine, with all that God has created and every person on the globe who ever lived that he loves *me*. His love is so very personal. Today, whether you have another soul in your life who loves you, you must know that God, who is over all, loves *you*. You are his treasure. He gave up heaven for *you*. He gave his life for *you*. He calls your name, and longs to speak his words of love to your heart and your soul. Dare to listen to the voice of love. Give thanks to the God of all grace, his love endures forever.

In God's Sanctuary

> Lord, who may dwell in your sacred tent? Who may live on your holy mountain? The one whose walk is blameless, who does what is righteous, who speaks the truth from their heart; whose tongue utters no slander, who does no wrong to his neighbor, and casts no slur on others; who despises a vile person but honors those who fear the Lord; who keeps an oath even when it hurts, and does not change their mind; who lends money to the poor without interest; who does not accept a bribe against the innocent. Whoever does these things will never be shaken. (Psalm 15)

Which of us can meet such criteria? Christ alone. How is it that God invites us as his children to come and dwell with him on high? We are made righteous by the blood of Christ. He has made the sacrifice for our sins. The very thought that without his sacrifice on our behalf we would not ever see the Lord ought to bring gratitude welling up in our hearts. Even so, with Christ as our example, and his Spirit filling our hearts, we cannot give up on being all that God would have us to be. We have been declared blameless because of Christ, but now in our day-to-day lives we must learn to walk in a blameless way. Though we fail often, we must continue to allow him to do the work in our hearts until our walk is indeed blameless. Do you speak the truth from your heart? Are you kind to your neighbor? Do you honor those who honor God? Do you keep your promises even when it hurts? Don't give up. God will complete the work he has begun in you until you are completely righteous if you will allow him to. The apostle Paul said he had to decrease and Christ increase within him. We do not stop being ourselves. We become all that we were intended to be when we allow God to complete his work in us. What is the reward? We will never be shaken. We get to dwell in the safety of the Master's sanctuary forever. What joy!

A Soul in Anguish

> Lord, do not rebuke me in your anger or discipline me in your wrath. Have mercy on me, Lord, for I am faint; heal me, Lord, for my bones are in agony. My soul is in anguish. How long, Lord, how long? (Psalm 6:1-3)

Do you get the sense that the psalmist has been struggling for quite some time? Perhaps he has been enduring a long illness or has been wrestling with depression for a long time. Whatever the cause, he is in agony in his spirit. He wants the struggle to be over, and I wonder if he is afraid to cry out to God because he has been at the throne of God begging for help for some time. There are times when we think we have had enough, and we can't figure out why God hasn't answered our prayers for relief. We call and call and God seems to be silent. We are in desperate need, and it seems as though God has left us alone to figure it out for ourselves. We may even get angry with God for not providing the relief we need. We wonder how long it will continue. There is definitely agony when we want the battle to be over, yet it rages on. We wonder where God is. Why does God sometimes take so long to answer our call? Only he really knows the answer to that. Only he knows the whole perspective. This I do know: He *can* deliver me, and he *will* deliver me in his time. He is with me, even when I do not see any evidence of that. He loves me, and does not enjoy seeing me in agony. I must trust in him. I must trust in his timing. I must believe that there is a reason for allowing this prolonged time of difficulty. I know that he is never too late. I pray that he will uphold me to the end. I ask that he would encourage me and help me to glorify him even in my pain. I praise him because of his unfailing love and thank him that I can come and pour out my heart again and again until the trial passes. I will trust in his unfailing love and wait for him to save me.

A Heart That Trusts

> When I am afraid, I put my trust in you. In God, whose word
> I praise—in God I trust and am not afraid. What can mere
> mortals do to me? (Psalm 56:3-4)

Can you think of a time when you were afraid? Were you alone or in the dark? Were you flying in an airplane or driving in a snowstorm? Was someone picking on you? The psalmist was often pursued by men who were looking to kill him, and this was his response, "What can man do to me? I will trust in God." I have never been in a situation like that, but I remember as a girl we got a call one night from an unknown caller who told us there was a bomb in our house. We quickly left the house and went to a neighbor's home to call the police. The police came and looked for a bomb. Finding none, they told us it was ok to go back inside. As a child, I wasn't all that excited about going back inside! If they had found a bomb, I might have been relieved it was gone but then fearful of whoever would do such a thing. Going back inside with no bomb found was pretty scary, though. What if there really was a bomb and the police didn't find it? I don't think I slept much that night! I didn't know then about trusting God, though I am sure I must have prayed. The psalmist has much to teach us here. He admits that he gets afraid. I used to be afraid of many things but being home alone at night was one of the worst. I would imagine every little noise was someone trying to get in to hurt me. I couldn't run the washer or dryer at night when my husband was out of town because I was afraid I wouldn't hear if someone was lurking outside! Yes, I was pretty pathetic! I was challenged when I came across this verse. The psalmist admits his feelings, but then he chooses to trust God instead of letting his feelings control the situation. It is easier to tell you this than to actually do it, but it is possible to control your feelings, especially if you wrestle with them before they get too out of control. In that moment, choose to trust God. The psalmist says he trusts God in whose Word he gives praise. This is a wonderful strategy for handling fear. Let God's Word come to your rescue. Think about what God's Word has to say instead of thinking about what is making you afraid and give him praise. Thank him for being with you, so you are not alone. Thank him for his protection and consider that even in the worst case situation—one that threatens to take your life—you will be safe with God. Physical death is only the gateway into eternity with our wonderful Savior, so what have we to fear?

God Hears My Voice

> Evening, morning and noon I cry out in distress, and he hears my voice. (Psalm 55:17)

God saves his people. He saves his people from sin and death, but he also saves his people from their trouble. I am so glad of that! What do we have to be saved from: a bad situation, a bad relationship, a bad health diagnosis, a conflict with a co-worker or family member, or a legal matter? David was having a serious problem with his best friend Jonathan. He was disappointed, because his best friend had let him down. What did he do? Evening, morning and noon he called out to God. I love the second part of that statement, "and he hears my voice." When we cry out to God, he hears us! God, who is enthroned forever, will come to our aid. Is there a difficult situation in your life right now? From what do you need to be saved: a stubborn sin, a situation you have gotten yourself into, an attack from the enemy or a relationship problem? Whatever your situation, call to the God who hears. Call to the One who is able to give light to your path and show you the way through the situation. He hears you. He knows your need. He will answer. He will help. If you are fortunate and do not have a struggle right now, call to the Lord on behalf of others you know who do. Stand in the gap for them, and ask God to rescue them from their trouble and show himself strong in their lives. Call to the Lord, and he will answer.

God Is Near

> We praise you, God, we praise you, for your Name is near; people tell of your wonderful deeds. You say, "I choose the appointed time; it is I who judge with equity. When the earth and all its people quake, it is I who hold its pillars firm." (Psalm 75:1-3)

I was listening to the news the other day and heard that there was a small earthquake in Chicago. There was no damage, and it didn't make big news because of raging snowstorms across the country. The quake was felt as far as Wisconsin. Having lived both in the Chicago area and Wisconsin, it made me think. Such a quake is a rare thing in that part of the country. I can't imagine being in a place that suddenly begins to shake. I think Christians sometimes take for granted the peace that is ours in Christ. Our God is sovereign over all. Nothing surprises him. Nothing is outside of his control. He doesn't ever nod off and leave his children unprotected. That said, we know from experience that God's children experience tragedy along with the rest of the world. The devastating quake in Haiti didn't just affect unbelievers. Believers' lives were also changed forever that day. What is the difference, then, for a believer in the midst of a time of uncertainty? As children of God, we know that he is with us. He will never leave us nor forsake us. He sometimes allows us to go through the storms of life, but we do not need to fear whatever may come, because our God is with us. Whatever we go through, he will use it for good in our lives. He will use it to bring glory to his wonderful name. Give thanks to God, for he is near. He is not up in heaven just watching what happens down here. He is with us. He gives us strength, wisdom, and courage in the midst of danger. He assures us of his unfailing love and promises to bring us safely through.

One Word from God

> One thing God has spoken, two things I have heard: "Power belongs to you, God, and with you, Lord, is unfailing love"; and, "You reward everyone according to what they have done." (Psalm 62:11-12)

What has God been speaking to you lately? The psalms are full of words that God had spoken to the psalmist. Here he tells us that he has heard that God is strong and loving. To understand the truth of those words will absolutely transform your life! Because God is strong, he is able to protect us from every foe; and because he loves us, we know that he will take care of our needs. To know this is good, but would it make any difference to you if God were to speak those words to you personally? Of course it would! If you are in trouble and God tells you that he is strong, wouldn't you be encouraged? More than the truth of the words spoken, our faith differs from other religions because our God is a personal God. When God speaks to me, I am encouraged by his words, but I am also so deeply touched by the knowledge that he is talking to *me*. He cares about *me*. I am reminded that I am his, and he loves me. When God speaks to my heart, I am reminded that I am not alone. My companion is the Lord of all! If he is speaking to me, then no matter what I am facing, it will be alright! I was speaking with a couple of friends yesterday about how these devotions came to be. I started writing a devotional a day in order to accomplish my goal of writing a devotional book that could be published. Where did that idea come from? I have struggled for the past couple of years knowing that God was leading me to write, but not doing it because I couldn't find the time—or the courage—to try something new. When I asked God what to do, he gave me this idea: Write just one each day, and share them with a few friends who could encourage me while the devotions encouraged them. God spoke to me, and his idea was good! One word from God can make a huge difference! So I ask again, what is God speaking to you?

Vessels of Redemption

> The Lord reigns forever; he has established his throne for judgment. He rules the world in righteousness and judges the peoples with equity. The Lord is a refuge for the oppressed, a stronghold in times of trouble. Those who know your name trust in you; for you, Lord, have never forsaken those who seek you. Sing the praises of the Lord, enthroned in Zion; proclaim among the nations what he has done. (Psalm 9:7-11)

I am currently taking an online class about world religions. We have studied Hinduism and Buddhism these past couple of weeks, and I am reminded why the words of this Psalm are so powerful. There will indeed come a day when God judges the earth. Whatever men and nations choose to believe about God and religion, one day the truth will be clear to all—Jehovah is God, Christ is our Redeemer. In that moment when truth dawns, there will be no turning back for those who rejected him in this life. Now is the day of salvation, friends. The days for telling the good news are growing fewer each day. Sometimes we take the coming judgment and wrath of God too lightly, I think. We pretend that we have lots of time to reach the lost, but I believe our time is short. Satan has deceived so many in our world with false religions and blinded many with lies that keep them from knowing the One who loves them, the One who can redeem their lives for eternity. How will they know unless we tell them? Take a moment to think about your family, your neighbors, your community, your country and beyond. How many people do you personally know or that your life touches who have been blinded to the truth of who God is and how much he loves them? We must get over our fear of being rejected and use the time we have to tell those whom God has given us to tell. We must remember that our good news has the power to impact lives for all eternity, so it is worth the risk we take in sharing. How will they know unless we share our story? Let us seek God today on behalf of the lost and begin to pray for opportunities to share the wonderful news of Christ's salvation. Let us pray that the Holy Spirit would remove the blinders from the eyes of those who cannot see and unblock the ears of those who cannot hear, so that they would receive the word of truth. Let us choose to be vessels of God's redeeming message to a lost and dying world.

The Apple of God's Eye

> Turn, Lord, and deliver me; save me because of your unfailing love. (Psalm 6:4)

How much does God love you? He loves you enough to give his only son's life to redeem you. He loves you with every cell of his body given for your salvation. He loves you with every drop of blood that was spilled at Calvary. If that is not enough, he loves you enough to pursue and capture your heart, so that you might know that he loves you. He loves you just as you are. You are his. He loves you and desires to bless you with every spiritual blessing in the heavenly realm. He loves you. He knows your name. He calls to you tenderly, "I love you, child. Come to me. Let me carry your burden. Let me heal your wounded heart. Let me fill you with joy for you are the apple of my eye. I love you." That's how much he loves you.

Like Gold Refined Seven Times

> "Because the poor are plundered and the needy groan, I will now arise," says the Lord. "I will protect them from those who malign them." And the words of the Lord are flawless, like silver purified in a crucible, like gold refined seven times. You, Lord, will keep the needy safe and will protect us forever from the wicked, who freely strut about when what is vile is honored by the human race. (Psalm 12:5-8)

We live in times like this, don't we? Those who are rich and powerful seem to have their way about everything. They do what is most advantageous to them and often do not care who is hurt in the process. Many leaders who say they are for the common man, often serve their own interests and have their own agenda. It is clear when you turn on the television for just a few minutes that the wicked are strutting their stuff in the face of all that is good. Have you noticed that most television shows seem to flaunt wicked behavior as though it is good and right? We who belong to God have a hope that is sure. There will come a time when God says it is enough, and he will arise and come to the aid of the weak and needy. What God says he will do, he will do. His words are flawless, like gold refined seven times. What a beautiful picture that is! Gold that has been purified is of great value and beauty. We can hold on to God's promise. We know he cares for those who are poor and needy. The wicked will not have their way forever. There will come a day when God will rescue us from the evil around us. Until then, we can hold fast to his priceless Word.

Seeking the Lost

> All people will fear; they will proclaim the works of God and ponder what he has done. The righteous will rejoice in the Lord and take refuge in him; all the upright in heart will glory in him! (Psalm 64:9-10)

These past few weeks I have spent a lot of time thinking about the fact that the Lord is going to return for his children, and that day is getting closer every day. Although men have been thinking that ever since Jesus returned to the Father in heaven, it is truer now than ever. Almost two thousand years have passed since Jesus left his disciples on earth, telling them he would return. That makes it easy to think it could be another thousand years before he actually returns for his church, but friends, the signs have never been clearer. Why is he taking so long? God has been patient about this last age for only one reason, I believe. He is waiting for all those who still need to come into the Kingdom. What are we doing while we wait? Some believers just live every day for today, never giving a thought to eternity. It is sad but true, and isn't that how the rest of humanity lives? One day, everyone will recognize that our God is the one true God, and they will finally understand all that he said. They will be afraid, because in that moment they will know that they made the wrong choice, but, it will be too late to change their minds. Yes, then they will see him for who he is and they will have to bow their knee, and then judgment will come. We who are righteous (not of our own accord but because of the redeeming work of Jesus Christ) can rejoice because we will finally see our God face to face. Oh what a glorious day that will be! Friends, we must learn to let our thinking be always in light of eternity. God is patient about Christ's return, because he waits for the salvation of those who have not yet believed. We who love him ought to join him in his work. We who love him ought to pray for the world around us (or maybe just our neighbors) that they would see the light of Christ and believe before it is too late. We ought to ask God to make our heart like his, seeing and seeking the lost with passion and compassion. Oh dear friends, I know that this life is so distracting sometimes. We must go to work and earn a living to provide for our families, and we must be busy living this life, but let's not neglect what is truly important in this life—to help as many as we can to know God. Let us rejoice today that he has called us to this task and he will lead us forward.

Cure for the Winter Blues

Praise the Lord. Sing to the Lord a new song, his praise in the assembly of his faithful people. Let Israel rejoice in their Maker; let the people of Zion be glad in their King. Let them praise his name with dancing and make music to him with the timbrel and harp. For the Lord takes delight in his people; he crowns the humble with victory. (Psalm 149:1-4)

The past few days they have been talking about the winter blues and the winter blahs on the news. Apparently, there is a difference between them, though the symptoms can be similar. In essence, we're talking about depression. They concluded the story yesterday by suggesting people get outside and play in the snow. That works for me! Yesterday, I took the students outside for recess, and we had a blast sledding down the hill behind the school. Everyone was smiling! It was fun! There was an added bonus— the sun was shining! We certainly need some sunshine after weeks of not seeing the sun. Actually, many people experience depression in the winter due to the lack of sunshine, and the cure is light therapy. The psalmist offers us another way to boost our spirits when we've got the winter blues. Praise the Lord. Sing songs of praise. Dance and make music. We sometimes don't realize we have a choice when it comes to feeling blue. It is easy to give into those down feelings, but we can choose another way. Choose to praise the Lord rather than complain. Praise him for his sovereignty. Praise him for the beauty of his creation. Praise him that spring will eventually come! Praise him that you have a warm house to be snowbound in! Singing and dancing are wonderful ways to lift the spirit! Don't give in to the winter blues, blahs or anything else! Let your heart be glad and rejoice in all that God is doing. Sharing stories of God's goodness is a wonderful way to lift your spirit and also the spirits of those who share with you.

The Lord Reigns

> The Lord reigns, he is robed in majesty; the Lord is robed in majesty and armed with strength; indeed, the world is established, firm and secure. Your throne was established long ago; you are from all eternity. The seas have lifted up, Lord, the seas have lifted up their voice; the seas have lifted up their pounding waves. Mightier than the thunder of the great waters, mightier than the breakers of the sea—the Lord on high is mighty. Your statutes, Lord, stand firm; holiness adorns your house for endless days. (Psalm 93)

After writing yesterday's devotional, I headed off to work. I always listen to the Christian station on the way to work, and they were talking about depression. A psychological study at a large secular university has discovered that people who believe in a God who cares about them tend to respond to treatment for depression more favorably than those who don't. Isn't that amazing! Depression can be like a mountain that feels too big to climb. It can feel like you are being sucked under large crashing waves with a strong undertow, and it often leaves a person feeling vulnerable and helpless. The good news for those who wrestle with depression is that God is with you. He has not left you alone to battle this unseen enemy on your own. He is able to lift you up out of the mire and set your feet on solid ground. Our God is mighty to save! Hallelujah! I do not trivialize the treatment of depression by saying that you can overcome it with singing and dancing. However, I have discovered for myself that you can choose to give in to the overwhelming sense of hopelessness, or you can stand on the promises of God and fight back in some positive ways. Today's Psalm reminds us that God is mighty, and he is King for all eternity. He is mightier than those raging waves and powerful storms of life that leave us breathless. We can allow our thoughts to focus on all that is wrong, or we can choose to think on all that we have in Christ. He is the one who redeems us from all manner of darkness. He will lead us into the light if we will but follow. He will grant us wisdom to know what we need to do to take the next step forward, and he will hold our hand while we do it! He is our mighty King, and he loves us. He knows our need and wants to help us know victory in this life.

A God of Salvation

The Lord has made his salvation known and revealed his
righteousness to the nations. He has remembered his love and
his faithfulness to Israel; all the ends of the earth have seen the
salvation of our God. (Psalm 98:2-3)

Our God is a God of salvation. His perspective is eternity. His desire is that none should perish but have everlasting life; however, he has given us the choice to follow him or not. God, who desires the salvation of his people, has done everything to provide the way of salvation. The Bible says that those who refuse him are without excuse. How did you experience salvation? Even if you grew up in church every Sunday, there had to be a time when you realized the truth of salvation for yourself, a time when the God who saves made himself known to you, and you entered into relationship with him. How marvelous it is that if we were all to sit down together and tell our stories each one would be different! Our God is personal. He calls each one by name. From the beginning of time he had a plan of salvation. Before Adam and Eve sinned in the Garden, God knew they would and had a plan ready. Do you remember the story? They were hiding from God, but he came seeking them. That is the amazing part of the story. God went seeking them. He is still seeking those who do not believe. He pursues us and pours his love upon us. He stirs in our hearts a desire to know the truth and opens our eyes and our hearts so that we can see the truth for ourselves. He makes his salvation known to us. God has done it all. What is left for us to do? We must make the choice to receive and believe the truth. Oh what a glorious moment it was when God, who had been pursuing me, finally had my heart! In that moment of surrender which followed weeks of wrestling with the truth, I was so full of joy I could have burst! I couldn't wait to tell someone what God had done for me! I wanted to sing and shout and dance for joy. It was a quiet, personal moment alone with God, but it was glorious! In that one moment of surrender my life was changed forever. I became his. He nurtured me and taught me how to grow. Salvation was only the beginning of a lifetime love relationship with the God of all creation. This love and desire for salvation is God's heart for his people. The work is his, but he wants us to be a part of that work by telling others what he has done for us. We can declare his praise and tell of the marvelous things he has done, and God will use it in the life of those who still need his salvation. Let us not keep quiet, but remember all that he has done for us and pass it on. Pray for the people in your life who do not yet know him. Pray that their eyes and ears would be opened. Pray that he would soften their hearts and help them to understand and accept the truth, and if he opens a door for you to tell your story, tell it. Let us declare the salvation of our God, for there are many who still need him.

Nothing Surprises God

The Lord reigns, let the earth be glad; let the distant shores rejoice. Clouds and thick darkness surround him; righteousness and justice are the foundation of his throne. Fire goes before him and consumes his foes on every side. His lightning lights up the world; the earth sees and trembles. The mountains melt like wax before the Lord, before the Lord of all the earth. (Psalm 97:1-5)

I sat in front of the television yesterday fascinated as the news commentators awaited a tsunami that was predicted to hit Hawaii as a result of an 8.8 earthquake that had hit Chile the previous day. They talked about the huge amounts of energy that were being transferred from the earthquake's epicenter out to the water producing the tsunami waves. I listened to the expert project what might happen and where, but it was interesting to see what really happened. Modern technology allows scientists to track the seismic activity much better than in the past, but so many other factors influence what the surge in energy will produce. Thankfully, there was not much to see. There was a rise in the water level and some tidal surges, but there wasn't a giant wave. As I marveled at the whole event, thankful that there was no devastation, I also thought about the fact that though the experts could project what they thought would happen based on prior knowledge, our God knew exactly what would happen, where it would happen, and when it would happen. Absolutely nothing surprises God or catches him off guard. Why does he let things like this happen? It is because sin still has an effect on the world. God will use every tragedy to bring about good. Are things in your life shaking, or are giant waves threatening to cover over you? Trust in the Lord. He is with you. He will strengthen you. He will rescue you in your time of trouble. He knows what you need and when you need it. There is nothing he does not know. Put your trust in him.

A Shelter in the Storm

My heart is in anguish within me; the terrors of death have fallen on me. Fear and trembling have beset me; horror has overwhelmed me. I said, "Oh, that I had the wings of a dove! I would fly away and be at rest. I would flee far away and stay in the desert; I would hurry to my place of shelter, far from the tempest and storm." (Psalm 55:4-8)

When I don't have words to describe what I am feeling, or I am feeling guilty for feeling the way I am feeling, I love to come to the Psalms. There I find another person who has dark times of struggle and anguish, and he helps me put my feelings into words to bring before the Lord. I have learned from the psalmist to be honest with God about my feelings, for he knows them already. I pour my heart out to him now when I am in anguish, and I know he will be faithful to comfort me and show me the way to go. Isn't it strange, though, that the place the psalmist chooses to go is the desert? What could be safe about a desert? Well, he tells us his place of shelter is there, so perhaps there is a cave in the rocks where he knows he will be safe from the elements. He is running from a storm, and the storm can't follow him far into the desert. My favorite part of these verses is the part about having wings to fly away. Wouldn't it be nice when things get difficult if we could just fly away to a solitary place to collect our thoughts and reign in our emotions? There are lots of times I would rather fly off into seclusion than face the storms in my life. Though I don't have wings, and I can't physically get away from my situation, I know that I have a safe place to run to when the storm is raging around me. Christ is my refuge and my strength. He is my shelter in the storm. When my heart is in anguish and everything is caving in around me, he is my solid foundation. He can calm the storm or give me courage to face it. He can soothe my troubled soul and bring my spirit to a place of peace and rest. When I am troubled, I run to him and place my head in his lap, pour out my troubles, and let him minister to me. He is always faithful.

In the Midst of Lions

> Have mercy on me, my God, have mercy on me, for in you I take refuge. I will take refuge in the shadow of your wings until the disaster has passed. I cry out to God Most High, to God, who vindicates me. He sends from heaven and saves me, rebuking those who hotly pursue me--God sends forth his love and his faithfulness. I am in the midst of lions; I am forced to dwell among ravenous beasts—men whose teeth are spears and arrows, whose tongues are sharp swords. Be exalted, O God, above the heavens; let your glory be over all the earth. (Psalm 57:1-5)

Have you noticed how many Psalms express anguish of the soul as the psalmist finds himself in difficulty? Oh, how I love the reminder in these verses that God fulfills his purpose for me! Just because we are walking in the will of God does not mean adversity will not find us. In fact, I find it quite the opposite. Sometimes when God is really moving in our lives, or is about to do something quite extraordinary, the lions come out of the woodwork! Satan wants to thwart any move of God in our lives, and he makes sure there is a battle to face. Praise God, we are not alone with the lions! Like Daniel in the lion's den, the angel of God is with us to subdue the lions and keep us safe from harm. God has a plan for your life, and no disaster of any kind can prevent his plan from being fulfilled. Now this doesn't mean we won't have difficulty. We know that, but God will use the difficulty to purify our hearts. The fires of fury will only bring about his glory in the end. God's love and faithfulness are never far from our situation, so we can find refuge in him. If you have a heart to follow him, why is everything so difficult? God's will is that he would be glorified in your life and that you would be a reflection of him to the world. Friend, I have found that in the darkest of situations I have learned the most about God. It is then that I have seen firsthand the love and faithfulness of the Most High. My faith grows exponentially when I have the opportunity to see him move mountains in my life. These are often opportunities for us to see just what our faith is made of, developing in us a confidence in God that cannot be shaken. Take heart if you are in the midst of a difficult time. God's love and faithfulness will come to your aid. He will fulfill his purpose for you, and you will find refuge in him. You are not alone. He is with you.

Between a Rock and a Hard Place

> Come and see what God has done, his awesome deeds for mankind! He turned the sea into dry land, they passed through the waters on foot—come, let us rejoice in him. He rules forever by his power, his eyes watch the nations—let not the rebellious rise up against him. Praise our God, all peoples, let the sound of his praise be heard; he has preserved our lives and kept our feet from slipping. (Psalm 66:5-9)

It is good to praise the Lord. God's Word tells us to give thanks in all circumstances, but sometimes that is just so difficult to do! How can you praise him when you have just received the worst news of your life? How can you praise him when everything seems to be falling apart? How can you praise him when he seems to be so far from your situation? It is easy to praise God when all is going well, but if you are in a place where you can't even remember what it is like for things to be going well, then it is not easy. In fact, it is extremely difficult, but there is a way! The psalmist often seems to be between a rock and a hard place. How does he do it? He remembers and recounts all that God has done previously to show his faithfulness. He keeps his focus on who God is to help him get his eyes off of the immediate circumstances. I don't know about you, but my nature is to just keep looking at what is going wrong, even though I know it keeps me down. I have to be deliberate in choosing to praise God and remember how many ways he has rescued me in the past. Like the psalmist, when I offer God praise for what I know is true in my situation and praise him for his faithfulness and tender mercies even when I cannot see them, then my heart is lifted, and he sets my feet on dry ground. Are you facing a sea that must be crossed? Are the waters raging, and you can't see your way around? Consider all that you know of God, and praise him. Praise him not for the bad situation, but his faithfulness to see you through. Praise him that he is a God of miracles. Praise him for his amazing love and his presence in your life, even if you cannot *feel* him with you right now. He is there and will make a way where there seems to be no way. He has done it before. He won't disappoint you, but remember, his ways are not our ways. Sometimes we can't possibly imagine how he is going to get us through. Do you think those Israelites in their wildest imaginations would have thought to ask God to part the Red Sea so that they could get across? No. That was God's way, but he didn't reveal the way through until the very moment that they needed it. Be encouraged today. God knows how to make a way for you too.

A Way of Escape

If the Lord had not been on our side—let Israel say—if the Lord had not been on our side when people attacked us, they would have swallowed us alive when their anger flared against us; the flood would have engulfed us, the torrent would have swept over us, the raging waters would have swept us away. Praise be to the

Lord, who has not let us be torn by their teeth. We escaped like a bird from the fowler's snare; the snare has been broken, and we have escaped. Our help is in the name of the Lord, the Maker of heaven and earth. (Psalm 124)

"If the Lord had not been on our side..." Is there a moment in your life when you can see the rescuing hand of the Lord pull you out of the raging waters, a time when the enemy threatened to get the best of you? This verse always takes me back to one summer day many years ago when depression threatened to swallow me up. I was alone, except for my three babies, and crying out of control. The name of a woman came to my mind, though we were not yet friends. I felt urged to call her. She prayed with me over an hour and a half on the phone, taking my cause before the Lord Almighty. She prayed against spiritual forces of darkness which had come around me like a flood with defeating thoughts of hopelessness. I remember as she finished praying I felt so free I bounced with joy! I know without a doubt if God had not intervened that day, I might not be here today. I am so very grateful that God is on our side. When we are engulfed and about to be consumed, he sends his mighty angels to come and rescue us and put our feet back on solid ground. Hallelujah! Be encouraged, friend, God is on your side and he is mighty to save. His hand can hold back the wave that is about to crash over you. He is able to release you from the tempter's snare and make a way of escape. He knows exactly what you need.

The Lord God Is a Sun and Shield

Better is one day in your courts than a thousand elsewhere; I would rather be a doorkeeper in the house of my God than dwell in the tents of the wicked. For the Lord God is a sun and shield; the Lord bestows favor and honor; no good thing does he withhold from those whose walk is blameless. Lord Almighty, blessed is the one who trusts in you. (Psalm 84:10-12)

What encouraging words we find in Psalm eighty-four! Do you know someone who would rather hang out with the wicked? It is only because they have not truly tasted of the goodness of the Lord Almighty. They have no idea what they are missing! We who love the Lord have only a glimpse on this side of heaven of what eternity with him will be like, for here we are still surrounded by sin, sorrow, and shame. If the only way you could get to heaven was to be God's doorkeeper, would you go? No question about it! Of course you would. It will be the best door you've ever seen! You would get to meet all the saints as they come and go. It might not be a glamour job here on earth, but for all eternity, it would be far better than the place of the wicked, wouldn't it? "The Lord God is a sun and shield." There will be no need for light in heaven because he is light, and his glory is even brighter than our sun which gives us light. Oh, what joy it will be to behold his glory! Today is only the second day in a row that we have had sunshine in over two months. As the sun shone brightly yesterday, people were actually giddy and smiling. There was so much energy that the children in my class could barely contain it! How much more wonderful the glory of God! My favorite part of these verses is the last verse. "The Lord bestows blessing and honor, no good thing does he withhold..." Have you ever felt like no one really notices how hard you work or the great job you are trying to do? You hear a lot of criticism, but praise is not easy to come by. God sees you and knows your heart is to glorify him in all that you are doing. He will see that you receive his blessing for a job well done. There is no praise on earth that could compare to the honor and blessing of the Lord God! It will certainly be worth the wait! Enjoy a few moments in the presence of God today. He loves you.

Can Good Come from the Rubble?

> You have rejected us, God, and burst upon us; you have been angry—now restore us! You have shaken the land and torn it open; mend its fractures, for it is quaking. You have shown your people desperate times; you have given us wine that makes us stagger. But for those who fear you, you have raised a banner to be unfurled against the bow. Save us and help us with your right hand, that those you love may be delivered. (Psalm 60:1-5)

Recently, there have been so many earthquakes that I wondered if there was more than the usual number, so I went to the USGS[3] website and was really surprised by what I found. There had been even more quakes in those months than were reported on the news. In fact, there were eight quakes in just that month alone, and a total of sixteen quakes in the previous three months, including one in Oklahoma (4.0) and one in Chicago (3.8). That roused my curiosity even more, so I compared it to how many quakes were listed in the previous year. There were only fourteen quakes in the previous year during the same time period, and I don't remember any of those quakes being so widely publicized. Maybe that was because they did not bring about the same devastation, and none of them were as great in magnitude as the 8.8 quake that had occurred in Chile. The following morning as I was reading in Psalms looking for some verses for this devotional, I came across Psalm sixty. I am sure I have read it before, but I don't think I ever gave it much thought. The Psalmist describes the quaking earth as though he has experienced it. Could there have been an earthquake in that part of the globe during the time of David? I don't think there is a natural disaster more frightening than when the earth quakes. It is unpredictable, so people cannot get out of the way. Even a mild shaking would shake me up, I think! There are so many questions we could raise here, but I want to focus on the outcome. Can God bring anything good out of the rubble? Yes! He is able to deliver out of the devastation. God is always thinking about eternity. If out of the rubble, there are many who come into the Kingdom, then there is much cause for rejoicing. Sometimes, when our life seems shaken and nothing is left but rubble, God is able to teach us something we could learn no other way. God is faithful. We can trust him.

A Miracle of Great Magnitude

I will consider all your works and meditate on all you mighty deeds. Your ways, God, are holy. What god is as great as our God? You are the God who performs miracles; you display your power among the peoples. With your mighty arm you redeemed your people, the descendants of Jacob and Joseph. (Psalm 77:12-15)

I was really shocked yesterday when we got in the car to head to church and heard a news report that over 40,000 people in Haiti have accepted Christ since the recent earthquake there! Praise the Lord! As I wrote the devotional yesterday morning, I knew God could and would use this devastation to accomplish good, but I had no idea the magnitude of the miracle! Though I would never wish an earthquake on anyone, I am so grateful that our God is still a God of miracles! His ways are indeed holy, and it is clear that his ways are not our ways. While I was verifying this fact on the radio station's news page this morning, I noticed that just this morning there has been another major quake, this time in Ankara, Turkey. This brings to mind Jesus' words in Matthew 24 where he tells his disciples that war, famine and earthquakes are signs of the end times. Let's continue to pray for the work God is doing in the world. May the outpouring of love from Christians continue to reach out to those in need, and may the hearts of the people be turned to the true source of salvation, our Lord Jesus Christ. As the day draws us closer to the times described in Revelation, let us join God in reaching the lost with the good news of a God who loves them and will provide for them. Let us rejoice in the salvation of so many!

Water from a Rock

> Tremble, earth, at the presence of the Lord, at the presence of the God of Jacob, who turned the rock into a pool, the hard rock into springs of water. (Psalm 114:7-8)

The Israelites had wondered in the desert awhile, following the Lord wherever he led. He gave them manna to eat each day. Their clothes and their shoes didn't wear out. They grumbled because they had no water, and he gave them water from a rock. All the amazing miracles they had experienced up to that point, and rather than come to God they grumbled to Moses. Moses was angry with them, but he took their request to God. God provided water for them from a rock! He turned the rock into a pool of water where they could be refreshed. That story holds so much of human nature, and a wonderful glimpse at the grace of God! How are we any different? Perhaps you have been in a spiritual or emotional desert for awhile and like the Israelites, you are so very thirsty. Are you grumbling about it to someone? We love to grumble, don't we? Unlike us, God looks past our human nature and sees our need. The people in our lives, like Moses, may tire of our grumbling and get angry or frustrated with us, but what can our grumbling change? Think about it. Grumbling only makes the difficult situation feel worse and worse, but God, who knows our need, can draw water from a rock! Bring your need to him, and he will refresh you. Our grumbling is evidence that we are not trusting God. God knew that the time in the desert was not easy. The Israelites' time there was only prolonged because of their lack of faith and their grumbling. Even so, God gave them what they needed. How much more will God provide what we need if we ask him and trust him to lead us! Are you desperately thirsty for some living water? God can quench your thirst in the most unlikely of ways if you trust him. He understands your situation and knows your need. The One who can draw water from a rock can help you in your time of need!

The Heritage of Those Who Fear Him

I long to dwell in your tent forever and take refuge in the shelter of your wings. For you, God, have heard my vows; you have given me the heritage of those who fear your name. (Psalm 61:4-5)

We learn from the psalmist to be honest with God about who we are and how we are doing. He knows anyway, but when we open our hearts to him and admit our need, there is freedom—freedom to admit when we are weary and need rest. I have promised to walk in his ways, but I have learned that I can do nothing without him. He is my strength. He is my hope. He has given me all I need to live a life worthy of him. He promises protection. He promises wisdom when I need it. He promises to make a way in the desert. He promises to lead me and to complete the work he has begun in me. He promises to forgive me when I fail and to bless me just because I am his. He promises me a place with him in glory and victory in the battle. Such is the heritage of those who fear him. *God, this morning I long to be in your presence, to feel your loving arms surround me and to be reminded that you love me and that you are with me. I am weary and discouraged and need a place of rest. Oh, I love that you draw me into your tent and wrap your arms around me! You are strong and mighty, Lord, but your tender mercies are like a healing balm to my soul. There is safety in the shelter of your wings. I am so thankful for your protection and blessing. You know my heart, Father, and you know my need. Thank you for your faithfulness. Amen*

Our God Reigns

> The Lord is King for ever and ever; the nations will perish from his land. You, Lord, hear the desire of the afflicted; you encourage them, and you listen to their cry, defending the fatherless and the oppressed, so that mere earthly mortals will never again strike terror. (Psalm 10:16-18)

Sometimes when we look around us or listen to the news, it can be easy to forget that the Lord is King. Even now, he reigns, though he has allowed the evil one to have influence on this earth. Our God reigns! He knows our hearts. He knows our needs. He listens to the cries of those who are afflicted. Hallelujah! I wonder how God has encouraged you lately. I appreciate when my friends encourage me during a time of difficulty, but it cannot compare at all to the experience of having the King of Kings encourage me. "How does he do that?" you wonder. Just when I need it, there is a passage of Scripture that speaks directly into my heart, and I know that God is telling me that he is with me and the circumstances will not overwhelm me. Sometimes it is just a gentle, uplifting thought as the Holy Spirit reminds me of a precious truth. Most times, the encouragement does not come in the form of a change in circumstances, but a change in me as I am reminded afresh who God is—the Lord Almighty, my King, my Redeemer, my Savior, my Rock, my Shield, my Strong Tower, my Help in time of need, and my Peace. I am so encouraged just to know that he listens to *me*! When I truly have need of a real person with skin on, he sends me one. How great is our God!

An Empty Vessel Waiting to Be Filled

> Lord, hear my prayer, listen to my cry for mercy; in your faithfulness and righteousness come to my relief. Do not bring your servant into judgment, for no one living is righteous before you...I spread my hands to you; I thirst for you like a parched land. (Psalm 143:1-2, 6)

I think one of the reasons I like Psalms so much is that the psalmist is so often in distress and crying out to the Lord for help. I don't feel so alone in my struggle when I see the psalmist so often in need of relief. He understands God and knows him so well that he is free to pour out his complaint before him. He isn't whining or grumbling, although at times he seems to be feeling a little self-pity, I think. He simply comes to God crying out for help, and then I love what he does. Almost always after he has voiced his need, he thinks about and remembers all that God has done before. He turns his focus away from the trouble and turns his eyes to the Lord. He speaks to God about how amazingly he has brought relief in the past, and his discouragement gives way to hope. Knowing God is faithful, he extends his hands to him in prayer like he is holding up an empty cup and asking the Lord to fill it with living water. There he waits on the Lord. He puts his hope in the One who is able to rescue, the One who is able to provide, the One who knows him and loves him, the One who has always provided a way before. Like the desert longs for a summer rain, so the psalmist waits for the Lord, and we know the Lord will answer in his time, because he is faithful.

Go with the Flow

The Lord Almighty is with us; the God of Jacob is our fortress. (Psalm 46:7)

There is a little stream that runs down the mountain I live on. Most of the time it is a quiet little stream with just a little trickle of water, but today it is like a raging river. Winter's furious snowstorms left us with such a pile of snow it is difficult to describe, and then the temperature suddenly went up into the fifties. Most of the snow that covered everything has melted away in such a short time that now there is danger of flooding. To add to that, today they are calling for a couple of inches of rain. The weather forecasters have said that all the moisture from the snow is likely to cause a significant rise in tornadoes in the Midwest, and the coastal areas can expect at least five hurricanes this summer. In our comfortable place in the world, there are few reminders that we are not as in control of our lives as we may think. People will talk about the causes of all this severe weather. Some will blame El Niño, some global warming, some Mother Nature, and some may even blame God. Well, I don't know what is to blame, but this I do know: Even in the severest of situations, God is with us and will help us at just the right time. We do not need to fear, because God will make a way. He will be our refuge and our strength if we come to him. He is faithful. Though the waters may be surging and threatening, God will bring us through. We can fight against the raging water, or go with the flow and see where it takes us. If God is with us, we have nothing to fear.

The Enemy Must Flee

> May God arise, may his enemies be scattered; may his foes flee before him. May you blow them away like smoke—as wax melts before the fire, may the wicked perish before God. But may the righteous be glad and rejoice before God; may they be happy and joyful. (Psalm 68:1-3)

I get a little uncomfortable sometimes with the psalmist's prayers against his enemies. He calls for their destruction, and I wonder if that is also God's heart. In the end the wicked will pay for their choices, of that I am sure. Here, though, the psalmist is talking about God's enemies. Who are God's enemies? In the beginning, when God created all of life, he had no enemies. Imagine that. When Lucifer, the most beautiful angel, wanted to be above God, his pride made him God's enemy. Satan was thrown out of heaven that day, along with one third of the angels that he had gotten to side with him. They, of course, made their own choice whom they would follow, but have you ever noticed when there is a trouble maker on the scene how many people he gets to join him before all is said and done. One wonders if at any point those fallen angels realized how wrong they were to side with Lucifer. While it is true that on earth even the vilest sinner can be redeemed by the blood of the Lamb if he repents, the fate of those fallen angels is sealed. They will suffer eternal punishment. Those wicked beings are not locked away somewhere waiting their fate. They have been given a time on earth, and they seek to add to their number as many foolish humans as they can sway. Although we may not ever see them physically, we can see their influence in our world every day. They stir up pride and dissension, arrogance and murder, slander and all kinds of evil. They speak lies into the minds of believers and unbelievers alike, trying to deceive and draw away from the Lord as many as they can. Even so, there is good news in these verses. The righteous are in stark contrast to the wicked. Those who are made righteous by the sacrifice of Christ on Calvary may rejoice and be glad because our reward is with the Father. We can be happy because he has overcome the evil one and is able to rescue us from the midst of a spiritual battle in the blink of an eye. When God enters the scene, the enemy must flee. This is cause for much rejoicing!

God Takes Delight in Us

> Listen to my words, Lord, consider my lament. Hear my cry
> for help, my King and my God, for to you I pray. (Psalm 5:1-2)

The signs of spring are all around. I have seen a couple of robins having a feast in my muddy yard. The daffodils and tiger lilies are about two inches tall, sprouting up nearly overnight. After such a long winter, these are signs of hope, signs of life that lift the spirit and bring joy to the heart. Our God is such an artist! He has created so much beauty around us to enjoy, and the most wonderful news is that he wants to enjoy it with us! He has not just put it together and left us to care for it. He longs for relationship with us. With all the people in the world, God is happy when I come to him and lay my requests at his feet. He enjoys listening to my voice declare my love for him. He is blessed when I tell him that I am trusting in his unfailing love and believe his Word. I have also come to understand that he is delighted when I linger in his presence, waiting for his still small voice to speak to my heart, happy to have him lead me through the day. This is what makes the Christian faith so much different from other religions. We serve a personal God who wants to have us know him as he knows us. We don't just follow rules or attend services. We have a God who delights in meeting our needs and loves to answer our prayers even beyond our expectations.

Share Your Story

> Come and hear, all you who fear God; let me tell you what he
> has done for me. (Psalm 66:16)

What is your story? I love to listen to the stories of how people first encountered God. Even those who have grown up in the church have a story to tell. Though they might not have a dramatic conversion story, there is still the story of how and when they encountered God. How did God reveal himself to you? I love that God is so personal that each of us have a very different story, though each one is about a personal relationship with the living God. I remember how excited I was (and a little scared) that God seemed to be trying to get my attention. I had believed in him as long as I can remember, but he seemed to be trying to tell me that he wanted more in our relationship. He met me just where I was. I felt his love and acceptance. I was so confused about what God would want with me that I went in the middle of the night to the men's dorm where the leader of the InterVarsity Christian Fellowship lived. I needed to know if it was really God trying to speak to me, so I knocked only lightly, telling God that if he wanted me to know it was him, then this guy would wake up. He did and later told me that he never wakes up so quickly or completely as he did that night. We went and talked in the Jay's Nest over coffee. He explained that God wanted me not just to believe in him but to surrender my life to him and to let him have total control over my life. We parted ways, and as I walked back to the dorm, I remember telling God that I didn't think my life was all that great of a prize to surrender, but if he wanted it, it was his. The next day when I awoke, I couldn't wait to tell somebody—everybody—about my encounter with God the night before. Since then, he has continued to lead and guide me. He has taken my broken life and made it new. He continues to give me a story to tell. Every day he draws me close and reminds me that I am his. Others are hungry to know this kind of God, this kind of love. How will they know unless we tell them?

The Dark Night of the Soul

> I cried out to God for help; I cried out to God to hear me. When I was in distress, I sought the Lord; at night I stretched out untiring hands and I would not be comforted. I remembered you, God, and I groaned; I meditated, and my spirit grew faint. You kept my eyes from closing; I was too troubled to speak. I thought about the former days, the years of long ago. I remembered my songs in the night... (Psalm 77:1-6)

Sometimes as Christians we get the idea that if we are doing the right things then everything should be going well. Something must be wrong if we are struggling, and we never want to admit to other believers that our faith is shaking, or we are discouraged. We put on our happy face around other believers, because no one else around us seems to be struggling. When I read Psalms, I am comforted by the fact that David struggled. Sometimes it was because he got himself in trouble, but sometimes not. Though he was God's man, a man after God's own heart, God did not spare him heartache and trial! What is more, David was honest with God about his struggles and always looked to God for the way through. Satan is very smart. He tries to keep us alone in our struggles, because he knows that there is power in corporate prayer. The prayers of the righteous accomplish much, but what about when we are weary and burdened down and too full of sorrow to lift our concerns to the One who can rescue us? Have you ever experienced the deep, dark place described above? When you are there, you are sure that no one else would want to join you in your plight. You cry to God, but he doesn't seem to hear. Your hope teeters on the edge of a dark chasm, and it feels like life will never be normal again. What does the psalmist do? He thinks about former days and remembers the songs he used to sing. He considers the faithfulness of God and reminds himself of the truth, even though it seems far off, and he keeps crying out to God until there is relief. Even when it feels like God doesn't hear our cry, he hears and loves us so much! He waits until the work of sorrow has been completed and not one moment longer to rescue us. Hallelujah! He is with us!

When God Steps In

> We have heard it with our ears, O God; our ancestors have told us what you did in their days, in days long ago. With your hand you drove out the nations and planted our ancestors; you crushed the peoples and made our ancestors flourish. It was not by their sword that they won the land, nor did their arm bring them victory; it was your right hand, your arm, and the light of your face, for you loved them. (Psalm 44:1-3)

The Old Testament is full of times when God rescued his people from their enemies. Some of my favorites are when God parted the Red Sea so Moses could lead the people out of Pharaoh's reach, when Gideon defeated an army of thousands with just 300 men, and when the walls of Jericho fell down after Joshua paraded the people around seven days in a row. The enemy was sure of winning and probably laughing at the Israelites' attempts to do battle—until God stepped in, that is! In each case the battle looked too big, and the enemy seemed too strong and well-equipped for there to be any hope of winning. Indeed it was! These men did not win because of their swords or smarts or their own effort. God stepped in. His right arm (his strength) and the light of his face brought about the defeat of the enemy. We do well to remember the events in history when God's people were rescued by him, for our battles with Satan are often intense and we may feel helpless against his attacks. He often uses situations that are too big for us to handle and his resources against ours can seem overbearing. We will never defeat him because of our own ability to fight. The battle belongs to the Lord! We must remember that we are in his hands, and when his light shines into our situation, victory will be ours! Be encouraged, friend, if you are in the midst of a battle that you cannot win. Our God is faithful and will show you the way to victory.

Who Am I That God Is Mindful of Me?

Clap your hands, all you nations; shout to God with cries of joy. For the Lord Most High is awesome, the great King over all the earth. He subdued nations under us, peoples under our feet. He chose our inheritance for us, the pride of Jacob, whom he loved. God has ascended amid shouts of joy, the Lord amid the sounding of the trumpets. Sing praises to God, sing praises; sing praises to our King, sing praises. (Psalm 47:1-6)

When I read verses like these, I get to thinking that perhaps heaven is going to be more like a football stadium celebration than a somber and quiet cathedral! The psalmist tells us over and over that God's people celebrated God with shouts and clapping and trumpets and other instruments and even dancing. I can't wait! What a celebration it will be! Our God is so awesome! We can praise him for creating a wonderful world for us to live on. In a seminar for science teachers, I learned that if the chemistry of the air we breathe were changed just a tiny bit, we wouldn't be here. If the earth were just a little bit closer to the sun, we wouldn't be here. If the earth were just a little farther from the sun, we wouldn't be here. If the structure of every living cell did not have a cell membrane to hold it together, nothing would be here. How many more ways can we see the awesomeness of our Creator who designed all of these things? For me, it is not just the big things God has done, like creating all things or sending Jesus as our Redeemer, but all of the small things he has done for me as well. I cannot contain my joy when I consider the fact that he came seeking me long before I ever realized that I did not know him. He lifted me out of a pit of despair and showed me the depths of his love. He has spoken words of encouragement and life to me at just the right moment until I could know without a doubt that he loves me. Who am I that God should do this for me? God pursues each of his children with fervor because of his great love. He tears down thick walls of resentment and unbelief. He heals wounded hearts and minds. He rescues the needy and gives them bread from heaven and water from a rock. What a mighty God we serve!

God Wants Our Hearts

> Listen, my people, and I will speak; I will testify against you, Israel: I am God, your God. I bring no charge against you concerning your sacrifices or concerning your burnt offerings, which are ever before me. I have no need of a bull from your stall or of goats from your pens; for every animal of the forest is mine, and the cattle on a thousand hills. I know every bird in the mountains and the insects in the fields are mine. If I were hungry, I would not tell you, for the world is mine, and all that is in it. Do I eat the flesh of bulls, or drink the blood of goats? "Sacrifice thank offerings to God, fulfill your vows to the Most High, and call upon me in the day of trouble; I will deliver you, and you will honor me." (Psalm 50:7-15)

As I read the words of this Psalm this morning, I didn't pay attention to the fact that this passage is a rebuke to God's people because I was focused on something else, but now the verses are down on paper and I need to write about them! Why is God testifying against his people? They are bringing plenty of sacrifices to him, but sacrifices are not what God is looking for from his people. In fact, he doesn't need anything from us! He has everything he needs. So what is it that God wants from us? The same thing he has wanted from the very beginning of creation— God wants fellowship with us! He wants us, not our sacrifices! The purpose of the sacrifices was to atone for sin, so that we could be restored to fellowship with the Lord. What God is saying in the above passage is that the people have it all mixed up. They are offering sacrifices for the sake of sacrifices and are missing God's heart. The one thing that God desires from us that he cannot get on his own is our hearts. He gave us free will because he wanted us to give ourselves to him freely. He wants it to be our choice to come into relationship with him. Imagine that! The God who has everything still wants us! He longs to have us know him and to bring to him our praises and our thanks, not our sacrifices. He would rather that we fulfill our promises and not need the sacrifice. Have you ever wondered what God would do with your life if you surrendered it completely to him? You know what I mean, no holding back. Let him have his way in every area of your life; he calls all the shots. Think about what God has done in the past with those individuals who have given him total reign in their lives. Amazing! What might he do with you or with me? Hey, I have an idea…let's find out!

God Gives the Increase

> May the Lord cause you to flourish, both you and your children. May you be blessed by the Lord, the Maker of heaven and earth. The highest heavens belong to the Lord, but the earth he has given to man. It is not the dead who praise the Lord, those who go down to the place of silence; it is we who extol the Lord, both now and forevermore. Praise the Lord. (Psalm 115:14-18)

"May the Lord cause you to flourish. May you be blessed by the Lord." This is my prayer for you today. Just a few words of blessing that speak volumes. Take a few moments today to pass on the blessing. Take time to pray for anyone and everyone who comes to your mind, asking God to bless them and to make them flourish. I've been wondering what it means for God to make you flourish. Clearly it means to get more of something, but what? We could ask God to bless one another financially to be able to meet the needs of our families. We could ask God to increase our faith. I wonder how that might change our lives if each of us had a greater measure of faith. We could ask God to increase our love for our brethren. That could have a great impact on the family of God. We could ask God to increase our effectiveness in reaching out with the Gospel and the Kingdom would grow. We could ask God to increase our numbers, having more people with whom to serve him and to praise him. We say so often, "God bless you." Do we say it without really thinking about the implications? Today, what would your life look like if God blessed you? Of course, he has blessed each one of us in so many ways, but if he blessed you today, what shape might that blessing take. Would a blessing today bring a word of encouragement or a healing touch? Would it bring salvation for a loved one or hope in a dark circumstance? Would it bring light into a dark situation or flood your heart with joy? Whatever the blessing you need today, whatever way you are needing God's increase, may he grant it to you immeasurably beyond anything you could ask or think, and may you be blessed as you pass a blessing on to someone else today.

Pray for the Peace of Jerusalem

> Pray for the peace of Jerusalem: "May those who love you be secure. May there be peace within your walls and security within your citadels" For the sake of my family and friends, I will say, "Peace be within you." For the sake of the house of the Lord our God, I will seek your prosperity. (Psalm 122:6-9)

All of us share a heritage with Jerusalem. We all have a connection, since we all trace our lineage back to the family of Noah. From his lineage all the people on the earth have been born. It is good to pray for the city of Jerusalem as God's Word tells us. This city's history is throughout the Bible. It is the city where God's people dwell. Today there is much war that affects Jerusalem, and God's people have been scattered all over the world. We can and should pray for this entire region, since history confirms its significance. There will be a day coming when God's chosen people turn to Christ as

Messiah. We can pray toward that end. As yesterday's devotional was about blessing, these verses also hold a blessing. We can speak this blessing on behalf of the nation of Israel, but it is also a wonderful blessing for all of God's children—peace. Peace, security and prosperity are wonderful words of blessing to give to another. I did not live in a home filled with peace. There was a lot of strife and much chaos. There was a lot of fighting and violence, so I did not understand the concept of peace. God has had to teach me as an adult how to live in peace, for he gives peace to those he loves. If we are unaware of this truth then Satan may easily rob us of peace we never knew we had. There is nothing more wonderful than peace in your heart! There is no way for Satan to counterfeit the peace of God. It is a gift only God can give, and he gives it freely to his children. When we know God's peace, then his peace can reign in our homes and our lives. The Bible tells us to seek peace and pursue it. When you are filled with peace, you are a blessing to everyone around you. Today, may God restore your peace, and may your life be so characterized by peace that others will take notice. Pray for the peace of Jerusalem, and pray for the peace of the children of God around you.

Delight in God's People

Keep me safe, my God, for in you I take refuge. I said to the Lord, "You are my Lord; apart from you I have no good thing." I say of the holy people who are in the land, "They are the noble ones in whom is all my delight." (Psalm 16:1-3)

"I'm no saint," you might hear someone say, and it would probably be true. However, we who belong to Christ are all saints of God, whether we act like it or not! Just recently I was sharing with my fourth grade class about Saint Patrick. They thought Saint was his first name! We talked about what it means to be a saint and the wonderful work that Saint Patrick did for Christ. Christians are often uncomfortable with the idea that we are saints because we know every failure and how many ways we fall short of the mark. However, we are declared saints not because of our work, but because of Christ's work in us. To be a saint, one need only say to God, "You are my Lord; apart from you I have no good thing." The greatness of our God calls us to be saints before him. The psalmist declares that he delights in the glorious saints who surround him. We could learn a lot from that! Delight in God's people around us, consider them glorious and celebrate the work of God in and through them.

Transformed by Joy

> Many, Lord, are asking, "Who will bring us prosperity?" Let the light of your face shine on us. Fill my heart with joy when the grain and new wine abound. In peace I will lie down and sleep, for you alone, Lord, make me dwell in safety. (Psalm 4:6-8)

I don't know about you, but when I see the spring flower bulbs start popping up, it brings such joy to my heart. I love winter, but there is something absolutely miraculous about the transformation from winter to spring. As the sun shines, life just seems to pop up everywhere all at once. The days are getting longer, we have seen more sunny days, and even the rain showers don't dampen our spirits because spring brings such a promise of hope! It can also be this way in our hearts. Sometimes we go through periods where it seems there is no growth—no life. It is dark and dull, and it seems like it will always be that way. The light of God's presence has the same affect on our spirit as the sunshine on spring flowers; suddenly life bursts forth from the hard frozen ground and we are filled with joy and hope once again. Doesn't joy have a marvelous impact on our day-to-day lives? There is spring in our step and a song on our lips. We delight in what we have to do and smile at others who cross our path. When joy fills your heart, you can't help but share it! We are transformed by it! Hallelujah! May the light of God's face shine on you today, filling your heart with great joy, for he is with you. His love brings beauty from ashes, dancing where there was only mourning, and flowers from the cold, hard soil of winter!

What's in a Name?

> The Mighty One, God, the Lord, speaks and summons the earth from the rising of the sun to where it sets. From Zion, perfect in beauty, God shines forth. Our God comes and will not be silent; a fire devours before him, and around him a tempest rages. He

summons the heavens above, and the earth, that he may judge his people: "Gather to me this consecrated people, who made a covenant with me by sacrifice." And the heavens proclaim his righteousness, for he is a God of justice. (Psalm 50:1-6)

When I read Psalms it is as though God himself is speaking truth to me, reminding me of who I am in relation to who he is. This particular Psalm begins with three different names for addressing God: the Mighty One, God, and the Lord. If you have never studied the many names of God used throughout Scripture, I would encourage you to do so. Each different name of God teaches us so much about who he is and helps us understand his character. God is the Mighty One. He speaks and all of creation must obey. I am comforted by the mightiness of God, especially when the enemy presses in hard against me. God is all powerful. There is no foe that he cannot conquer. There is no problem too big for him, because he is Almighty! One word from him and the seas rise up. Another word and the raging seas are quieted. Because my God is Almighty, I know I am safe in his hands. Even when he allows me to go through trials, I know he is the One who measures when it is enough. The trials we face are not trivial to God, and he does not place us in the midst of trials arbitrarily. There is always a work to be accomplished for his glory. The Lord is another name the psalmist uses to address God in these verses. He is almighty, but the name Lord also tells us that he is sovereign over all. He reigns over all. When we call him Lord, we acknowledge that he is our Master, the One who leads us in the way we are to go. We will follow him because he is Lord. We also see in this passage that he is our judge. Everyone will face judgment one day. Can you imagine standing before a holy God knowing you rejected him your whole life? I cannot. Even when I understand and acknowledge God as my judge, I am comforted, because he has called me his own and provided for me a Savior, a Redeemer who has already paid the penalty for my sin, so that I can stand before the judge righteous by the blood of Christ.

God, Our Savior

Help us, God our Savior, for the glory of your name; deliver us and forgive our sins for your name's sake. (Psalm 79:9)

God our Savior is perhaps the most wonderful name for God that there is! As we consider all that the Lord has done for us, we are most grateful that he has saved us from eternal judgment and forgiven our sins. Christ came to earth to show us the way to the Father, but more than that, he made the way open for us by giving himself on the cross to pay the penalty for our sins. Can you imagine how he felt riding on that colt into Jerusalem almost two thousand years ago, knowing that the people who were praising him would reject him and cry out that he be crucified just a few days later? The people awaited a Savior, but they didn't understand that God would not only save them from their situation but the whole world from sin. They were so short-sighted that their worship of Christ as Savior was pitifully shallow. I wonder if we are like that sometimes too. We want him to rescue us, but we want him to do it our way, and when he doesn't, we reject him and think he has let us down. As we worship our Savior today, let us worship him in spirit and in truth. We have the joy of knowing that Christ's suffering brought redemption to the world. He is indeed our Savior. Let us celebrate the Savior's great sacrifice and offer him our praise and thanksgiving. *Oh God our Savior, how grateful we are for the high price you paid for our redemption! Forgive us for so often misunderstanding the work you are doing. We love you. Amen*

Jesus Is the King of Kings

Endow the king with your justice, O God, the royal son with your righteousness. May he judge your people in righteousness, your afflicted ones with justice. May the mountains bring prosperity to the people, the hills the fruit of righteousness. May he defend the afflicted among the people and save the children of the needy; may he crush the oppressor. May he endure as long as the sun, as long as the moon, through all generations. May he be like rain falling on a mown field, like showers watering the earth. In his days may the righteous flourish and prosperity abound till the moon is no more. May he rule from sea to sea and from the River to the ends of the earth. May the desert tribes bow before him and his enemies lick the dust. May the kings of Tarshish and of distant shores bring tribute to him. May the kings of Sheba and Seba present him gifts. May all kings bow down to him and all nations serve him. (Psalm 72:1-11)

Jesus was King of Kings when he walked upon this earth, and he is still the King of Kings as he prepares for the final battle with evil. He reigns forever and ever! Everything that is will bow down to him, though now many refuse to recognize his sovereignty. The day is not far off when he will judge the people of the earth and crush the oppressor for all time. God's people misunderstood him when he came to earth the first time. I wonder if God's people will do a better job at recognizing him at his second coming. Will our hearts be ready or will be looking in the wrong places? Because we look at the past with 20/20 vision, we wonder how the same people could cry out, "Hosanna!" in worship of the King on Palm Sunday, and then just a few short days later be crying out, "Crucify him!" We often misunderstand God's ways, don't we? Scripture is clear that his ways are not our ways. We are often arrogant enough to think we know better than God. Where would we really have been two thousand years ago? Would we have been with Jesus in the Upper Room to celebrate the Last Supper with him, or would we have sided with the crowd to have Jesus crucified? Do we acknowledge that he is King of Kings today, or are we still the king of our own castle? Does it make a difference to us that Jesus is the King over all kings? It should. It should give us hope and confidence. It should give us clear purpose and direction. It should give us a message to share that we cannot hold back.

When God Chooses to Use Us

But God is my King from long ago; he brings salvation to the earth. (Psalm 74:12)

As I left for work yesterday, I kept thinking about the Lord as our King, for he is not just the King of Kings; He is *our* King. The concept of king is foreign to us perhaps. Having a President who is supposed to be of the people, by the people and for the people leaves us often thinking we get to decide. We vote for our leaders, and when they let us down, we don't have any trouble getting rid of them, but a king is a king until he dies. What the king says is law, and his subjects must obey. Our King has brought salvation upon the earth. Hallelujah! Our King's boundaries are endless! Our King is limitless! Our King is eternal! Our King has conquered his enemies. Consider a king's soldiers. Do you think they struggle trying to decide what to do? Not at all!

The king's soldiers follow the king's orders whatever they are. They serve the king with their very lives, and so must we serve the King of Kings. We do not need to fret over what we ought to do; we need only to obey the voice of our King. What possible help could he need from us? He who created all things and holds them in place, he who makes rivers where there are none or dries up ones that are there, does he really need our help? Probably not. OK. Definitely not! Our King invites us to join him in the quest. He knows the blessing we will experience when we follow him in obedience. We will be filled to overflowing with joy when he uses us to bring salvation to the heart of a friend or acquaintance, or even a complete stranger. He chooses to use those who will follow and obey him, not because they must, but because they want to. Will we choose the life of obedience to the King?

One Nation under God

> Return to us, God Almighty! Look down from heaven and see! Watch over this vine, the root your hand has planted, the son you have raised up for yourself. Your vine is cut down; it is burned with fire; at your rebuke your people perish. Let your hand rest on the man at your right hand, the son of man you have raised up for yourself. Then we will not turn away from you; revive us, and we will call upon your name. Restore us, Lord God Almighty; make your face shine on us, that we might be saved. (Psalm 80:14-19)

God's people are described here as the root he has planted. If you have ever taken a root from a vine to replant, it usually isn't much to look at. In fact, often you might wonder if it will grow at all because it looks so small and pitiful. Our Father is an expert vinedresser. Imagine what that vine was like after spending forty years in the desert! I have had plants near to dead that when planted in the right place, have grown wonderfully. God's people have disappointed him so often, haven't they? He rescued them, and they would follow him for a while. How quickly they turned away to other gods and other peoples. We wonder how they could be so foolish not to see the Father's love for them. Why would they wander? We are not so very different from them. We pursue God with all of our hearts when we need him, but how quickly we get distracted with other things, other people, or even just living life. Our nation has been so blessed. Many of our founding fathers knew and trusted God. They built this nation upon godly principles and called us a nation under God. Now that phrase offends people. We are a nation that has wandered so far from our roots. Oh, how we need God to revive us and to restore us to himself. We need him to shine his glorious light upon us that we might be saved. Pray for our nation today, that God might pour out his Spirit once again in our land, drawing the hearts of the people back to him. Revive us, O God!

He Gave Himself

He sent Moses his servant, and Aaron, whom he had chosen. They performed his signs among them, his wonders in the land of Ham. He sent darkness and made the land dark— for had they not rebelled against his words? He turned their waters into blood, causing their fish to die. Their land teemed with frogs, which went up into the bedrooms of their rulers. He spoke, and there came swarms of flies, and gnats throughout their country. He turned their rain into hail, with lightning throughout their land; he struck down their vines and fig trees and shattered the trees of their country. He spoke, and the locusts came, grasshoppers without number; they ate up every green thing in their land, ate up the produce of their soil. Then he struck down all the firstborn in their land, the first fruits of all their manhood. He brought out Israel, laden with silver and gold, and from among their tribes no one faltered. Egypt was glad when they left, because dread of Israel had fallen on them. He spread out a cloud as a covering, and a fire to give light at night. They asked, and he brought them quail; he fed them well with the bread of heaven. He opened the rock, and water gushed out; it flowed like a river in the desert. For he remembered his holy promise, given to his servant Abraham. He brought out his people with rejoicing, his chosen ones with shouts of joy; he gave them the lands of the nations, and they fell heir to what others had toiled for--that they might keep his precepts and observe his laws. Praise the Lord. (Psalm 105:26-45)

Jesus celebrated the Passover meal with the disciples knowing it would be his last meal with them until the resurrection. He would become the very bread of heaven sent from God. His blood would be poured out for our sins. As we remember his sacrifice and all he has done for us, let us be filled with gratitude, and serve him with glad hearts.

Let Us Offer a Sacrifice of Praise

Those who sacrifice thank offerings honor me, and to the blameless I will show my salvation. (Psalm 50:23)

There are many who understand better than I what God meant here about sacrificing thank offerings. When I looked it up, I found that it was given as part of a peace offering, and it was more than just being thankful for what God has done. It was sacrifice. A sacrifice by definition costs something. David said he would offer God no sacrifice that had cost him nothing. This particular sacrifice was given in thanks to God for all he had given them, and it comprised three different types of bread. Some say this suggests the implication that we give thanks to God with body, mind and spirit. Christ paid it all for us. He gave his life that we might be set free from sin and be made holy for God in order that we could know God. What is left for us to do? We must accept Jesus' sacrifice offering and repent of our sins. There is a song I have sung with these words, "All that I can do is thank him…"[4] He has paid it all, so all that is left for us to do is thank him. We typically talk about giving thanks at Thanksgiving, but Easter is a wonderful time to offer thanks to God for all he has done for us. I think this goes beyond merely having a thankful heart, though most assuredly it must begin there. What sacrifice is there to merely being thankful of heart? Perhaps we need to offer our thanks at the altar of God, sharing openly with God's people a testimony of what the Lord has done for us. How might we encourage other believers as we share our story of how God redeemed us, and how he yet blesses us each and every day? All through the Bible we see the command to tell others what God has done, so the next generation will know him and praise him. Why are we so shy about sharing our story with others? Has the cost become too great? If we share, someone might judge or misunderstand. Maybe my story isn't as good as your story, so I should be quiet and let you share yours.

Perhaps we are just afraid to speak in public. Whatever the reason, we have lost the art of telling God's story. We must remember that our testimony blesses and honors God. He wants us to tell others what he has done for us. He wants to use our story to be part of someone else's story. Our fear is perhaps what makes it a sacrifice. Jesus paid it all, should we not honor him by telling others what a wondrous thing he has done in our lives?

Only the Eternal Will Last

No one can redeem the life of another or give to God a ransom for them—the ransom for a life is costly, no payment is ever enough—so that they should live on forever and not see decay. For all can see that the wise die; that the foolish and the senseless also perish, leaving their wealth to others. (Psalm 49:7-10)

What no one else could do, Jesus did. Jesus paid the ransom for my life and yours. That payment was his very life. He suffered ridicule and an agonizing death on the cross, so that our debt could be paid. Though our bodies will one day decay, our spirit will live forever with him if we have accepted his wonderful gift of salvation. There is no man or woman on earth who can make their way to heaven by their wealth, power or prestige. There is only one way, and that is through the redeeming blood of Jesus Christ. Why is there only one way? The world certainly does not agree or like that Christians believe theirs is the only way to heaven. The reason is found in the verses above. The ransom for a life is costly. No other human being has ever led a sinless life. No other sacrifice compares to the sacrifice Jesus made on the cross for all who would believe. Our time in this world is but a blink of an eye in comparison to eternity. We must spend our time here wisely, for only the eternal will last.

He Lives!

The Lord lives! Praise be to my Rock! Exalted be God my Savior! (Psalm 18:46)

It is so difficult for me to imagine having the Lord to walk with and talk with in a physical body like the disciples did. On the other hand, I can not fathom the grief of losing him to the cross, not understanding his plan. The sorrow seems much too great to even consider. Though I have lost loved ones to death, Jesus was the long-expected Messiah. When he finally came, what a blessed relief it must have been. The Savior had come! Everything was going to change. It certainly did, but it changed in ways the young disciples could not even have imagined. Though Jesus explained to them what must happen, I think they really had no idea what he was telling them until the whole ordeal was over and he was gone. Their Lord was gone! From Friday afternoon until Sunday when they got the news that he had risen, it must have been agony. Though he had told them he would rise again, they really weren't looking for him. They believed he was gone forever. What a glorious moment for each of them when they knew the truth! He lives! The Lord lives! They saw him and walked with him again, and even though it was only for forty days, it was enough to restore their faith, to restore their hope, and to renew their purpose. Jesus is alive! There must have been dancing and shouting and great celebration! The experience of the resurrection changed them forever! They began to understand. Jesus had conquered death! He was indeed the Savior, the long-awaited Messiah! It was true! It was all true! I wonder. Do we live like Jesus is alive? Do we really understand that our Savior lives? Does the resurrection make any difference at all in our lives? Death has no victory over God's people! Hallelujah! He is alive!

Confidence in God

> I will sacrifice a freewill offering to you; I will praise your name,
> Lord, for it is good. You have delivered me from all my troubles,
> and my eyes have looked in triumph on my foes. (Psalm 54:6-7)

David was rescued by God many times, and many times God had given him victory over his enemies. From the time David was a young boy, he had learned to trust the God who was with him in times of trouble. The hours he spent tending sheep and singing his songs of praise to God were never wasted. In those quiet moments of worship, David got to know God, so that later when he faced many trials, he already knew that God would help him, protect him, and sustain him. David said when he faced Goliath, that he had learned of God's faithfulness to provide protection when he faced lions and bears that would attack the sheep. If God had given victories then, he would surely go before him in greater battles. What confidence David had in his God! Do you ever wonder how a person can have that kind of confidence? It doesn't just happen by accident. David loved and worshiped his God every moment of the day. He knew how to meditate on God's Word and he trusted God in things both little and great. David did not simply know about God, he knew God and loved him. His childlike trust continued on into his adult life because at each place of testing he chose to put his trust in God. He believed that God loved him and was on his side. He wanted his life to glorify the Lord, and his choices reflect that. Is there trouble in your life right now? Come before the Lord and offer him your praise. Put your faith on the altar and choose to trust the God who loves you more than anything. He will be faithful and will lead you to victory.

Be Still My Soul

> Yes, my soul, find rest in God; my hope comes from him. Truly he is my rock and my salvation; he is my fortress, I will not be shaken. (Psalm 62:5-6)

I don't know about you, but my soul is not always at rest in God. Sometimes I get anxious because circumstances seem so out of control. My emotions can so easily get the best of me, and my trust in God seems so very small. I have learned from the psalmist that at those times, I need to talk to myself. As the psalmist speaks to his soul telling it to be at rest, I have learned that finding rest and keeping peace are more a matter of choice than emotions. I do not have to give in to raging emotions. I can stand on the Word of God as my rock and my refuge and command my soul to be at rest. I realize these words are much easier for me to speak, and even believe, than to actually do them. It seems there is a brief window where our emotions are manageable, and beyond that they veer out of control. I must recognize early, and sometimes often, that I am losing it, and in that moment come running to my refuge, the God who loves me. On the way, I remind my soul that my rest and my peace are with God alone. He will meet my need. He will guide me on the way. He will see me through. He will help me in my time of need. I will trust his unfailing love. I will trust his will for my life. I will rest in the knowledge that he is in all, over all, and though all. He is my rock.

Homesick for Heaven

How lovely is your dwelling place, Lord Almighty! My soul yearns, even faints, for the courts of the Lord; my heart and my flesh cry out for the living God. Even the sparrow has found a home, and the swallow a nest for herself where she may have her young—a place near your altar, Lord Almighty, my King and my God. Blessed are those who dwell in your house; they are ever praising you. Blessed are those whose strength is in you, whose hearts are set on pilgrimage. As they pass through the Valley of Baca, they make it a place of springs; the autumn rains also cover it with pools. They go from strength to strength, till each appears before God in Zion. (Psalm 84:1-7)

I heard a sermon once about being homesick for heaven. The preacher expounded on the fact that we are strangers in this world, and our true home is in heaven with God. Those who love him have a longing to be with him. We are on a pilgrimage, and the journey is often very difficult and long, though not compared to eternity. The Valley of Baca was part of the journey. It was a difficult place. Those who love God do not let the valley be their focus. It says here they make it a place of springs. Perhaps there are so many tears that it would make pools in the desert, but God's children keep their eyes on their King, the Lord Almighty, for he is their strength. As they journey the difficult road, they remember that he is their strength. He will bring them through, and when the difficult road is at an end, they will finally reach his dwelling place. We may get discouraged along the way, but God will lift us up. He blesses those who draw near to him. Let us keep our focus on him and continue on in our pilgrimage praising the Almighty God who leads us onward.

A Flowing Fountain

You answer us with awesome deeds of righteousness, God our Savior, the hope of all the ends of the earth and of the farthest seas, who formed the mountains by your power, having armed yourself with strength, who stilled the roaring of the seas, the roaring of the waves, and the turmoil of the nations. The whole earth is filled with awe at your wonders; where morning dawn, where evening fade, you call forth songs of joy. (Psalm 65:5-8)

These two sentences are so packed with encouragement that as you meditate on them today I am sure God will bless you over and over again. God's Word is like a flowing fountain, isn't it? You drink it in, but it never dries up! It is always there ready to refresh your weary spirit! Praise God for his living Word! We don't always like the way God answers our prayers, do we? Sometimes he gives us what we ask for and sometimes he does not, but he always answers us with righteous deeds and out of the utmost of love for us and for our loved ones. He always answers us with eternity in mind—somehow, not just for today, not just for us, but for those who see us, those who wonder about the God we serve. Our Savior is the hope of the whole world! He saves us from death. He saves us from our sin. He saves us from trouble. He saves us from ourselves even! He pursues us with his tender heart, drawing us into his gentle arms where he can minister to our broken, bleeding spirit. He knows our need, and he who formed the tallest mountain has the strength and the grace to form in us what is lacking today. He longs to complete the work he has begun in us, but unlike the mountains and the seas, he will not cross the boundary of our will. We may decide if we want God's help today. He will not intrude where you have not given him permission to work, but how amazing it is when we allow him to calm the raging seas in our lives! Oh, when we allow him to calm the turmoil swirling in our hearts, he is able to fill us to overflowing with songs of joy! Oh, how he longs to fill us with his songs of joy as we rest in him and find all of our strength in him whatever storm we face.

He Longs to Lead Us

Remember the wonders he has done, his miracles and the judgments he pronounced, you his servants, the descendants of Abraham, his chosen one, the children of Jacob. He is the Lord our God; his judgments are in all the earth. He remembers his covenant forever, the promise he made, for a thousand generations. (Psalm 105:5-8)

I have heard from so many of you how God is using these short devotionals to encourage you and strengthen your faith, and that has been such a blessing to me! To see God using the words he has given me to encourage and strengthen the faith of others is humbling and at the same time glorious! How powerful are the words of God! It is utterly amazing to think how often I sit down to write and think I have nothing to say, and then I open Psalms searching for something to share. Sometimes I still sit there wondering how there could possibly be anything more to say, and then I just start writing and the words seem to come pouring out! The Spirit of God knows so well what we need! When we open up a devotional and God just speaks to our hearts through those words, it is clear that he knows us. He loves us. He longs to lead us in the way we should go! When we look to him and seek his face, we will always find strength and courage to face whatever trials may come because he is with us! I love when he so clearly reminds us that he is with us! When we stop and think about all he has done, our discouragement quickly flees, because we are able to see his faithfulness. Then we know once again that he has not forgotten nor forsaken us. Though today we may not understand why he has brought us to this particular path on the journey, we can rest in the knowledge that he is here. He knows that we need him so desperately, and in one quiet moment we are comforted because the Most High God has reminded us of his wondrous love. *Bless the Lord, O my soul! And all that is within me bless his holy name!*

Ready for the Test

> Search me, God, and know my heart; test me and know my anxious thoughts. See if there is any offensive way in me, and lead me in the way everlasting. (Psalm 139:23-24)

As a teacher, I know how I feel when a student comes to me and says, "I know my spelling list, teacher, give me the test!" There is confidence in those words, and although I know they may not be as ready as they think they are, they have spent time preparing for the test, and I know they will likely do well. Teachers love to have students who are eager to learn. These students make the difficult job of teaching worthwhile. I wonder how God feels when we come to him in such a way. I wonder if he smiles and thinks to himself, "She is not quite as ready for this test as she thinks she is." It must delight the Lord just that we have come to him trusting him enough to be transparent with him. Confident, not in ourselves, but in the Lord, knowing that the work he is doing in us must be completed. This simple prayer acknowledges to God that we trust him enough to have him examine our hearts, even the places we do not see. We are completely yielded to him, wanting him to expose any unrighteousness that he might see in us that we have hidden even from ourselves. This simple prayer says to God that we are not afraid to have him examine our life—not because we think we are perfect, but because we want to be holy as he is holy—so we yield to the test. Since I have struggled with anxiety, this simple prayer means so much to me. It gives me the words to tell God that I know I struggle with anxious thoughts, but I want his help to overcome them. I know God's testing is not for his sake, but for mine. It helps me to see how much—or how little—I have grown. It keeps me relying on my Savior, because I know he cares for me. When I am most vulnerable with God, I find out how gentle and loving he is. I wouldn't trade that for anything!

Are You Flourishing?

> The righteous will flourish like a palm tree, they will grow like a cedar of Lebanon; planted in the house of the Lord, they will flourish in the courts of our God. (Psalm 92:12-13)

I grew up in the small city of Lebanon in Pennsylvania, and I graduated from Lebanon High School. We were called the Cedars of Lebanon, and our school mascot was a cedar tree! Cedar trees are very tall and evergreen. They are strong trees that can withstand much. As long as I live that image will come to mind whenever I read this Psalm. The imagery of these verses is amazing, isn't it? If you have been to a place where palm trees grow, you know how beautiful they are. They are also tall and strong, and they bear much fruit. God's people, the righteous, will continue to grow and flourish even when they are old. Flourish means so much more than just to grow. It means to grow profusely! It means to thrive. I bought a small palm tree the other week, and it is growing in my house. The leaves are already turning yellow! For a palm tree to grow, the conditions need to be just right. They need warm sunshine and enough rain to keep them watered. As God's children, we ought to be encouraged by these verses. With God to guide us, we will continue to grow, bear fruit, and be strong even into old age. As we drink deeply from the Word of God, and reach daily for the warmth of the Son, we will grow and keep growing tall and strong. Are we bearing fruit? We should be. If not, we can if we will let God continue the work of growth in our lives. Growth is not an end in itself. We do not grow for the sake of growing, but that we reach full maturity and bear much fruit. Bearing fruit is a natural part of the growth process. As we grow, we must give what we have been given to others so that they will grow too.

He Lifts My Burdens

> I removed the burden from their shoulders; their hands were set free from the basket. In your distress you called and I rescued you, I answered you out of a thundercloud; I tested you at the waters of Meribah. (Psalm 81:6-7)

Oh how we need God! How often do we call to him in our distress and find him faithful to answer our prayers? There are so very many things in life that can bring us distress. medical issues, relationship issues, issues with our kids, issues with our parents, issues at work, issues with our neighbors, issues with addictions, and the list could go on. Those things that distress us can be like a burden around our neck, weighing us down until we can barely function. When we are in distress, there is usually no easy answer, no quick fix, and the fact that there appears to be no immediate solution adds to the burden, doesn't it? I have to admit, I actually get a little lost when I am in distress. I get confused about what I know is true. I spend a lot of energy trying to figure out solutions or ways to deal with problems for which there are no real solutions. I can get pretty weighed down too, before I finally remember that the burden I carry is not too heavy for God! He longs to lift my burden and ease my distress if I will let go of it and let him have it. Why is it so hard to let go sometimes? Why do we long to be released from our burden but hang on to it with all our might? Maybe it is just me who struggles with issues of control. I can see that the problem is too big for me. I know that it is not too big for God, but I am too often afraid to give it to him because that somehow feels like a loss of control. Yes, that is exactly it! I cannot keep control of a situation and let God have control at the same time! I have to believe God loves me and will manage my situation in the best way before I can let go. I have to trust him. He is trustworthy. I am the one who struggles with trust. He is able to help me even to release my burden to him. He is able to reassure me that my burden is safe with him. He will lift it from my shoulders, and I can rest in his loving arms. Oh, the peace that comes when we finally choose to let go and let God have the situations that cause our distress!

Look to the Lord

> I lift up my eyes to you, to you who sit enthroned in heaven. As the eyes of slaves look to the hand of their master, as the eyes of a female slave look to the hand of her mistress, so our eyes look to the Lord our God till he shows us his mercy. (Psalm 123:1-2)

Oh God, I am so grateful that I can look to you and know that you care about me. You know my needs. You know my heart. You know the solution to every problem I will ever have. You promise wisdom, Lord, to those who ask for it. You grant grace and mercy when we need it. You long for us to turn to you, O God, and how it pleases you when we obey the calling of your voice! Oh Lord God Most High, I lift my eyes to you today, seeking your guidance and your help. I seek your direction, Lord, because I want to follow the path you have laid for me. Lord, I know that too often I let my eyes get turned to other things, and I am easily distracted. Help me to keep my eyes firmly fixed on you. I look to you today, Lord, for the help I need. I ask for your blessing, Father, so that I might be a blessing to others around me. As I encounter problems today, let my eyes turn to you for your wisdom and your peace that passes all understanding. I love you, Lord, and long to serve you with an undivided heart, seeking only to do your will. Please glorify yourself in my life today. Amen

Refiner's Fire

> For you, God, tested us; you refined us like silver. You brought us into prison and laid burdens on our backs. You let people ride over our heads; we went through fire and water, but you brought us to a place of abundance. (Psalm 66:10-12)

God refines his people like silver. I grew up near the Cornwall Furnace where they once refined iron ore into steel. The refining process is slow and the heat intense. It is amazing that the psalmist is commanding the people to praise God in light of such testing, but that is what he is saying here. Of course, we understand that the time of refining and testing is already in the past tense, and the people of God have been brought to a place of abundance. It is much easier to praise God when the refining is done! Why is all this refining necessary anyway? I have a silver necklace that my husband bought in Mexico. I treasure it even though it is not refined. Its luster is dull and it doesn't have the beautiful finish of other silver jewelry that I have. Without refining, we are still a treasure to God, but just as silver becomes more valuable after it has gone through the refining process, so are we more fit for God's service when the impurities of sin are burned off through the refiner's fire. Oh, how often I would have jumped out of the fire because the heat was so intense! Oh, how many times I thought I would not get through the process! Praise God! Our times of refining do not go on without end! We can look forward to the place of abundance! We can praise God that the impurities that kept us from glorifying God with a pure heart have been removed, and we can praise God that he is like the skillful silversmith. He knows just how much time to keep us in the heat and when it is enough. God is a skillful craftsman. He sees us as the finished treasure! Praise God for His refining work in our lives. If you are in the midst of the fire, hold tight; it will be worth it in the end!

Rescued from the Flood

> Save me, O God, for the waters have come up to my neck. I sink in the miry depths, where there is no foothold. I have come into the deep waters; the floods engulf me. I am worn out calling for help; my throat is parched. My eyes fail, looking for God. (Psalm 69:1-3)

When I was a little girl, a hurricane on the eastern seaboard had brought heavy rain to our area, and just down the street from my house the water was more than a foot deep in the street. My dad owned another house which stood right along a channel that normally had just a few inches of water in it. During this storm, a wall of water had come raging past, leaving more than three feet of water, mud, and debris on the first floor of the homes on that street. The people had to be rescued by boat from their rooftops! It was shocking to see how much filth and damage was left behind when the water receded. The clean up took months. I remember my dad telling us not to go in the water because the current was so strong it would have carried us away. Life can get like this for us sometimes too. All of a sudden you find yourself inundated with problems or situations that have gone from a small stream to a raging river overnight. You cry out to God to save you, but you cannot see him, hear him, or feel him near. Just when you need him, he seems to be gone. What can you do? The psalmist is always honest with God about how he is doing, and he always remembers the truth he knows. God is near, whether he can see him or not, and God has always been faithful and rescued him before. No situation is too big for God. I find it so easy to get focused on the raging flood waters that seem to be getting higher and higher. Fear can carry me away just like the current unless I get myself on something solid where I can hold on until help comes. In fact, there have been times when I couldn't hold on any longer, and the current of events threatened to sweep me away! It was then I learned that even when I cannot see, hear, or feel God nearby, he is, and he is holding on to me even when I am worn out and too tired to hold on to him. He has always been faithful to rescue me in due time. I rest in this truth and know that he will be faithful. He will save me. He is with me in the midst of the flood. He is the solid rock to which I cling.

God's Faithfulness in Your Time of Affliction

Your hands made me and formed me; give me understanding to learn your commands. May those who fear you rejoice when they see me, for I have put my hope in your word. I know, Lord, that your laws are righteous, and that in faithfulness you have afflicted me. May your unfailing love be my comfort, according to your promise to your servant. (Psalm 119:73-76)

When we find ourselves with health issues, it is often confusing and scary. The outcome is never guaranteed, and doctors don't know everything about anything. It is certainly a comfort to know that God knows everything about everything! He formed us and made us. He knows not only every hair on our heads but every cell in our bodies. He can cure anything in a moment with just one word. I think that is why sometimes it is difficult for us to understand why he doesn't always do that. I am pretty sure it would take at least one book and someone a whole lot more knowledgeable than me to explain the answer to that dilemma! Nevertheless, there are some things we do know that can encourage us in these situations. First, God knows our situation, and he is with us. If we are afflicted with a health issue, God has allowed it in our lives for some reason we may never fully know. He will see us through, giving us the strength we need to meet the challenge. He promises to guide us and give us wisdom, and he will give us as much grace as we need; his unfailing love will be our comfort. We live in a fallen world. Sickness and disease are a part of the world in which we live. Christians are not immune. Who can understand why God allows some to be healthy and some spend their lives battling health issues? For today, we must trust God through whatever situation he has placed us. He is our hope and our strength. Whatever we are going through, God will use it somehow for eternity. The Word of God tells us that in comparison to eternity, these struggles are light and momentary. Take a moment today to lift up those who are facing battles with health today.

Seek the Lord

> Blessed are those whose ways are blameless, who walk according to the law of the Lord. Blessed are they who keep his statutes and seek him with all their heart--they do no wrong, but follow his ways. You have laid down precepts that are to be fully obeyed. Oh, that my ways were steadfast in obeying your decrees! Then I would not be put to shame when I consider all your commands. I will praise you with an upright heart as I learn your righteous laws. I will obey your decrees; do not utterly forsake me. (Psalm 119:1-8)

We are so blessed! God has given us so much. If we just started listing every blessing God has given us, we could write for days! Reading the words at the beginning of Psalm 119, we might get the idea that we deserve the blessings God has given us. "They are blessed whose ways are blameless."

Do you know anyone who is blameless? Not on this planet! All of us have sinned and fallen short of the glory of God. We are blameless because of the blood of Jesus Christ which has cleansed us from all unrighteousness. In him, we are considered blameless. Praise God! We are blessed if we keep God's statutes and seek him with all our hearts. Have you ever stopped to wonder what it means to seek God with all your heart or if you were doing that? I was so moved by that question that I did a word study on the word *seek* and found it very interesting and quite challenging! This word *seek* is not like hide and seek where God is hiding from us and we have to seek him! Quite the opposite! God longs for his children to seek him, so that he can lead us in the right way. He longs to bless us. He longs to reveal more of himself to us, so that we will know him in the same way that he knows us. I have found so many verses throughout the Bible that indicate that God's people should be seeking him and several which indicate that most are not doing that. Seeking God is the opposite of what Adam and Eve did in the Garden after they had sinned. They hid from God, because they were ashamed of their sin. Sadly, we still do that today. We know we fall short of the mark, so we keep our distance from God because we fear he will reject us, or we choose not to seek God because we are afraid. We are not afraid of God so much as we are afraid he might ask us to do something we don't want to do. We sometimes choose not to seek God because we are just too busy, and we are sure God will understand. He does. He understands that we are busy doing a lot of things he has not told us to do, so we are not available to him. Friends, this is a critical truth. If we are too busy to have time with God, we are too busy! We often fail to seek God because we do not know what that is or that we should be doing it. Seeking God is not hard, but it does take time. It also takes a heart willing to obey whatever and wherever he leads. It is difficult to even describe the blessing there is to those who seek him with all their hearts! For those who seek him find him, and those who find God will know the greatest intimacy with him possible on this side of heaven. With intimacy comes faith that is stronger, confidence in him that is unshakable, and an understanding of spiritual truths that will encourage us to draw even nearer to our God. You won't know what you are truly missing until you choose to seek him with all your heart. Today is a good day to start!

Replace Your Complaints with Praise

> Why, my soul, are you downcast? Why so disturbed within me?
> Put your hope in God, for I will yet praise him, my Savior and
> my God. (Psalm 43:5)

There are times when I know I gravitate to being a little like Winnie the Pooh's friend Eeyore. Once you have battled with depression, there are times when it will come knocking at your door to see if you will entertain it again. If you are honest, you have to admit it is tempting. When your soul is downcast, there is a shadow covering everything. You are sure there are good reasons to feel a little down, and so you give in to it. The psalmist is wise, though, and does not keep going on this slippery slope. No, he speaks to his soul, the core of his being, his spirit, and he asks what is there to be so disturbed about. Whatever it is that has you looking down, stop it. Look up! Put your hope in God. Think about the many ways he has blessed you. Think about the fact that he is with you and he will lead you on this dark road. Remember that he loves you and will lift you up when you fall. You are his. It won't be long before a song of worship is filling you lips with praise instead of complaints.

God's Treasured Possession

> Praise the Lord. Praise the name of the Lord; praise him you
> servants of the Lord, you who minister in the house of the Lord,
> in the courts of the house of our God. Praise the Lord, for the
> Lord is good; sing praise to his name, for that is pleasant. For the
> Lord has chosen Jacob to be his own, Israel to be his treasured
> possession. (Psalm 135:1-4)

Do you ever take time to ponder the fact that God chose you to be his treasured possession? Sometimes, I think, we get it backwards and think that we are Christians because we chose God. Oh, we may have said yes to God, but if we are his, it is because he has chosen us. He pursued us, wooed us, and drew us to himself. It is only when he reveals himself to us through his Holy Spirit that we are even able to understand that he is God. When you think about your faith story, can you identify the ways in which God got your attention and how he began to stir in your heart until you surrendered to his saving grace? When I was a teenager, my family did not attend church. My dad had had a disagreement with his pastor long before I was old enough to remember and never set foot in a church again except for weddings and funerals. There were two churches within a block of our house, though, and I can remember lying in bed every Sunday morning hearing the sound of the church bells calling to me, "Come to my church. Come to my church." Sometimes I did get up and go. When I left home to attend college, I found myself with a Christian roommate. We lived on a floor with several other Christian girls who invited us to come along to the InterVarsity Christian Fellowship meetings. They even encouraged me to bring my guitar and play along as they sang. I began to sense the nearness of God and had many questions. Being too shy to ask my questions, I just kept quiet. As I watched and interacted with all those Christians, God answered every one of my questions through the conversations of others, and I never had to say a word! How amazing to know that God wanted me to be his child so much that he pursued me until I understood his call! Praise the name of the Lord! He called you by your name and drew you to himself. Hallelujah! We are his!

The Purpose-Filled Life

> Though I walk in the midst of trouble, you preserve my life. You stretch out your hand against the anger of my foes, with your right hand you save me. The Lord will vindicate me; your love, Lord, endures forever—do not abandon the works of your hands. (Psalm 138:7-8)

On our journey through Psalms, we have seen some common themes reoccurring in many of the verses. When God's people are in trouble, he saves them. He deals with their enemies, and his love for them never fails. We also see again and again that God has a purpose for our lives. Several years ago Rick Warren wrote a book that became popular in Christian circles called *The Purpose-Driven Life*[5]. It came out in book form and then in a variety of devotional type books and has been a great evangelism tool, because people long to know that their life has purpose and meaning. We need to know that there is a reason we are here on this earth. We have heard that people without a vision (purpose) perish. Why is it, then, that so few people really seem to know what their purpose is? We grow up and get a job, but that does not always mean we know our purpose, does it? The disciples were fishermen before Jesus called them, but he made them fishers of men. Since my first day of school, I have wanted to be a teacher, and even when I was raising my babies I was busy teaching Lamaze classes and Bible studies. However, every day I am sensing a greater purpose for which God is preparing me. I see that in the lives of others as well. Our purpose in life is much more eternity centered than vocational, I think. It is much more about how our life touches others than about making a name for ourselves. Can it be that our purpose is the very same purpose of those early disciples—to be fishers of men (and women)? Well, I may never be a great fisherman, but could it be that all of the abilities and talents God has given me are supposed to be used to draw others around me to Jesus? Could it be that until I discover how to do that in the life situation God has place me, I may never know the joy of living a life filled with purpose? How can we discover our true purpose? There is only one way that I know—ask the One who created you. It is he who will fulfill his purpose in you.

The Earth Is the Lord's

The earth is the Lord's, and everything in it, the world, and all who live in it; for he founded it on the seas and established it upon the waters. (Psalm 24:1-2)

As I am writing this, it is Earth Day, so I thought it appropriate to remind us that the earth we are to be taking care of belongs to the Lord. Oh, if we could really and truly grasp the full depth of understanding that the earth is the Lord's and everything in it! This verse says that all who live on the earth belong to him. When I watch the children building with Legos at recess, sometimes it brings this fact home to me a little more. Whatever they build fills them with so much joy! They love to come and show me what they made and how it works! When it is time to put away the toys, they want to know where they can put their creation so that no one else will mess with it. Even on such a small scale, we can see that creating something gives us the feeling of ownership, doesn't it? That is what the second verse says above, God founded the earth. He created it. It is his. Being good stewards of this earth was God's idea in the Garden of Eden, but it is nice that for at least one day out of the year the rest of the world joins us in thinking about how we can care for the earth. It is too bad that most of God's creatures here on this earth do not know him as their creator. *God, we love you! We are so thankful for this earth you have given us on which to live. Forgive us for not taking better care of it. Forgive those, Lord, who do not acknowledge you as their creator. Open the eyes of the blind, Lord, and let them see you in all your glory. Open the ears of the deaf, God, that they might hear your majestic voice declaring your love for them. Give understanding, Father, to the foolish and help them to recognize your grace and mercy and turn to you. Amen*

God Keeps His Promises

The Lord is faithful to all his promises and loving toward all he has made. (Psalm 145:13b)

Yesterday as we were getting ready for a charity auction, we saw a double rainbow! The first bow was visible from one side to the other. It was such an awesome encouragement to us! Our God is a God who keeps his promises! Hallelujah! He promises to never leave us nor forsake us. Hallelujah! He promises to protect us in time of trouble. Hallelujah! He promises to keep us safe from our enemies. Hallelujah! He promises to guide our steps and light our path. Hallelujah! He promises to give us wisdom when we ask. Hallelujah! He promises to meet our needs and to care for us. Hallelujah! Our God is a God who keeps his promises.

Keep Your Eyes Fixed on Jesus

But my eyes are fixed on you, Sovereign Lord; in you I take refuge—do not give me over to death. Keep me from the traps set by evildoers, from the snares they have laid for me. Let the wicked fall into their own nets, while I pass by in safety. (Psalm 141:9-10)

In the twenty-eighth chapter of Deuteronomy, the Lord tells his people, "I have set before you life and death, therefore choose life." Sadly, often

God's people choose death over life, not physical death necessarily, but spiritual death. As followers of Christ, we must realize how important it is to keep our eyes fixed on the Lord, to take refuge in him and nothing else. Technology has changed since Old Testament days, but the human heart has not. We are so prone to seeking after the wrong things or the wrong people, aren't we? We do not have to look very far to name a handful of successful Christian ministers who have fallen because of choices leading to death— death of a ministry, death of a relationship, etc. In any conversation where these people are mentioned, Christians tend to judge them very harshly, as though they could never make such a mistake. Do you think any one of those ministers set out to make a stupid choice? No, but it happened. Why? The verses above give us some perspective on this. There are going to be snares and traps for all of us, but those of us in leadership roles are particular targets of the enemy. If he can ruin a whole ministry, a whole church, or a whole family, he will. No one is immune. We can avoid such pitfalls if we always remember to fix our eyes on Christ. We do that naturally when things are going poorly, but we must also remember to stay close to the Lord when times are good. When times are very good, we better keep on the alert, because surely there will be some testing ahead!

Bloom Where You Are Planted

It was you who set all the boundaries of the earth; you made both summer and winter. (Psalm 74:17)

When winter is over and the spring flowers begin to bloom, I start looking on the hillsides for trillium. I love that God is so creative! There are so many unique varieties of flowers and plants. Even more, I love that God is a lover of beauty. I know that because he decorates the woods and meadows with so many beautiful wildflowers. They come up every year unattended, planted only by the Creator! Trillium is the most beautiful, delicate wildflower I have ever seen! Looking at it, you are sure it would need to be tended and cared for. I understand you can't just take some and plant it anywhere. It grows best wild, so you have to go where it grows to enjoy it, and I had never seen it growing wild until I moved to the mountains. Whenever I see the trillium growing wild, I am reminded of God's love of beauty and the wonderful care he takes of his creation. It blesses me to see such beauty there on the hillside, put there by God simply to be enjoyed. Perhaps God sees me in this same way. Perhaps when he looks at me, he smiles and is blessed just to see me blossoming where he has planted me.

Letting Go of Perfectionism

> Out of the depths I cry to you, Lord; Lord, hear my voice. Let your ears be attentive to my cry for mercy. If you, Lord, kept a record of sins, Lord, who could stand? But with you there is forgiveness; so that we can, with reverence, serve you. (Psalm 130:1-4)

How glad I am that when I cry out to the Lord, he not only hears my voice, but he brings me comfort and encouragement! I am learning to be content with myself, not in a complacent sort of way, but to accept the fact that I am going to fail and make mistakes. Daily there are ways that I just do not hit the mark of righteousness, but I can come to the Lord and be forgiven. I can surrender again those things that cause me trouble and know that he will forgive me. He will help me. It is not God who expects me to be perfect; it is me. God has made a way for my failures to be forgiven, so I can let go and continue to move forward. This is not to say that I ought to think it is ok to do wrong or fail to live up to the holiness of God. It never is! When I do fall short, though, I have a Savior who forgives me. He is the righteousness I need, and he will finish what he has started in me.

Guard Your Words

> I call to you, Lord, come quickly to me; hear me when I call to you. May my prayer be set before you like incense; may the lifting up of my hands be like the evening sacrifice. Set a guard over my mouth, Lord; keep watch over the door of my lips. Do not let my heart be drawn to what is evil so that I take part in wicked deeds along with those who are evildoers; do not let me taste of their delicacies. (Psalm 141:1-4)

How often do we say things that we shouldn't? If you are like me, it happens way more than you want to admit! What comes out of the mouth is a reflection of what is in the heart. James tells believers to control our tongues. This is much easier said than done, isn't it? I am getting better at it as the years go by, but still when I am tired or not feeling well, my lips quickly give way to harshness. My words become critical and complaining and seem to escape from my mouth before I can stop them. Is it hopeless then? I don't think so. I think the key is in the first two verses. When we know that we are in a vulnerable condition, we must call to the Lord and ask for his help. We must pray instead of grumble. We can voice our complaint before the Lord and let him purify our thoughts. When I lift my hands to him in surrender of my will to his, it is amazing how trivial those things that irritate me become and how quickly my heart can be refreshed. The key is to recognize our own shortcomings and cry out to the Lord before the words we might speak have a chance to form on our lips. One second's hesitation may be too late. The key to taming the tongue lies in our hearts and in our minds. If we want what comes from our lips to only glorify God, then we must pursue pure thoughts and a pure heart. At the first sign of trouble, we must call out quickly to the One who is able to redeem even our lips, turning our grumbles and complaints into praise before him. The wicked speak their minds freely, not caring whom they hurt in their paths. This should not be so of God's children. Let us desire his holiness all the way from head to toe.

God's Grace Is Enough

> Awake, Lord! Why do you sleep? Rouse yourself! Do not reject us forever. Why do you hide your face and forget our misery and oppression? We are brought down to the dust; our bodies cling to the ground. Rise up and help us; rescue us because of your unfailing love. (Psalm 44:23-26)

We know that God never slumbers nor sleeps, but have you ever felt that he must have dozed off while your situation got out of control? For our family, it was a health issue. Our son had been born with a problem in his bladder that affected his kidney function. The doctor had scheduled a test to help us determine how well his kidneys were working, and I will never forget that day. The phone call came telling us that our little boy's kidneys had gone from almost a hundred percent function down to fifty-four percent! In a moment everything changed, and when you get done crying and run to God, you have to wonder if he fell asleep. How did it get so bad so quickly? I cried most of the day. The situation was not hopeless, but there would be some adjustments to make. I went to choir practice that evening, though I did not feel much like singing. After the director warmed us up with some familiar songs we had been practicing, he handed out a new piece and asked us to sight read it. I did not get past the first two measures! The song began with "My grace is sufficient for thee." I sat there in my chair, tears rolling down my face, and in that moment I knew that God had not been sleeping. He was with us and cared about our pain. He understood the situation and a mother's love for her child. His gentle reminder to me as the choir sang blessed me more than I can express. In that moment I knew whatever happened it would be ok. God's grace would be enough. He would see us through. His love reached down to me through the choir that night, and I will never forget it. His grace is sufficient for our every need.

Cast Your Cares on Him

In you, Lord my God, I put my trust. I trust in you; do not let me be put to shame, nor let my enemies triumph over me. (Psalm 25:1-2)

What do you do with your burdens? Do you keep them to yourself and carry them through life? Do you share them with others you meet along the way? This reminds me of John Bunyan's book *Pilgrim's Progress*[6]. Christian has a burden to carry until he gets to the city of God. Only God can remove the burden. Have you ever noticed that people handle their cares differently? Some people don't seem to have any cares, while others are so weighed down with cares that life is always hard. Do you think some people have more cares than others, or does it only seem that way because of how they handle them? I spent many years so burdened down with not just my cares but everyone else's burdens as well. Sadly, I found comfort in letting others know how burdened I was, as though it somehow would help. It did not. We do have a choice, though I did not realize it at the time. Those who are God's may cast our cares on him because he cares for us. We have a choice. We can carry our cares around, letting them burden us down, or we can cast them onto the Lord. Given the choice, why are we sometimes still so burdened down? The answer is here in this verse, "I trust in you..." As I wrestled with this, I had to admit that sometimes I carried my cares around because I was not able to trust God with them. This was not because he is not trustworthy. He is, but I was not able to trust him. Trust has been an issue for me, and it was easier for me to carry my cares myself rather than deal with my inability to trust. What a wonderful relief to learn to trust him, because he is completely faithful. Because he cares for me, I can cast my cares on him. I no longer have to carry them! Hallelujah! I will put my trust in him!

When Trouble Comes Your Way

> Listen to my prayer, O God, do not ignore my plea; hear me and answer me. My thoughts trouble me and I am distraught because of what the enemy is saying, because of the threats of the wicked; for they bring down suffering on me and assail me in their anger. (Psalm 55:1-3)

Have you ever noticed that when you are tired or not feeling particularly well that Satan likes to send trouble your way? The enemy does not fight fair. He doesn't wait until you are at your best. When you are in a weakened state, he will often come and add to your misery. He will stir up strife in your home or your workplace. He will help you keep your focus off God and onto yourself. He will do what he can to get you to grumble and complain or to lash out at the people around you. Sometimes when we are vulnerable, we do not even stop to recognize the source of our trouble. However, when we stop and cry out to God for help like the psalmist, he is faithful to come to our aid. Even when we are weary and weak—or especially when we are weary and weak— God loves to come and give us the help we need. When we are weak, he is our strength. When we are weary, he will hold us up. When we are distraught, he will calm our hearts and bring us peace in the midst of turmoil. When we invite him into the situation, he will protect our hearts and our minds and give us hope rather than despair. He will not just give us strength; he *is* our strength. He will not just give us victory; he *is* our victory. He will give us wisdom to help us know how to walk through the troubled waters, and he will lift us up when our feet slip. He is our help in time of trouble.

Great Is Thy Faithfulness

> Give thanks to the Lord, for he is good; his love endures forever.
> Let Israel say: "His love endures forever." Let the house of Aaron
> say: "His love endures forever." Let those who fear the Lord say:
> "His love endures forever." (Psalm 118:1-4)

It is a good day to give thanks to the Lord! He is so good! All of us have been and are being touched by his love every day. Even when we are experiencing trouble, we can praise God that he is with us and will comfort and encourage us. Some have said we should thank him for all things, even the trouble. I am not sure I agree with that, but I do believe that in the midst of trouble, we can certainly give thanks that he promises to see us through. We can praise him for his help and rejoice that the troubles we face in this life are so minute compared to the glory we will know when we see him face to face. We can be thankful that there is nothing that we go through in this life that has not passed through the hands of God first. If he has allowed it, then we also know that he will use it to bring about some good in our lives. The good might be that we become more mature in our faith learning to trust him in all things, or it might be that we see for ourselves the unfailing love of Christ and how great is his faithfulness. Because God is good, we can trust him and never have to fear.

A Bit Repetitive

> Therefore let all the faithful pray to you while you may be found;
> surely the rising of the mighty waters will not reach them.
> You are my hiding place; you will protect me from trouble and
> surround me with songs of deliverance. I will instruct you and
> teach you in the way you should go; I will counsel you with my
> loving eye on you. Do not be like the horse or the mule, which
> have no understanding but must be controlled by bit and bridle
> or they will not come to you. Many are the woes of the wicked,
> but the Lord's unfailing love surrounds the one who trusts in
> him. Rejoice in the Lord and be glad, you righteous; sing, all you
> who are upright in heart. (Psalm 32:6-11)

Lately, I have been worried that my devotionals are all beginning to sound alike. I wondered if it matters that there seem to be so many reoccurring themes, and then I began reading Psalms and found that is exactly what the psalmist does. I stopped to ask myself if I get bored when reading Psalms. I don't. Why? Every day I find something there to encourage me and strengthen my faith, so I never get bored. I find that I need to hear over and over again about God's unfailing love, because I tend to forget so easily. I need to be reminded a lot that I need to rejoice and be glad, since I am often discouraged and tend to complain a lot. Although I love to sing, I need to be reminded to sing especially when I do not feel like it, because he inhabits the praises of his people. When I sing and praise, my spirit is lifted, and I am encouraged. I even need to be reminded to pray, because too often when I encounter struggles my natural instinct is to try to figure it out myself. I still forget to ask God first sometimes even after all these years of following him. As a teacher, I know that just like I do not give up on any of my students, but keep working with them to help them learn the things that they have trouble with, so God will continue to instruct me. He won't give up on me and will complete the work he has begun. I may be wrong, but I figure if I need all those reminders, maybe there are others who do also.

When God Is Silent

> My God, whom I praise, do not remain silent; for people who are wicked and deceitful have opened their mouths against me; they have spoken against me with lying tongues. With words of hatred they surround me; they attack me without cause. In return for my friendship they accuse me, but I am a man of prayer. (Psalm 109:1-4)

What do you do when God is silent? Have you experienced times in your life when you have been calling out to God, but it seems he is not there or he isn't listening? It is the loneliest feeling in the world to feel that God has forgotten you! What do you do? If there is ever a time when faith is essential, it is in those times when you cannot hear God, and he seems to be absent. This is a not a time to give up on prayer. Continue to pray, asking God to work in your situation. Continue to ask for his help and guidance, and then, begin at the beginning with what you know to be true of God, especially that which will help you in this particular situation. Remind yourself that God has promised to never leave you nor forsake you, so even though you cannot see or feel him, he is there. This is not a time to go by your feelings! God has promised to give you wisdom when you ask in faith, so trust him to do just that, even if he does it in an unexpected way. Remember all of the times that God has come to your rescue in the past, and thank him for it. Thank him that even though you cannot hear him, you know he is there and will help you according to his Word. When God is silent, he is often testing our faith. Will we trust him, or will we give way to fear? Will we trust his Word, or will we find something or someone else to trust? When God is silent, we must learn to be silent too. Don't go barging forward, but wait for his lead. Stand on the truth. Remind yourself of the truth, and wait. Wait upon the Lord. He will not fail you!

The Plans of the Enemy

> I say to the Lord, "You are my God." Hear, Lord, my cry for mercy. Sovereign Lord, my strong deliverer, you shield my head in the day of battle. Do not grant the wicked their desires, Lord; do not let their plans succeed. (Psalm 140:6-8)

As I read these words, I am thinking about an attempted car bombing in New York City this week. I am so grateful that God did not permit those terrorists to succeed in their plans! Last night on the news, they thanked and honored the veterans who stand guard on the streets of New York City as they man their vendor carts. On the busy streets of New York, imagine that anyone noticed something out of place! Yet they did, and as they cleared the area, people cooperated and worked together to help everyone be safe. The bomb was diffused after what must have seemed endless moments, and the people of New York are safe once again. We can thank those who were alert enough to notice the wrong car in the wrong place or the smoke coming out of it. We can thank those patrolmen who cleared the area so well, but I believe with all my heart if God had not opened their eyes to see it, the terrorists might have succeeded. Today, let us pray for our nation. May God forgive us for wandering from his ways. May God protect us from terrorist enemies who come to destroy our land and our spirit. May God draw this nation back to himself. We need a move of God in this nation. *Lord, hear our prayers.*

Experiencing God for Yourself

As we have heard, so we have seen in the city of the Lord Almighty, in the city of our God: God makes her secure forever. (Psalm 48:8)

I love to take a walk through my yard every day to see what new flowers are growing. Spring is such a wonderful season to be reminded of the wonder of life. Just a few weeks back things were covered with snow and everything looked bleak. Today the mountain is turning green, and all of my trees and plants are bursting with life. I am especially excited because I have some new irises that a friend gave me two years ago. They didn't bloom last year, but they are just about ready to open and I can hardly wait! She told me that they are midnight blue, a deep shade of purple—almost black. I am so eager to experience them for myself. Just like with God, it is not enough to simply hear about all that God has done or is doing in the lives of others, we must experience him for ourselves if there is to be any real and lasting growth in our spiritual lives. No matter how great the pastor's message is on Sunday, we won't really grow just by hearing it. We must experience the truth by putting it into practice in our lives. When we not only hear what God is doing, but see for ourselves how God is working, our faith grows like the flowers in spring! God makes us secure in his truth as we learn to practice it. We can rest in the joy of knowing that he is our God and he is with us. We know that he will lead us and protect us. How wonderful to know the Savior's love!

When Struggle Draws Us Close to the Savior

I cry aloud to the Lord; I lift up my voice to the Lord for mercy. I pour out before him my complaint; before him I tell my trouble. When my spirit grows faint within me, it is you who watch over my way. In the path where I walk people have hidden a snare for me. Look and see, there is no one at my right hand; no one is concerned for me. I have no refuge; no one cares for my life. I cry to you, Lord; I say, "You are my refuge, my portion in the land of the living." Listen to my cry, for I am in desperate need. (Psalm 142:1-6a)

It was the summer of 1977 that I traveled to Japan on a summer mission trip. How uncharacteristic of me to go on such an adventure by myself! I sensed a calling from God to go, and when my finances were not coming in, I put it in his hands. I told the Lord that if he wanted me to go, then he would have to provide the finances because I didn't have any. It was the night before I was scheduled to leave when I received a phone call telling me that there was a donor who would pay for me to go! God wanted me there! It was a wonderful adventure! Not all of it was easy though. I was assigned to a church in a small village near Osaka where no one spoke much English. The translator came by train from two hours away! My only time to speak English was at the weekly teachers' meetings. God used me that summer to share the Gospel with most of my students, but God also used that summer to teach me how to rely on him. My mentor shared this Psalm with me when I was having a particularly difficult time, and it became so very real to me. When it felt like there was no one to care for me, God did. He heard my cries and listened as I poured out my heart to him. He reminded me often that I was in the place where he had called me that summer. He wanted me there, and he was with me. Oh such precious lessons to know that God cares about my tears. He knows when my lonely heart is breaking. He knows me. He knows what I need. I needed to learn to depend on him more than I needed another person to talk to. He wanted me to learn that he is my refuge, and when I am in desperate need, he is there. What priceless lessons! I could not have learned them better anywhere else than the place God had for me that summer. He loved me enough to put me in a place where my deep struggle would draw me closer to him. What wondrous love is this!

The Lord Is Near

The Lord is righteous in all his ways and faithful in all he does. The Lord is near to all who call on him, to all who call on him in truth. He fulfills the desires of those who fear him; he hears their cry and saves them. The Lord watches over all who love him, but all the wicked he will destroy. My mouth will speak in praise of the Lord. Let every creature praise his holy name for ever and ever. (Psalm 145:17-21)

Oh God, my God, how I praise your holy name! Indeed you are righteous in all your ways! There is none like you. You bless those who trust in you. You rescue those who cry out to you. You watch over all who love you, and I know your heart breaks for those who have refused your gracious gift of grace. Lord, today may your Word penetrate into our hearts, minds, souls, and bodies. Let every fiber of our beings praise you, O God, because you are worthy of praise!

I heard a statistic yesterday on the news, and though I can't remember it exactly, they said that most Americans believe that there is a God, and many believe that God answers prayer. The percentage of people in America who believe we should not have a National Day of Prayer was very small. American Christians need to recognize that there is a war going on in America, and it isn't terrorism. Terrorism is a problem, but America will suffer more because we have gotten confused about democracy. Our country was founded on the belief that the government is of the people, for the people and by the people. When did it become of the politicians, by the politicians and for the politicians? Our nation was founded on the principle that the majority rules. When did we become a nation run by small interest groups and individuals who challenge everything our nation was founded upon that is good and right? Christians, there may come a day that speaking the truth becomes illegal in America, but until it does, we who love God and call upon his glorious name need to pray fervently for this nation. God hears the prayers of those who love him.

Joy Comes in the Morning

Sing the praises of the Lord, you his faithful people; praise his holy name. For his anger lasts only a moment, but his favor lasts lifetime; weeping may stay for the night, but rejoicing comes in the morning. (Psalm 30:4-5)

I came across this verse last night as I began reading a new Karen Kingsbury novel, and it took me back to a time when I was so broken the tears seemed to never stop. There may have been some post partum depression going on, but I remember feeling like I might never experience joy again. In the middle of a season like that, like when the spring rains never seem to quit, it seems like it will never end. It is difficult to imagine a time when you weren't filled with tears. The time of grieving after the sudden death of my older brother was like that. I cried at everything, anything. I came across this verse on a cross stitch design that my mother had given me at some point, and I clung to its promise. Joy comes in the morning. Hallelujah! It soon became clear that this did not mean tomorrow morning! Like a night when you are having trouble sleeping seems to go on forever, so the dark night of the soul can go on for a seemingly endless time. There is good news, though. Eventually, every night gives way to morning. Morning will come! There is hope. When the night seems never ending, know that morning will come sooner or later. I learned that God does not allow us to be in those seasons one moment longer than is necessary to accomplish his purposes. He does not enjoy seeing his children struggle, but there are times when it must be so. The Bible is clear on that. If the only reason is that we can somehow share in his sufferings, then that is enough. Hold on to the hope that it is not forever. Soon weeping will give way to joy unspeakable. God will see that it does. Remember that he loves you, he knows your need, you are his beloved child, and joy comes in the morning.

Motherhood is Not for Sissies

> He settles the childless woman in her home as a happy mother
> of children. Praise the Lord. (Psalm 113:9)

I have learned so much from my mother about being a mother and a woman of God. She has encouraged me so often and reminded me of what is important. I am so thankful for my mother! Life as a mother is rarely easy, is it? This week, I observed a young mom whose little one had gotten the best of her. This little one has mastered the art of the power struggle, and is making the life of her mother very difficult. As I looked on, I thanked God that he was with me when I was in that place, and I prayed for that young mom who was weary and distraught as another woman pulled her aside and sought to comfort and encourage her. Oh, how difficult it can be to be a mother!

There are lots of books out there about motherhood, but who has time for books when you're in the middle of mothering! I can recall learning a lot of dependence on the Lord during the years of young motherhood. There was one lesson I learned that I wished I had learned sooner: how to be a happy mother of children. As with much of life there is a choice in mothering. Whatever our circumstances in mothering, we can choose to enjoy our children or not. I was eager to be a mother and loved children, but when my own came in 1987, 1988, and 1989, I spent a few years quite overwhelmed to say the least. Sadly, my being overwhelmed robbed me of the joys of motherhood for a time. As I sought the Lord, he reminded me to enjoy them. I learned to take my Bible out to the picnic table and watch them play as I spent time with the Lord. I often took them to the lake where I could watch them play for hours. They were happy. I was happy, and I again began to enjoy them. May our mothers be blessed today, and Lord, bless the children you have called us to be a mother to. What a precious gift!

Consider What God Has Done

I remember the days of long ago; I meditate on all your works
and consider what your hands have done. (Psalm 143:5)

What is your story? It is always good to stop and remember what God has done in our lives. Sometimes we remember because we are in need of encouragement. Sometimes we remember because someone else needs to know what God did for us. When we stop to remember all that God has done, we can gain perspective on what is going on now. In the Old Testament, God often had his children stop and make an altar after a significant event. Why? So whenever they saw it, they would remember what he had done for them there. Why? Because we tend to forget, don't we? When we forget, we lose sight of how big God is. We forget the depth of his love for us. We forget what we used to be and how far he has brought us. Whenever we stop and think about—which is what it is to meditate on something—what God has done, it takes us back there. It becomes new again, and we are reminded of the wonder of God's saving work in our lives. Remembering what he has done for me often gives me hope for the lives of those I love who do not know him yet. I remember that it was he who pursued me. He surrounded me with everything I needed to consider his plan for my life, and he helped me to come to the place of surrender. He did it all, and I just had to accept. If he did that for me, he can reach my loved ones too. Sometimes life is discouraging, and just stopping to take a few minutes to think over all that God has done can give us courage to go on. We are reminded that God is in control, and it will be all right somehow. Consider all that God has done for you and rejoice in his magnificent love and grace today.

Hope for the Hopeless

> Blessed are those whose help is the God of Jacob, whose hope is in the Lord their God. He is the Maker of heaven and earth, the sea, and everything in them—he remains faithful forever. He upholds the cause of the oppressed and gives food to the hungry. The Lord sets the prisoners free, the Lord gives sight to the blind, the Lord lifts up those who are bowed down, the Lord loves the righteous. The Lord watches over the foreigner and sustains the fatherless and the widow, but he frustrates the ways of the wicked. (Psalm 146:5-9)

If you awoke this morning in need of encouragement, you have come to the right place! As I opened God's Word this morning, I came across these verses and knew they must be shared today. Friends, our God reigns! He is our Mighty Redeemer who rescues us from every kind of trouble. He loves us with an everlasting love, and he has promised to never leave us nor forsake us. It is his joy to bless his children with peace, and he has promised to be our strength when we are weak. Our God is faithful, even when we are faithless. He offers us hope, even when our hope has dried up. He comforts us when everyone else around us has forgotten our struggle. He lifts up those who have fallen and carries them, if necessary, until they are able to walk again. He opens the eyes of those who cannot see and heals those who are broken-hearted. Our God reigns! Sometimes it doesn't feel that way in this life, especially when the challenges in our path draw our focus away from him. Look to God today, whatever your need. He is waiting for you to come into his presence where he can pour his love into you and restore your soul. May he bless you today in a very personal way. He loves you.

Even Kings Will Bow in Worship

> May all the kings of the earth praise you, Lord, when they hear
> what you have decreed. May they sing of the ways of the Lord,
> for the glory of the Lord is great. (Psalm 138:4-5)

A day is coming and is perhaps not far off when all the peoples of the earth will recognize the Lord for who he is. Many will feel foolish for having convinced themselves that he was not God. Many will fear him because of their wickedness, for in that moment in time, they will know that the Day of Judgment has arrived. I wonder, though, if there are any kings alive today who already recognize the King of Kings. Are there any who realize that it is God who sets kings in their places of honor? It is God who rules over all things. How wonderful it will be when all those who love God are together in one place praising him and singing songs declaring his glory! When I attended Creation, a Christian music festival, with about 60,000 other people, the worship was so awesome! That many voices lifted in praise is an amazing experience, a taste of heaven. I look forward to joining with the angels in worship of my King. How magnificent is his glory! Perhaps today as you spend a few moments in worship of your Lord, you might imagine the glorious day when every knee shall bow and every tongue confess that Jesus Christ is Lord. Imagine an angelic choir singing of his glory, for his glory is great!

Sweeter than Honey

> The law of the Lord is perfect, refreshing the soul. The statutes
> of the Lord are trustworthy, making wise the simple. The
> precepts of the Lord are right, giving joy to the heart. The
> commands of the Lord are radiant, giving light to the eyes. The
> fear of the Lord is pure, enduring forever. The decrees of the
> Lord are firm, and all of them are righteous. They are more
> precious than gold, than much pure gold; they are sweeter than
> honey, than honey from the honeycomb. By them is your servant
> warned; in keeping them there is great reward. (Psalm 19:7-11)

We moved to the mountains of Pennsylvania a few years ago, and I was surprised to find such a vastly different culture. One notices very quickly that there are not many who obey the road signs here. There don't seem to be any police in the local area to enforce the traffic signs, so most people ignore them. Funny thing is that same attitude can be seen even at the Christian School where I teach. When I first arrived I found it very curious that there were signs up everywhere about keeping particular doors closed at all times, and I noticed no one seemed to pay much attention to the signs. God has given us his Word to guide our way, but if we do not heed the signs, we will not have the life God intended for us to have. When you start talking about rules and precepts and ordinances, there is the danger of falling into legalism. Legalism is bondage to the rules. We can tell from this passage that is not what God intended. The psalmist isn't keeping God's laws and statutes because he has to; he is keeping them because he loves the King of Kings! He wants to follow the ordinances laid out by God because he loves God. God has made these rules to govern our lives so that we can live at peace with him and with one another. When we begin to respond to God's Word as though it were a treasure map leading us to a great treasure, we will not find it a hardship to follow! God's statutes and ordinances are like pure gold, sweeter than honey, and following them will lead us to great reward.

God: Our Refuge

> In you, Lord, I have taken refuge; let me never be put to shame; deliver me in your righteousness. Turn your ear to me, come quickly to my rescue; be my rock of refuge, a strong fortress to save me. Since you are my rock and my fortress, for the sake of your name lead and guide me, for you are my refuge. Into your hands I commit my spirit; deliver me, Lord, my faithful God. (Psalm 31:1-5)

In these few verses, David refers to God as his refuge three times. Psalm 46 tells us that God is our refuge and strength a very present help in trouble. A quick search of Psalms found forty-three references about God being a refuge for his people. Do you ever find yourself in a situation where you need a refuge? Most often, for me, it is because of a spiritual battle that brings me to the Lord seeking refuge. The forces of darkness never seem to give up trying to tempt and try God's people. When we are weary, they are not. We may lack the wisdom and knowledge to know how to handle this adversary, but God does not. One word from him and we can be completely hedged in by a fortress of heavenly beings standing ready to protects us. God is our refuge when we are in trouble. Is there any trouble in your life today? Take refuge in the Lord God, our rock and our strong tower of defense. Have you been falsely charged? Take refuge in the God of all truth. He will come to your defense. Whatever your trouble, God is a faithful refuge.

Consider His Word

> When I consider your heavens, the work of your fingers, the moon and the stars, which you have set in place, what is mankind that you are mindful of them, human beings that you care for them? You made them a little lower than the angels and crowned them with glory and honor. You made them rulers over the works of your hands; you put everything under their feet: all flocks and herds, and the animals of the wild, the birds in the sky, and the fish in the sea, all that swim the paths of the seas. Lord, our Lord, how majestic is your name in all the earth! (Psalm 8:3-9)

Matthew Maury was a Christian oceanographer and naval officer. He believed in and studied God's Word as well as the oceans. It was this passage in the eighth Psalm that led him to discover the ocean currents, like the paths in the seas described in these verses. If God who created the seas said there were pathways in the seas, then he believed that they would be there. Scientific evidence proved him correct, and Matthew Maury became known as the "Pathfinder of the Seas." While it is true that the Bible is not a science book, whenever God mentions scientific truth in his Word, it is the truth. We may not understand it, but it is true nevertheless. "When I consider…" Matthew Maury's time spent considering God's Word led to a wonderful scientific discovery. Take time to consider his truth, his creation, his commands and his promises. How often does he speak to us through his Word to encourage and strengthen our faith and to lead and guide us in his way? Every time we go to his Word to seek him, he will meet us there! What have you discovered in God's Word lately?

Revive Us Again

> Will you not revive us again, that your people may rejoice in you? (Psalm 85:6)

As I write this, we are approaching an election. It is a good time to seek the Lord about this nation. We are a nation who no longer seeks God. We are very close to losing our freedom of religion, I think. As long as there are still a few of God's people here who love Him and are willing to intercede for this nation, perhaps there is hope of revival. Nothing is too difficult for God. It may not seem so at times, but God still seats those who are in places of leadership. He has allowed wicked men to rule in the past so that the people's hearts would be turned back to him. The special interest groups have wielded a lot of power in our nation, but we have weapons of warfare that God has given us that will lead to victory. We must pray without ceasing for God to bring his salvation to this nation. As citizens, we have a right to vote too. Perhaps God's people have silently stood by watching this nation turn its back on the Lord our God. If we do not stand for what is good and true, who will do it? Let us pray, let us believe in God's unfailing love, and let us vote for those who stand for truth. May God raise up godly men and women to lead this nation, those who would be willing to fight against the current of moral decay and self-serving leadership.

Making Deals with God

> I call with all my heart; answer me, Lord, and I will obey your decrees. I call out to you; save me and I will keep your statutes. I rise before dawn and cry for help; I have put my hope in your word. My eyes stay open through the watches of the night, that I may meditate on your promises. Hear my voice in accordance with your love; preserve my life, Lord, according to your laws. Those who devise wicked schemes are near, but they are far from your law. Yet you are near, Lord, and all your commands are true. Long ago I learned from your statutes that you established them to last forever. (Psalm 119:145-152)

In what situations do you find yourself making deals with God? It is usually a desperate time, isn't it? The psalmist tells God he will obey him if God will only answer him. God's Word is everlasting. It never fails. Every promise is still as true today as the day it was written, because God is true to his Word. If we want to depend on God's promises, ought we not also to depend on his commands to guide us through life. I suppose it is human nature that wants to hold God to his promises yet still live independently of him. It can never be so! God's promises are always true, not only when we obey God; however, God's promises are for those who love him. Those who love him will desire to follow him by obeying his commands and statutes. His decrees will rule our lives if we love him, and then when we cry out to him late at night or before dawn or anytime before or after, God will hear our cry. He will answer our call in his perfect time and in his perfect way. Whatever life brings us, our God is always near to those who love him. We do not sense him with us always. Nevertheless, he is there, and we can count on his faithful leading all along the pathways of life, because God is faithful. I long to be as faithful to God as he has been to me! May God grant you a sense of his nearness today. His promises are sure. Trust in his Word whatever your need.

Pray for our Nation's Leaders

> Therefore, you kings, be wise; be warned, you rulers of the earth. Serve the Lord with fear and celebrate his rule with trembling. Kiss his son, or he will be angry and your way will lead to your destruction, for his wrath can flare up in a moment. Blessed are all who take refuge in him. (Psalm 2:10-12)

I was reading an interesting article the other day about faith in America. Actually, the article said that there are now many more Christians living in other parts of the world than here in America, and that will change the face of Christianity in our day. While churches in America are struggling, the church in Africa, for example, is growing and thriving. I worry sometimes at how far America has come from its early dependence on God. Like individual people, only the nation that follows God can experience his blessing. Take time today to pray for our nation. Pray for our president and our leaders, not only that God would lead them, but that they would come to know him. He is our hope. He is our refuge in the storm. Nothing is impossible for him. He can restore our nation and bring revival to our land. Let us find refuge in him once again.

He Hems Us In

> Before a word is on my tongue you, Lord, know it completely. You hem me in behind and before, and you lay your hand upon me. Such knowledge is too wonderful for me, too lofty for me to attain. Where can I go from your Spirit? Where can I flee from you presence? If I go up to the heavens, you are there; if I make my bed in the depths, you are there. If I rise on the wings of the dawn, if I settle on the far side of the sea, even there your hand will guide me, your right hand will hold me fast. (Psalm 139:4-10)

Sometimes I do not know what my next word is, but God does. What an amazing thought! My God knows before I even speak what my concerns are. He knows when I am going to say something I will regret later and will lead me a different way if I let him. He hems me in. I guess sometimes I don't like to be hemmed in. Sometimes I am foolish enough to want to go my own way, and then being hemmed in feels like a cage from which I need to escape. Most of the time, though, knowing that God has hemmed be in allows me to feel secure. God's protection is around me, so I am completely safe. That does not give me permission to be reckless, and it does not mean I will not have difficulties. The Bible is completely clear on that point, but it does mean that wherever I am today, whatever I am doing, God is both before me and behind me. He is with me. I am so grateful for that knowledge, though I must admit that in the course of my day I often forget this fact. Wherever I am, God is with me and has promised to guide me with his very own hand! Have you noticed that there are some roads in life that we must walk alone? It isn't that there are no people around us, but there are times that we may be in the midst of a trial that others just don't see or don't understand. Even those closest to us cannot go with us on some of the journeys that God takes us. During those times, we may feel lonely and isolated. We long for people to stand with us, but there are none who can. In those times, we must remind ourselves that we are not alone. We are never alone. The Lord God Almighty is with us. He will never leave us. He will guide us and give us strength. He will encourage us and protect us. His hand is upon us. What an amazing and wonderful truth! Draw near to him today, because he cares for you.

A Light to Guide Us

> The Lord is my light and my salvation— whom shall I fear? The Lord is the stronghold of my life—of whom shall I be afraid? (Psalm 27:1)

We are heading to Lake Erie on a fieldtrip with the elementary children today. We'll be seeing a lighthouse and the maritime museum which is loaded with the history and records of many wrecks upon those rocky shores. The lighthouse is always a symbol to me of the light of God in our lives. In the midst of every storm or foggy day when we cannot find our way, he is there shining his light to guide us. His light will guide us safely to shore where we can find our refuge in him. I am always amazed to think about the lonely life of the lighthouse keeper, who daily attends the light, making sure that it is prepared to do its work when visibility is poor. Each night he makes sure the light is glowing brightly to light the way. Perhaps we are the keepers of the light in God's kingdom, since his light goes forth from us to a dark world. Those who see the light in us are drawn to it and can be guided to a safe haven in Christ. Today let your light so shine before men—and women and children—that they might be drawn to the Light of the World.

God is Good

> Give thanks to the Lord, for he is good; his love endures forever. Who can proclaim the mighty acts of the Lord or fully declare his praise? Blessed are those who act justly, who always do what is right. Remember me, Lord, when you show favor to your people, come to my aid when you save them, that I may enjoy the prosperity of your chosen ones, that I may share in the joy of your nation and join your inheritance in giving praise. (Psalm 106:1-5)

Have you given any thought lately to how good God is? What difference does it make in your life that God is good? We say these words often, but have they penetrated our hearts, minds, and souls? Do we see life through the knowledge that God is good? We got word yesterday that a young man who was in my daughter's eighth grade class died this week because someone entered his apartment to rob him, and he was hit on the head. He died in his sleep. What a terrible tragedy! How is it possible to see the goodness of God in such a situation? Is it possible? Yes, it is possible, but only in light of eternity. This young man is with Jesus now. He does not have to live one more minute in this sin infested place. I am quite sure that if given the choice, he would not want to return here from his place with God. For those who grieve his loss, where is the goodness of God? On this side of heaven we may never know why such a terrible thing happened, but if God is good, then we must believe that he allowed this for a reason. We must believe that he can somehow use this tragedy to bring about good, perhaps the salvation of loved ones or friends who can now see their own immortality. How can we praise him during a time of great sorrow? We can praise him because he will bring us through. We can praise him because he will bring good out of every bad situation. We can praise him because he is worthy of all our praise. Even when we do not understand him or his ways, we can praise him because he is our Creator and Redeemer, and he will lead us on. Our praise cannot compare to the wonderful greatness of our God. Isn't it amazing that God loves our praise anyway! Praise him today because he is good.

The Lord's Return

> The Lord says to my lord: "Sit at my right hand until I make your enemies a footstool for your feet." The Lord will extend your mighty scepter from Zion, saying "Rule in the midst of your enemies." (Psalm 110:1-2)

According to the twenty-second chapter of Acts, the verses above are referring to Jesus Christ upon his ascension into heaven. Christ is still seated upon the throne at the right hand of God the Father, awaiting the moment in time when the Father sends him back to earth for his saints. Sometimes in this life we can lose sight of the fact that the final battle with evil is yet to come. It is always encouraging to remember that the final days are in the Father's hands. The only reason we are still here on this earth awaiting the return of Christ is that all of those may yet believe who are called into God's kingdom. If we are still here, then there must be some who have not yet received him as Lord and Savior. Though we look forward to the coming day of the Lord's return, he has entrusted us with the gospel and has called us to speak the truth boldly that others might believe and be saved. Scripture is clear that no one knows the day or the hour of Christ's return, but when we observe the news it seems clear that the day is drawing closer. Even so, today, we who serve Christ upon the earth have a job to do—until he comes, we must be about the task of drawing others to Christ. However inadequate we feel for this task, this is the task he has given us, but he has not left us alone to do it. His precious Spirit was sent to reside within us and to empower us to do the work we have been called to do. The Spirit will lead us and give us the words to speak if we allow him. Will you be about the Father's business today?

Sing to the Lord a New Song

I will sing a new song to you, my God; on the ten-stringed lyre I will make music to you, to the One who gives victory to kings, who delivers his servant David... (Psalm 144:9-10)

I was startled yesterday when a coworker told me her brother had sung one of my songs in church, and everyone was really blessed by it. Wow! No one else except me has ever sung a song I have written! I have written a few songs over the years, but the ones that are the most special to me are the ones that come spontaneously in praise and worship to the King. The best place for that is in the car. I just turn the radio off, and instead of praying, I sing to the Lord whatever is on my heart. The praise hasn't originated with someone else; it comes from my heart to his. Usually these songs don't stick in my brain, so once they are sung to the Lord, they are gone. It is a personal moment of praise to my God. There is no analyzing the music or wondering if someone else will like it or not. It is just a melody of praise to the Lord. I don't take credit for being able to do that either. It is God who has put the song in my heart in the first place, and it is such a joy to sing for him. Not everyone is a singer, but God has filled us all with his love of creating. He has given us many reasons to praise him. As he is doing a new work in you, perhaps you will find a new song to sing to him! Use whatever way God has given you to let the joy of the Lord bubble out of you into something new.

Heaven Is a Wonderful Place

> The Lord is in his holy temple; the Lord is on his heavenly throne. He observes everyone on earth; his eyes examine them. The Lord examines the righteous, but the wicked, those who love violence, his hates with a passion. On the wicked he will rain fiery coals and burning sulfur; a scorching wind will be their lot. For the Lord is righteous, he loves justice; the upright will see his face. (Psalm 11:4-7)

I am convinced that heaven is going to hold many surprises for us. Here we can only imagine the throne of God in his holy temple. Oh, we do have a glimpse at the tabernacle in Scripture. The ninth chapter of Hebrews tells us that the earthly tabernacle that was built for the Lord was a copy of the heavenly one. How much more glorious the true tabernacle of God, created not by man but by God himself! When we worship the Lord, we are drawn into his presence in that heavenly place, though we cannot see it with our earthly eyes. Can you imagine your first glimpses when you cross over into that heavenly realm? Keeping our focus on the things promised for all eternity can enable us to endure the sorrows of this sin-filled world. Even so, when we think of heaven and long to look into our Savior's eyes, do we wonder who will be there with us? This verse tells us that only the upright will see his face. I am so grateful for the grace of God that redeems me from all unrighteousness, so that I might be one of those upright ones. I know that it is only his work on the cross for me that makes it so. There is nothing good in me that he did not place there. If it were not for his saving grace, I know that I would suffer the fate of all the demons of hell in fiery condemnation. How many people whose lives I touch today may never know that wondrous grace of God? How many who still live in darkness, controlled by the evil one, do not know that Christ died for them? May we be sensitive to the leading of the Holy Spirit today to pray for those around us who need Christ, and may we obey the call to carry the good news to all those who will hear.

A Journey Worth Taking

> My soul is weary with sorrow; strengthen me according to your word. Keep me from deceitful ways; be gracious to me and teach me your law. (Psalm 119: 28-29)

Have you read John Bunyan's *Pilgrim's Progress?*[7] The main character wears a burden of sin upon his shoulders but is completely unaware of it until he reads a book he has found. He begins a journey to the Wicket Gate to find deliverance. On the way, he meets all sorts of characters who would dissuade him and encounters obstacles that would prevent him from going further. A Christian allegory, the story reflects the difficulty we often have in this world. We can be weighed down by sin and be unaware of it. On our journey with God, we are often distracted by so many things, and Satan makes sure there are a lot of temptations along the way to prevent us from following the narrow path God has for us. We can become weary and susceptible to Satan's tricks to derail us. The easy way can look pretty inviting when you come to a fork in the road! How can we persevere when the road is difficult? Find strength in his Word. Consider his ways. Hold fast to his statutes. Run in the path of his commands. The journey in this life may be long and sometimes very difficult, but the glory of spending eternity with God far outweighs the struggles of this life.

A Hope Worth Sharing

> Save me, O God, by your name; vindicate me by your might. Hear my prayer, O God; listen to the words of my mouth. Arrogant foes are attacking me; ruthless people are trying to kill me—people without regard for God. Surely God is my help; the Lord is the one who sustains me. (Psalm 54:1-4)

I just finished reading Randy Alcorn's book *Edge of Eternity*[8]. On the same line as *Pilgrim's Progress*, the main character finds himself on a journey to the city of the King. He has difficulty choosing the right road because most of the other people are going the other direction. The people he meets along the way who are going the other way are often verbally abusive and threatening. Most do not want to hear about the place of the King, nor do they want to be told which road on which to travel. We live in that kind of world today, don't we? The world expects us to buy into their philosophy that all roads lead to God and that we need to be tolerant. Christians are not tolerated very well, but we are supposed to tolerate everyone else. The truth is that we are not merely to tolerate everyone else but to love them. Sometimes that love involves telling them the truth. When we speak the truth, not everyone—in fact, most people—really don't want to hear it. They simply do not know what they do not know and are blinded by this world's empty promises. They lash out because they are not ready to accept the truth about themselves and their need for a Savior. We do not know, though, which person along our journey is ready to respond to God, so we must tell them as God so leads. I am certainly glad that God is my help! He is the One who sustains me. He gives me courage and grace when I need it. He leads me on the right road and encourages me when I am weary. He is my hope and has given me a hope worth sharing.

The Sun Rises and Sets to Glorify the Lord

> In the heavens he has pitched a tent for the sun. It is like a bridegroom coming out of his chamber, like a champion rejoicing to run his course. It rises at one end of the heavens and makes its circuit to the other; nothing is deprived of its warmth. (Psalm 19:4b-6)

Have you seen a good sunrise or sunset lately? Isn't it just one thing that makes you stop and notice the beauty of creation? When I spend time meditating on just this one aspect of creation, I am in such awe of the power of God! The sun gives us light and heat—not too much, nor too little. If we were just the smallest bit closer to the sun, it would be too hot to sustain life. If the earth was just the smallest bit farther away from the sun, it would be too cold, and ice would cover the planet. The earth rotates on its axis and we have day and night. It revolves around the sun and we have a year. Through the sun, God has given us a way to measure time. Why do we need time?

There is no time kept in eternity. I think it is to measure down the days until he will fulfill his prophesies and we will be with him forever in eternity. Time is the grace he has given us to turn to him and be saved. If there were none of those things, how about the beauty of the sun as it rises and sets or sneaks out from behind a cloud! It speaks so loudly of the glory of God and the wonder of his creation. Thank God today for his creation of the sun.

God's Word to Light the Way

> I wait for your salvation, Lord, and I follow your commands. I obey your statutes, for I love them greatly. I obey your precepts and statutes, for all of my ways are known to you... (Psalm 119:166-168)

I am always inspired by the psalmist's devotion to the Word of God. He knows God's Word, loves God's Word, meditates on God's Word, and keeps God's Word. God's Word gives him courage and hope. God's Word guides his way and reminds him of God's unfailing love. God's Word keeps him from stumbling, and reminds him that he is loved. God's opinion of him matters more to him than the taunting of his enemy. God's Word is a treasure to him, so he praises God for it many times a day. God's Word is the way we get to know God, and God's Word assures us that God knows us and cares about us. Are you finding joy in God's Word as you meet him there? Spending time with God in his Word is so much more than just completing a task on our list or something we are devoted to doing. It is like our oasis in the desert! When we come to God's Word, he meets us there! He will use his Word to strengthen and encourage us. Like food to our bodies, his Word is nourishment to our spirit. Satan works very hard to keep us out of the Word, because he knows that we become weak and discouraged easily without it. Don't let him have victory in your life! Take a few moments to meet with God in his Word today. He loves you and is waiting for you there!

Let No Sin Rule over You

> Direct my footsteps according to your word; let no sin rule over me. Redeem me from human oppression, that I may obey your

precepts. Make your face shine upon your servant and teach me your decrees. Streams of tears flow from my eyes, for your law is not obeyed. (Psalm 119:133-136)

All of the psalmists' verses seem to come back around this one theme, keeping God's Word. Have you struggled with keeping the precepts of God? These few verses give us insight into the solution. Pray. Ask God to help you to walk according to his Word. Ask God to show you how to conquer those sins that still master over you. He has the wisdom you need and wants you to be free from bondage to sin. He can and will guide you as you look to him. Stay focused on his Word. If God's Word is our spiritual food, how many of us are starving for lack of it? We cannot gain all of the spiritual nourishment we need simply by listening to a sermon on Sunday. We need to look to God daily in his Word in order to be strengthened to face the challenges of the day. What would the body of Christ be like if we all grieved the presence of sin in our lives like the psalmist does here? We cannot keep God's laws on our own. We need his help. That is why he has given us the Holy Spirit. What we think about sin is very important. If we look past it and think it is not important or not possible to have victory over, then we will remain locked in sin's grip; but if we take God at his word and seek his help, we can find victory. He will help us. There is great joy in life when we walk in the ways of God.

Our Spiritual GPS

But I, by your great love, can come into your house; in reverence I bow down toward your holy temple. Lead me, O Lord, in your righteousness because of my enemies—make your way straight before me. (Psalm 5:7-8)

Have you ever laughed at a Family Circus comic where the little children make paths all over everywhere before they end up somewhere not far from where they started? We laugh at how true it is, but it makes me wonder if sometimes we do that with God. He has a plan for our lives and would make straight the path before us, but we get sidetracked and distracted and run all over the place doing everything along the way. We can't figure out exactly why our life is not producing or does not seem to be jiving with his, but we keep going round and round in circles until we either get worn out, or we stop and ask God for some direction. Although the path God has for us is not always straight, God rarely has us going in circles! We do that to ourselves. Thank God for the invention of the GPS! It gets more people to the right places without getting lost. Isn't it wonderful that when you do make a wrong turn, it warns you to make a U turn and helps you to get back on track? Too bad we don't have one of those for our spiritual life! Oh, but we do! God's Word is our guidance system, but we must learn to listen and to follow as he leads. Unlike that GPS in your car, you can't just turn it on and get directions. God will speak to us through his Word, but we must keep tuned to his voice, or we can soon find ourselves running around in circles again!

Victory over Depression

> He reached down from on high and took hold of me; he drew me out of deep waters. He rescued me from my powerful enemy, from my foes, who were too strong for me. They confronted me in the day of my disaster, but the Lord was my support. He brought me out into a spacious place; he rescued me because he delighted in me. (Psalm 18:16-19)

I am surprised by how many people struggle with depression. Most Christians I know would be reluctant to tell anyone that they struggle with depression, because Christians aren't supposed to have those problems. We have the Lord. While it is true that we have the Lord, it is not true that Christians don't struggle with depression. Depression can come like a tidal wave and knock you down suddenly, or it can be more like a lingering rain where the waters rise and rise until you feel you are drowning, and it is too late to get to shore. There are probably as many reasons for depression as there are people who struggle with it. These verses always take me back to a time when God reached into my life and lifted me out of a suffocating depression. During that time, I learned a lot about myself and how I think. I also learned the reality that God himself is my support. He was willing to rescue me because he delighted in me. Have you ever just meditated on that little phrase, "... because he delighted in me?" God, the creator, redeemer, and sustainer of all things delights in *me*! Not just when I am victorious and on top of the world either, but even when I am bowed low and inundated with depression, he delights in me and wants to lead me to a safe place. There is no instant cure for depression. You have to learn to think differently and perhaps make changes in the way you do things. There may be a need for counseling and medication to help in the process of sorting all that out, but the greatest relief and joy can come in the knowledge that you are not alone. God is with you. He delights in you and will be your support.

He Goes before Me

> All the days ordained for me were written in your book before
> one of them came to be. (Psalm 139:16b)

Sometimes when we consider this verse, it is in the context of how many days on this earth God will allow us to live. God has already established the length of my life, but I find comfort in this verse today knowing that even before I was born, God knew what I would have to face today. He knows whether it will bring joy or challenges. He knows the right decisions I will make and the wrong ones. He already knows everything that is coming. He knows every aspect of my life. I can rest assured that he is with me. There is nothing I will ever face that is beyond his knowledge, and his Word reminds me that everything that happens in my life he will use for my good somehow, because I love him and am called by his name. Whatever comes, God is with me already working on my behalf. He will lead. He will provide. He will guide and encourage. He will instruct me and show me how to walk in his ways if I ask him to do so. My life is an open book to God, and he knows what is coming in every chapter. He does not put me in a bubble where I am untouched by life's challenges. Instead, he uses every event of every day to train me and help me to grow into the person I was created to be. I can rest in the knowledge that God already knows everything about everything, and he is with me every moment.

What Wondrous Love Is This

> I call on you, my God, for you will answer me; turn your ear to
> my prayer. Show me the wonders of your great love, you who

save by your right hand those who take refuge in you from their foes. (Psalm 17:6-7)

I have walked with God a long time, though for a long time I walked in a sort of blindness I was not even aware of until God began revealing himself to me in a new way. God began to shower me with love like I had never known. I was the fifth child of nine. My mother shared with me the story of her pregnancy with my twin brother and me. She still had a baby in diapers and her abdomen began to grow so fast that she was convinced she had a tumor! She shared with me that she would have preferred a tumor to twins! My mom was already overwhelmed with four children. It was my dad who wanted enough kids to make a baseball team. She assured me that she was glad I was her daughter, though those early years were a real challenge. I have wrestled with feelings of being unloved and unlovable my whole life. I knew in my head that my parents loved me, but my heart missed the memo! I believe those early days in my mother's womb left a wound of rejection in my spirit. Let me tell you how God healed my wounded heart. Day after day, he would shower me with tangible love gifts. I could see and understand for the first time in my life that God not only loves the world, but he loves *me*. This revelation transformed my life! I began to see myself as the apple of God's eye, his precious daughter. It was not an epiphany, but rather months of God's demonstrations of love in very personal ways that changed my thinking. He loves me so much that he was willing to do whatever it would take to help me to understand his great love. My dear friend, he loves you too. You are the apple of his eye, his dearest treasure. Today may he open the eyes of your heart to see and receive his wondrous love!

In God I Trust

In God, whose word I praise, in the Lord, whose word I praise— in God I trust and am not afraid. What can man do to me? (Psalm 56:10-11)

"...in God I trust." That was not always true of me. There was a time when it would have been more true to say, "In me I trust." Growing up in an alcoholic home, I learned that I was the only one I could really count on, for many times when I needed help or attention, the attention was focused on the alcoholic, my dad. It is so very hard to unlearn the kind of self-reliance and lack of trust that comes from this type of situation, but I am so very thankful to God for revealing to me time and time again how faithful he is. Step by step, one experience at a time, God helped me to learn to trust him. First, he put me into a situation where I had to come to the place of understanding that I could not trust even me to help. God is so very good at impossible situations! He showed me in his Word that he wanted and deserved my trust. He was a patient teacher and gave me many opportunities to see his faithfulness until I grew to the point of trusting him with both big and small things. In God I trust. It is true today, and will be for eternity because my God is so very faithful, and he loves me. In whom do you place your trust?

Walk in the Light of His Countenance

> Righteousness and justice are the foundation of your throne; love and faithfulness go before you. Blessed are those who have learned to acclaim you, who walk in the light of your presence, Lord. They rejoice in your name all day long; they celebrate your righteousness. For you are their glory and strength, and by your favor you exalt our horn. Indeed, our shield belongs to the Lord, our king to the Holy One of Israel. (Psalm 89:14-6)

We all have loved ones who do not know Christ and are often at a loss to help them understand their need of him. Thank God for his Holy Spirit whose job it is to convict the world (and our loved ones) of their sin! We can only point the way. How do we do that? It is perhaps not as difficult as we make it out to be. Righteousness, justice, mercy and truth are several of the character qualities of our God. Do our loved ones see Jesus in us? Do they see mercy in us when they have wronged us or we have been wronged by someone else? Does his righteousness reign in our lives? No, we are not perfect. That is for sure, and our loved ones see us as we are, faults and all. Sometimes I think that is why we feel we cannot share the truth of God with them. We know how far we fall short, and we don't want to be hypocrites. We must remember that telling the truth is not about us or how often we have failed. It is about the Almighty God who created us and knows our every flaw and yet loves us and longs for us to know him. It is about Jesus Christ who willingly died upon the cross so that we could be restored to the Father and can spend eternity with him. When our loved ones point out that Jesus died because of *our* sin, we must not get defensive or pretend it isn't true. God doesn't love us because we are good. He loves us because he is good. He doesn't love us because we are perfect. He loves us because he is perfect, and his perfect love casts out every fear. His perfect love transforms the lives of those who will trust only in him. He is our strength and our shield, our hope in this life, and the promise of life everlasting. May his love guard your heart today, and may others see the light of his presence upon your face and be drawn to him.

A Softened Heart

Sing to the Lord a new song, for he has done marvelous things.
(Psalm 98:1)

It has been so very dry that I have not been in the garden weeding lately. Well, actually I have tried several times and have given up because it was just too difficult to weed in dry, packed soil. Over the past several days, we have had about three inches or more of rain, and the earth has just soaked it up. I knew I needed to get out there to do my weeding while the ground was moist. Although we had lots to do yesterday, I felt compelled to get the gardens weeded that I am preparing to mulch and plant. I was out there with a shovel, turning the soil and pulling out the weeds. It was just perfect! When I lifted the clumps of dirt I had shoveled, the soil just fell apart and I was able to easily pull out the clover and other weeds that have made themselves at home in my garden. As I worked, I was reminded again how much weeding my garden is like God working on my heart. Lately I have been struggling with a broken heart, and there have been many tears. I know there is no way to rush the grief process, but I get frustrated when the smallest thing can get the tears rolling. I am always in a hurry to get through seasons of grief and sorrow, but there is no rushing it. As I worked in the perfectly moistened soil, I thought how easy it was to remove the weeds, and was reminded that seasons of tearfulness often accompany a time when God removes the things from my heart that inhibit growth. The tears soften the soil of my heart and get it ready for God to work, and when the time is right, he removes the weeds. I was amazed how much ground I was able to cover when the soil was so well prepared as compared to other days when it was hot and dry. I listened as the Holy Spirit reminded me of lies that I have let infiltrate my thinking and the truth that stands against them. I was so blessed and encouraged that except for the stiffness, I actually quite enjoyed the task! Praise God for his faithfulness, for he has done marvelous things!

Forgive My Hidden Faults

> But who can discern their own errors? Forgive my hidden faults. Keep your servant also from willful sins; may they not rule over me. Then I will be blameless, innocent of great transgression. (Psalm 19:12-13)

Do you find that even after years and years of walking with Christ there are often some things that still cause you to stumble? As a perfectionist, I wrestle with the knowledge that I am only human every day. Often we don't admit our weaknesses even to ourselves, never mind admitting them to others. We get defensive when others try to help us see an area we still need to bring under the lordship of Christ. If we could only admit to one another, "This is something I am still struggling with." Instead, we try to hide our imperfections and pretend we have it all together. The prayer in this Psalm is one I so often need. *Lord, help me not to allow any sin to rule over me or have influence in my life. Guard my tongue, Lord, so that all I say will honor you and be a blessing to those who listen. Lord, may even my thoughts be those that glorify your name. Forgive me for grumbling and complaining when I could be praising you or encouraging another. Strengthen me in my weakness, O God. Rule over every fiber of my being, for you are my Rock and my Redeemer. Amen*

Every Victory Is from the Lord

> The king rejoices in your strength, Lord. How great is his joy in the victories you give! You have granted him his heart's desire and have not withheld the request of his lips. You came to greet him with rich blessings and placed a crown of pure gold on his head. He asked you for life, and you gave it to him—length

of days, for ever and ever. Through the victories you gave, his glory is great; you have bestowed on him splendor and majesty. Surely you have granted him unending blessings and made him glad with the joy of your presence. For the king trusts in the Lord; through the unfailing love of the Most High he will not be shaken. (Psalm 21:1-7)

King David surely has a way with words! He is not ashamed to declare his praises to God, and he knows that it is God who has given him all that he has. Every victory is from the Lord. Every blessing has come from God alone. I have not been called by God to be a king. Nevertheless, I find myself in these words, praising God for all of the victories he has given me. I rejoice for he has indeed given me the desire of my heart and has blessed me with joy and peace. There is even a crown awaiting me when I reach my heavenly dwelling! He has made me glad with joy in his presence. How wonderful to celebrate the goodness of the Lord in our lives!

Relief from Distress

Answer me when I call to you, my righteous God. Give me relief from my distress; have mercy on me and hear my prayer. How long will you people turn my glory into shame? How long will you love delusions and seek false gods? Know that the Lord has set apart his faithful servant for himself; the Lord hears when I call to him. (Psalm 4:1-3)

If all that you knew of the person who wrote these words was the words alone, what would know of him? The writer of this psalm is in distress and is crying out to God. Other people are perhaps mocking him for his faith in God and he is responding to them with a statement of faith: God will hear when I call on him. We discover from these verses that the man (or woman) of God is not immune to trouble. God's people sometimes get into difficult situations in life. Those who think being a Christian is all harps and music haven't walked long with God. Not only do we have times of distress, sometimes that distress comes as a result of others. It was really hard for me to accept that not everyone I meet is going to like me! In fact, there are those who are going to hate me just because I follow Christ! The Bible tells us that we are blessed when we are persecuted because of Christ; this allows us to share in his sufferings. When life is filled with distress, what can we do? Follow the psalmist's example and call out to God in faith. Know that he will hear your call and come to your aid, though it may not be in your timing or in the way you want him to. Be ready to speak the truth to those who taunt, and then, hold fast. Trust the Lord to be faithful. Know that nothing is ever wasted with God. When we are in a difficult situation, God will use it somehow to bring a blessing. God does not take our suffering lightly. He promises to be with us and to strengthen us. He will see us through.

Unwavering Devotion

> Vindicate me, Lord, for I have led a blameless life; I have trusted in the Lord and have not faltered. Test me, Lord, and try me, examine my heart and my mind; for I have always been mindful of your unfailing love and have lived in reliance on your faithfulness. (Psalm 26:1-3)

Do you have this kind of confidence in God? This psalm of David seems a little over the edge. We wonder if David is consumed with pride. How can he think that he has led a blameless life? Do you wonder what God thinks of David's prayer? Don't we do this with God sometimes too? We are in trouble and we come to God telling him what a great servant we have been and then tell him we deserve to be rescued. I do know this: David was a man God honored. David put his trust in the Lord alone. I think David's confidence was not in himself but in his God. David learned to trust God as a young boy and never wavered in his devotion. We know that he was not a sinless man, but his heart's desire was to follow after God. He wanted to walk in purity before the Lord. What I love about Psalms is the honesty the psalmist brings to God. His relationship with God is such that he can be real. He can express what is truly in his heart and know that his God loves him no matter what. It is this kind of intimacy with God that is worth pursuing. This kind of intimacy allows us to come as we are before him and know that he loves us no matter what. We know that we can tell him what is on our hearts, and he will listen. He will lead us. Oh, the confidence that comes from knowing God! Do you have enough confidence in God to ask him to examine your heart and mind? It is not confidence in ourselves we need, but confidence in him. If we know him, we know that he will examine us with love, he will lead us in love, and he will even correct us in love when we need it. What sweet fellowship comes when we know God so well that we are willing for him to know us as we are!

An Everlasting Kingdom

> Your kingdom is an everlasting kingdom, and your dominion endures through all generations... (Psalm 145:13a)

We human beings often lose sight of eternity. We are so focused on today and right now that we do not spend much thought on God's perspective of eternity. Our God never changes. He is the same now as he was when Noah was building the ark. God always has the perspective of eternity, and all he does is for the sake of someone's eternity. This does not mean God is not concerned about our todays, but whatever is going on in our now, God wants to use for the benefit of someone's eternity. If we keep a perspective of eternity when we are living our todays, we may find strength, encouragement and hope. Since my mother went home to be with the Lord, we have been sorting through her belongings. One thing that I wanted to have was a large, oval picture of my mother's grandparents. It had been presumed sold at a yard sale years ago, but as we were going through Mom's things that had been in storage, there it was! It was such a blessing to me to find the picture! Why? My mother's grandmother was a beautiful Christian woman. Her love for God is why my mother became a Christian. I wonder how my life and the lives of my children have been influenced by my great-grandmother's prayers and the promises the Lord made to her. I want to be a Christian whose life has influence for generations to come. I am so glad that God was, is, and is to come!

God: Our Fortress

> Praise be to the Lord my Rock, who trains my hands for war, my fingers for battle. He is my loving God and my fortress, my stronghold and my deliverer, my shield, in whom I take refuge, who subdues peoples under me. (Psalm 144:1-2)

As a shepherd, David learned from God about trust and courage. He learned that God was faithful to help him when predators came in to steal the sheep. As a king, David used all of those lessons the Lord had taught him as a boy and trusted God to lead him to victory in every battle he fought. He understood that God's wisdom was far above his own and knew that God would lead him if he sought God's counsel. He came to know God as his fortress (a protection from the enemy), his stronghold (a place of security), his deliverer (the one who would rescue him), his shield (protection from the flaming arrows of the enemy), and his refuge (protection from danger or distress). Even when the only weapon David had was a sling shot and five smooth stones, he was fully armed because God was with him. We face spiritual battles every day whether we recognize them or not. Life can be hard. Sometimes we are even our own worst enemy! God can help. God wants to help. He wants to train us to think his way and to follow his direction. This takes training and a willingness to allow God to teach us, because we just don't think like he thinks! When we have training from God, the battles we face in life will not rage out of control. We will have confidence in God and in our ability to follow his leading. We will know we are not alone, because our God is a strong fortress, our protection, and a refuge to which we can run.

The Name of the Lord Is a Strong Tower

> Your name, Lord, endures forever, your renown, Lord, through all generations. For the Lord will vindicate his people and have compassion on his servants. (Psalm 135:13-14)

There is a song I like to sing:

> The name of the Lord is a strong tower. The righteous run into it, and they are saved. The name of the Lord is a strong tower. The righteous run into it, and they are saved. Blessed be the name of the Lord. Blessed be the name of the Lord. Blessed be the name of the Lord, Most High.[9]

Throughout the Bible there are many names used for God. Each one signifies different attributes that are true of him. You can learn so much about God by studying his names. The truth is that there is no other name under heaven by which we can be saved. We often add "in Jesus' name" to the end of our prayers without really considering why. At the name of Jesus, every knee will bow and every tongue will confess that Jesus Christ is Lord. One day soon, everyone who ever lived will recognize the name of Jesus as the Messiah. What a wonderful day that will be! From all the way back to Adam and Eve until the current day, those who love God and call upon his name will find a love that never fails. Every servant of God who has ever called on his name has found him to be faithful.

He Is My Portion

You are my portion, Lord; I have promised to obey your words. I have sought your face with all my heart; be gracious to me according to your promise. I have considered my ways and have turned my steps to your statutes. I will hasten and not delay to obey your commands. (Psalm 119:57-60)

Sometimes when I am reading through Psalms, it becomes pretty obvious that most of us still have a lot to learn about prayer. Just these few lines from Psalm 119 are packed with a powerful prayer. Is God your portion? The Lord has given us all of himself. He is everything! In response, the psalmist gives back to God obedience, devotion, and a willingness to follow him. I am challenged by these words today. Am I obeying God's words? Am I seeking him with all my heart? Have I taken time lately to consider my ways and line them up with God's ways? Do I hasten to obey God, or do I obey in my own good time? It can become so easy to just drift in our relationship with the Lord instead of being deliberate. Take time today to seek him with all your heart and with no distractions. Dare to ask him how you are doing. Time is never wasted that is spent in the presence of God!

Answer the One Who Taunts

May your unfailing love come to me, Lord, your salvation according to your promise; then I can answer anyone who taunts me, for I trust in your word. Never take your word of truth from

my mouth, for I have put my hope in your laws. I will always obey
your law, for ever and ever. (Psalm 119:41-44)

Life has been pretty difficult lately, not just for me, but for many of my friends.
Just because we belong to Christ does not exempt us from experiencing the
pains of life. In fact, often these trials cause us to grow and challenge our
faith. I do not know what people do who do not have the unfailing love of
the Lord to see them through difficult days. If it were not for God's faithful
promises, difficult days would be impossible to get through! Thanks to the
Lord who has given us his Word and his truth to support us and encourage
us when life's challenges sit on our doorstep for a while! Have you noticed
that Satan does not wait until a crisis is over before he hovers, waiting for an
opportunity to draw us away from the Lord? No, he taunts, jeers, accuses,
and mocks us. When we are weary with a struggle, we often forget that we
don't have to listen to him. We need to respond with a word of truth, "I
belong to Jesus Christ. You have no authority in my life. Get lost!" Don't
let the devil add to your struggle. Focus on the truth you know. Let the
Holy Spirit bring to mind the promises of God, and be encouraged by his
unfailing love.

Enthroned in God's Presence

Increase the days of the king's life, his years for many generations.
May he be enthroned in God's presence forever; appoint your love
and faithfulness to protect him. Then I will ever sing in praise
of your name and fulfill my vows day after day. (Psalm 61:6-8)

There is so much to learn from King David about walking with God. As
we read through Psalms, we can see that David trusts God enough to share
with him how he is feeling and dealing with many different situations. David
wanted to serve God and to please him in all he did, and though he wasn't
perfect, his life reflects the kind of intimacy with the Lord that inspires us.
What is the key ingredient in a life of intimacy with the Lord? David asks to
be "enthroned in God's presence forever." This is the key. God promises to
never leave us nor forsake us, and he is faithful to his Word. So, in truth, we
are all in God's presence all the time. However, for many years I lived my

life oblivious to the presence of God. Even in prayer and Bible study, I was doing all the right things completely unaware of the presence of God with me. As a result, I became weak, powerless, afraid, and lonely. There came a time when God rescued me from that way of living the Christian life. He drew me to himself and through Psalms showed me that David was who he was because he lived every day in the presence of God. David spoke with God and acknowledged his presence in every aspect of his life. He trusted God to lead him in big things and in small things. When David was alone, he could be found singing praises to his God and speaking with the Lord about all that was going on in his life. My life was transformed when I began to practice walking in the presence of God like David did. Instead of just coming to God sometimes or when I thought about it or just when I awoke or was going to bed, I started inviting God to be a part of every aspect of my day. I soon began to sense God's presence with me all the time. He was there all along, but until I became aware of his presence, it was like he wasn't there. With a sense of God's nearness, we become filled with courage to face hard things, because we are sure of his help. Aware of his presence, we are empowered to choose his way and find greater victory, and when we become aware of his presence in our lives, we may be physically alone, but we never need to be lonely again. He desires to be our constant companion, and oh what joy there is in the presence of the Most High God!

Distant from God

I have strayed like a lost sheep. Seek your servant, for I have not forgotten your commands. (Psalm 119:176)

How the psalmist so skillfully tells it like it is! He loved God with all his heart, and yet there were times that even he drifted away from his relationship with God. Has that ever happened to you? Have you ever just stopped and suddenly realized that you are not really sure when it happened, but you have become distant from God? No one wakes up one morning and decides, "I am going to take a break from God today." No, when we pull away from God it happens slowly, unconsciously, and for many different reasons. Sometimes we just get too busy, so we skip our time with God. Even the bullet prayers throughout our day seem to come fewer and farther between. Sometimes we get pulled into a crisis in life. We draw near to God and lean on him throughout the crisis, but then when the crisis is over, we drift away. Whatever the reason, the psalmist points the way back for us. If you have ever felt like a lost sheep, there is only one solution. Call out to God. He is still the seeker of lost sheep. Hallelujah! Our God is faithful. He is ready to bring us salvation—even from our own wandering—for when we feel distant from the Lord, it is never he that has wandered away! How wonderful that the solution can come in just one moment as we draw near to him once more. His loving arms beckon us to come.

Living in the Last Days

> From you comes the theme of my praise in the great assembly; before those who fear you I will fulfill my vows. The poor will eat and be satisfied; those who seek the Lord will praise him—may your hearts live forever! All the ends of the earth will remember and turn to the Lord, and all the families of the nations will bow down before him. (Psalm 22:25-27)

As I was looking through a catalog to find a new Bible study book for my Sunday school class, I came across a title that intrigued me: *Living with Discernment in the End Times*[10]. I can get so discouraged sometimes when all around me people seem to be fighting one battle or another. Some of my friends seem to have multiple situations going on in their lives, and it makes me stop and wonder why. That Bible study book covers the books of 1 and 2 Peter and Jude which discuss what life will be like in the end times. Ever since the generation after Christ people have been thinking their generation was the last one, but we certainly can say that our generation fits the description better than any other so far. We know that the last days on earth will hold much catastrophe, and Revelation describes many things we cannot even imagine. So what? What difference does it make? The passage above reminds me that time on earth is short. There is a day coming—perhaps not too far off—when every knee shall bow and every tongue confess that Jesus Christ is Lord. What might our lives be like if we could catch a sense of urgency about our calling in Christ! This life on earth is not just about us, or even us and our families. Our purpose here is to declare the glory of God and share the good news of Christ wherever we go. May we be faithful in fulfilling our calling, because that day is drawing near.

Forgotten Promises

> I will come to your temple with burnt offerings and fulfill my vows to you—vows my lips promised and my mouth spoke when I was in trouble. I will sacrifice fat animals to you and an offering of rams; I will offer bulls and goats. (Psalm 66:13-15)

Have you ever made promises to God when you were in trouble hoping that he would work in your favor? Most of us have at one time or another. Most of us too, have quickly forgotten our promises when the trouble has passed. It might be that we make promises that are impossible to keep, or we get back to the business of living and then forget them. Whatever the reason, do you think it matters to God? Maybe we shouldn't make promises to God in the first place, but usually when we are promising God something, it is a last ditch effort to try to fix a situation that is humanly unfixable, isn't it? When God gives us the miracle we've been asking for, we often forget those desperate moments and go on just as before. The psalmist has not forgotten his promise. He comes with a grateful heart to God, and in the presence of his people he declares what God has done for him. He keeps his word to God and remembers to give glory to the Lord in the form of a testimony before the congregation. Oh, how the body of Christ might be encouraged if we would overcome our fear of speaking up and share what he has done!

He Can Redeem My Failures

> Do good to your servant according to your word, Lord. Teach me knowledge and good judgment, for I trust your commands. Before I was afflicted I went astray, but now I obey your word. You are good, and what you do is good; teach me your decrees. Though the arrogant have smeared me with lies, I keep your precepts with all my heart. Their hearts are callous and unfeeling, but I delight in your law. It was good for me to be afflicted so that I might learn your decrees. The law from your

mouth is more precious to me than thousands of pieces of silver and gold. (Psalm 119:65-72)

What has the psalmist learned from his failure? He has learned that God is good, that God's Word is good, and he is ready to learn from God how to walk in his ways. No one likes to fail. I don't know about you, but I often have trouble with the idea of failure. When I experience failure, I spend a lot of time beating myself up because I think I should be beyond failure. I don't like to disappoint the Lord, but even after many years of growing in the Kingdom, I still fail. I want to walk in God's ways. I want to do what he wants me to do and say what he wants me to say, but I often fall short. When I do, I struggle to move forward. There is a lot to learn from the psalmist. He acknowledges his failure and sees it as an opportunity to learn from the Lord. He knows God is good and his precepts are worth keeping. Failure is a sure reminder that we still need Jesus—every day, all the time. We cannot live this life without the help of the Holy Spirit. Failure is not something to celebrate, but if the result of failure is that we draw closer to the Lord, then maybe it is not so bad. I know that when I fail, it also helps me to be more patient with others around me who make mistakes. God is good. He can redeem every failure if we look to him.

A Desperate Plea

I love you, Lord, my strength. The Lord is my rock, my fortress and my deliverer; My God is my rock, in whom I take refuge, my shield and the horn of my salvation, my stronghold. (Psalm 18:1-2)

What a glorious declaration! You can feel the confidence and love the psalmist has for his Lord. You may have trouble relating to God with such intimacy, faith and confidence. You must realize that these words of love and confidence can only be spoken truthfully by the soul who has first known desperation and despair. If you read all of Psalm 18, you will see that the psalmist has been assaulted by many enemies and is desperate. In his desperation, he calls out to the Lord, and the Lord rescues him and exalts him to a place of honor above his enemies. There is confidence that comes when you have been desperate, have called out to God, and he has rescued you. It is an unshakable knowledge that God is indeed a fortress of protection for you. Once these words of the psalmist have become personal for you, you are changed forever. He is indeed your rock, your deliverer, your shield, your stronghold, and the enemy never has the same power to intimidate you again. Call out to him in your time of trouble, and you will find him faithful!

Feeling Forsaken

> My God, my God, why have you forsaken me? Why are you so far from saving me, so far from my cries of anguish? My God, I cry out by day, but you do not answer, by night, but I find no rest. (Psalm 22:1-2)

At one time or other most of us have been in the place where God seems sadly absent. If you have not, then you will. You may recognize these words as those spoken by Jesus in his last moments on the cross. Had God really forsaken Christ? Yes, when he bore our sin, God had to look away from him. Does he ever turn his back on us? No. There may be times when we are not aware of his presence near us and we may not *feel* him near to us. We may indeed feel that he has forgotten us or turned his back on us because of our sin or our pain or our ugliness, but Christ has already paid for our sin. Though we may be completely unaware of him, he is there, ever watching, waiting for the moment he will again make himself known to us. Keep reading in Psalm 22, and you will see the psalmist remembered this truth. The third verse says, "They cried to you and were saved; in you they trusted and were not disappointed." There may be times when God seems far away and deadly silent. When we have caused this distance because of our sin, we have only to confess and be restored. When we are in this place of feeling forsaken and it is not of our own doing, then, like the psalmist, we remember the truth. We walk by faith not feelings. We praise God and thank him that he has promised to never leave us nor forsake us. We focus on the knowledge that he *is* there whether we feel him or not. We trust in his Word and stand on his truth, and sooner or later, he will again reveal himself to us.

The Lord is My Shepherd

The Lord is my shepherd, I lack nothing. (Psalm 23:1)

In our culture, we don't really relate very well to God as a shepherd. We might not know that sheep are very stupid animals. They will get into dangerous situations, because they are not aware of the dangers. They need a shepherd, someone to guide them, protect them, look out for them, and keep them from being eaten by predators that lurk. How wise the psalmist! He has learned that we, like sheep, often foolishly get ourselves into trouble because we do not look where we are going and often forget that the enemy of our souls is lurking, waiting to devour us when we wander away from the Shepherd. Yes, we have a Shepherd, the Lord our God, who wants to protect us from the enemy. He wants to guide us to safety and provide all that we need. If we will only follow him, we will not be in want. That is not to say that we will not want things. We will. In this culture, we want too much! We won't be in need of any good thing, though. We will have what we need. We will be cared for, looked after, and safe in the Shepherd's care.

Seeking His Face

Such is the generation of those who seek him, who seek your face, God of Jacob. (Psalm 24:6)

I remember a time long ago when I finally had everything I wanted—a loving husband, three beautiful children, a nice house, a good church—but I was empty and depressed. It didn't make sense, but in desperation I went to God and asked for help. I remember reading these words about seeking the Lord. Actually, it wasn't these words, but a similar verse that says those who seek the Lord will find him. I thought I had already found Him. I loved God. I was challenged by the word *seek*, so I did a word study to gain a deeper understanding. I looked the word up in the dictionary[11]. The first two meanings were enough to get me started:

1. to go in search or quest of: to seek the truth.

2. to try to find or discover by searching or questioning: to seek the solution to a problem.

So, I set out to *seek* God, to go in search, to try to find or discover him in a new way. I looked in the concordance and found every verse in the Bible that used the word *seek*. I learned a lot that day. I had given my life to Christ, but I really hadn't learned to seek him. The promise that those who seek him will find him really had an impact on me, so I began to seek him in earnest. I will never regret it either! As I began to seek his face, he began to reveal himself to me in new ways, drawing me into a more intimate relationship with him than I ever could have hoped for. Take time to seek the Lord today. You will be glad you did.

Weary and Broken

> Praise the Lord, my soul; all my inmost being praise his holy name. (Psalm 103:1)

My mother often told the story that when I was almost 2, she was standing with me in front of a calendar with a picture of Jesus on it. I got all excited, jumped up and down in her arms and said, "Je-sus" –my first word. I will have to take her word for it, but such natural praise has not always been so natural for me. When my three children were all under the age of 5, I struggled with depression to the point of despair. God gave me the wisdom I needed to experience wholeness again. He put a song on my lips…

> *Bless the Lord, O my soul*
> *Bless the Lord, O my soul,*
> *Bless the Lord, O my soul;*
> *And let all that is within me*
> *Bless His holy name!*

I didn't feel like praising God. My soul was weary and broken, and I spent a lot of time feeling sorry for myself, but I began to sing. The Bible tells us that he inhabits the praises of His people. I know it is true! He met me at my point of need. As I sung, telling my soul to praise him, peace began to fill my spirit. That little praise chorus helped to lift me out of a dark pit. Though that was not the only prescription for my pain, it was the beginning of healing and helped me to be open to God's further work in my heart. The praise didn't heal me, God did. When we praise God, we are not rehearsing all that is wrong with our lives. When we praise God, we acknowledge that he is God and that he is good. We choose to trust him; having our hearts opened to him in praise, he is able to do the work in us that needs to be done. Don't underestimate the power of praise!

God's Still Small Voice

> The voice of the Lord is powerful; the voice of the Lord is majestic. The voice of the Lord breaks the cedars. (Psalm 29:4-5)

Just yesterday in our Sunday school class we began a study of Isaiah. We read in the sixth chapter that Isaiah actually saw the Lord and heard his voice. Can you even imagine the glory of that moment? I remember years ago being struck with these words in John 10:4 "…his sheep follow him because they know his voice." They know his voice! I am one of his sheep and I don't know his voice. I went right to the Lord in prayer and asked, "Lord is this true? Can your sheep hear your voice? If it's true, will you teach me to hear your voice too? I want to hear your voice." Well, I didn't hear him right then, but I looked up "God's voice" in my concordance, and I was amazed by how many references there were for hearing God's voice all through the Bible. I began to seek God fervently. I asked him to teach me to discern his voice, and he taught me how to listen. You know the verse about his still small voice? These words in Psalm 29 say God's voice is big. We want God to speak to us with his big voice or to write us a letter or send us an email. We want to hear from God—or do we? If we actually hear from God, then we have to follow him. We have to do what he says. If we can't hear him, we can figure out what we want to do on our own. We are off the hook, right? We might be off the hook, but we miss out on the most amazing and personal relationship with the living God if we never learn to listen to his voice. I had to learn to be still before I could hear God speaking quietly to my heart. That was not easy. I was most comfortable with lots of noise. It took courage and discipline to turn off the noise and choose to be still and listen, but I never want to go back to not hearing. How amazing that the God who created the universe wants to talk to me—and to you—if only we will listen.

Stand Firm

They are brought to their knees and fall, but we rise up and stand firm. (Psalm 20:8)

My family just spent a week at the beach. It was great fun playing in the ocean waves! It was difficult, if not impossible, at times to stand firm when a large wave crashed into me. Then my nephew gave me some valuable lessons from his experience. "Stand sideways," he said, "so you can brace yourself and not get knocked over." I also learned for myself that I shouldn't turn my back on those waves, because they were constantly changing, and a big one could come along at anytime. It became apparent that in order to not get knocked down, I needed to get myself out passed the breaking point of most of the waves. There the ocean was much easier to handle. Life circumstances can often be like those waves. We can stand firm. We can let nothing move us if we keep firmly grounded in the Word of truth. If we know that what we are doing is not without purpose or reason, we can keep going. If we keep alert to the temptations that can cause us to stumble, we can avoid having them get the best of us. Sometimes, instead of running away, we have to go further in past the breaking point before we can find rest. So then, stand firm in the work you are doing, and he will sustain you.

Take Every Thought Captive

May these words of my mouth and this meditation of my heart be pleasing in your sight, Lord, my Rock and my Redeemer. (Psalm 19:14)

Wow! That is a powerful prayer, isn't it? How often do you tell God you want the words you speak to please him? What kind of talk pleases God? Grumbling and complaining? No. Words that tear down? No. I think this is one we cannot do without the help of the Holy Spirit. For our words to be pleasing to God they should be truthful and uplifting. The thing about words, though, if you haven't noticed, is that they escape from our mouths too often before we can evaluate them by God's standards. I think that is why the second part of this verse is there. What exactly are the meditations of your heart? What do you think about? What do you hope for? For some help with making our thoughts pleasing to the Lord, we can go to Philippians 4:8 "…whatever is right, whatever is pure, whatever is lovely… if anything is excellent or praiseworthy— think on these things." I remember when God convicted me about this verse. I was so depressed and disgruntled that I could not think of one thing that fit God's criteria! That is when I learned to take every thought captive unto Christ. I had to make a conscious effort to stop every thought, consider if it met God's standards, and correct my thinking to be in line with God's word. It was not easy. I wasn't very good at it, but I learned one thought at a time. Now thinking God's way is much more natural for me, and the more I think God's way, the more the words that come out of my mouth are also more pleasing to the Lord. May God help us to make our thoughts and words pleasing to him.

When I Am Afraid

Though an army besiege me, my heart will not fear; though war break out against me, even then I will be confident. (Psalm 27:3)

If I were David, I might be tempted to think I had plenty of reasons to be afraid! When he tended sheep as a boy, he had wild animals to fear. As a young man, he faced Goliath. As a man, Saul pursued him time after time seeking to kill him because David was God's man. Yet, David says he is not afraid because God is his stronghold. This truth is so hard to get a hold of sometimes! Do you have fears? Are you intimidated by people? Are you afraid of what people think about you? From David we learn that even in times when there might be a legitimate reason to fear, if we know that God is with us, we do not need to fear. He is our salvation in time of trouble. He is bigger than any giant we might face. Knowing the truth and appropriating it are two different things, though. How could David say this and really mean it? David knew God and trusted him. He didn't just know about God. As a boy tending sheep, he spent time talking with God, and God had been faithful in protecting David over and over. Though my fears were not as legitimate as David's, there was a time when I was tormented by many fears. Philippians 4: 6 says, "Be anxious for nothing but in everything by prayer and supplication with thanksgiving, make your requests known to God and the peace of God…will guard your hearts and minds in Christ Jesus." I realized that I was disobeying God if I allowed my fear of failure, my fear of what other's think, my fear of being alone, or any other fear control my life. I learned that I couldn't just tell myself not to be afraid, but if I spent more time with the Lord, he could equip me to handle my fears. I learned to bring my fears to him and let his peace guard my heart and my mind. I learned that I didn't have to give in to fear, but could instead stand on the Word of God. He has been faithful, and fear no longer controls my life.

Walk in Freedom

> I will walk about in freedom, for I have sought out your precepts.
> (Psalm 119:45)

We celebrate the freedom that we have in this nation. We are indeed grateful for our freedom, but even more important than political freedom is our freedom in Christ. The fifth chapter of Galatians tells us that it was for freedom that Christ set us free. Sadly, many think our freedom is so that we can do whatever we want. No, we are free to do the right thing. We are free from sin, so that we can live in a way that pleases God, and our freedom was purchased with the blood of Christ our Savior. I have to confess that I do not always walk in the freedom that Christ purchased for me. I struggle with addictive tendencies and do not always walk in the victory that is mine in Christ. The psalmist helps us to understand the right way to walk in freedom. He can walk in freedom because he has sought out God's precepts. Everything God teaches us in his Word is so that we can enjoy a life of freedom, if we will only follow!

When We Fail

> Blessed is the one whose transgressions are forgiven, whose sins are covered. Blessed is the one whose sin the Lord does not count against them and in whose spirit is no deceit. (Psalm 32:1-2)

Yesterday in Sunday school, we were talking about failure. Why is failure so difficult for some of us to admit to? We must admit that in our times of failure we often grow the most, and it is only when we sin that we can truly understand the forgiveness we have in Christ. Only when we fall short can we really see how deeply we need Jesus. Christians frequently get uncomfortable talking about sin because we think we should have mastered it by now, but in all of us there are still sins that tempt us and lure us away from Christ. The reason for this is that we are human! We were born with a sin nature, and though Christ has purchased our freedom from sin, the actually living out of that truth is much more difficult sometimes than we pretend. Our pride gets in the way of admitting that we still struggle with sin. We can become convinced that we are the only Christian who still has a problem with sin. In reality, all of us must wrestle with temptation. If we are without sin, it is only because Christ has declared us righteous by his work on the cross. I am so thankful that I can still bring my sin to the cross! There are still things in my life that he must redeem if I will allow him to do so. Just because others don't see our sins doesn't mean they aren't there! God sees. We know. We forget that we are not alone in this. If I admit my sin to you, you might use it against me, but if we could begin to share our struggles, perhaps we all might have the encouragement we need to succeed! Just a thought....

The Majesty of the Mountains

Before the mountains were born or you brought forth the whole world, from everlasting to everlasting you are God. (Psalm 90:2)

Can you imagine the world before mountains? I can't. I live in the mountains. The beauty and the majesty of the mountains help me to understand the glory of God. This week my husband and I were traveling home from a business trip to South Carolina. I was moved in my spirit as we drove through the mountains in northern South Carolina and southern North Carolina. The beauty is breathtaking! We stopped along the way to view a waterfall. As we walked up the long path to the top, I wondered if it would be worth it. I had taken us out of our way to see this, and I didn't want it to be for nothing. We were not disappointed! It wasn't until we got all the way to the top that we stood before the majestic display of God's handiwork. It was glorious! As I stood there, I could not help but think what an amazing God we have. He was the One who formed this mountain. He was the One who invented the waterfall. We were not alone. There was a steady stream of people who had also taken time to come and see this beautiful display of natural beauty. It is good to be reminded how big God is. When you stare down into a chasm that is so big you can't see the bottom, you have to pause and think about the fact that God sees. God knows the top from the bottom. He knows the beginning from the end. How amazing is that!

The Righteousness of Christ

> The Lord has dealt with me according to my righteousness; according to the cleanness of my hands he has rewarded me. For I have kept the ways of the Lord; I am not guilty of turning from God. All his laws are before me; I have not turned away from his decrees. I have been blameless before him and have kept myself from sin. The Lord has rewarded me according to my righteousness, according to the cleanness of my hands in his sight. (Psalm 18:20-24)

This is a psalm of David which he sang after the Lord delivered him from the hand of his enemies. Perhaps David's righteousness was far above my own. When I read the words to this Psalm, I wonder how it could be true. Do the words not echo a heart filled with pride? There was a time when I would have read these words and connected with them, thinking them true of myself, but then I had a major dose of reality hit my life. I fell far short of the mark, but it was not until then that I truly began to understand the grace and mercy of God. Yes, God sees me as righteous, but it is not my righteousness he sees, it is the righteousness of Christ. I am blameless before the Lord only because of the redemptive work of Christ in my heart. Nevertheless, because of Christ's atonement for my sin, my heart longs to walk in his ways, to follow his decrees, and to live the righteousness he purchased for me. He cleanses my life with his own, and I am made new.

An Undivided Heart

> Teach me your way, Lord, that I may rely on your faithfulness; give me an undivided heart, that I may fear your name. (Psalm 86:11)

This prayer from Psalm 86 becomes more personal to me every day. The more I know God, the more I understand that his ways are just not my ways. (Isaiah 55:8), and the more I learn about myself, the more I understand that my heart is often divided. I want my heart to be completely devoted to Christ, but too often I find that other people and other things can crowd into that spot. To have an undivided heart does not mean that you don't care about other people or other needs. The things, people, and demands of life in general can often rival in importance to our relationship with the living God. We know he will understand, so we sometimes ignore him to care for what seem like urgent needs. I want my heart's desire to be to love and serve Christ—all day, every day. In all that I do and in every relationship I have, I want Christ to have preeminence, but I have discovered that this single-minded devotion doesn't (at least for me) come naturally. It is easier to sometimes ignore God because he is invisible and is not demanding my time and attention. That doesn't mean he doesn't want it or isn't disappointed when I let other things crowd him out of my life. When I allow God to truly teach me his ways, I find balance. I find peace. I find wholeness and satisfaction, and I find that there is time for the other important priorities in my life. Rarely, if ever, does it work the other way around. Have you discovered that you can only learn God's ways if you ask him to teach them to you? His ways are so far from the natural way we humans tend to do things! His ways are worth learning. They are not burdensome or heavy. Walking in his ways really does lead to peace, joy, and contentment that you can get no other way.

Living for God's Glory

> But God will redeem me from the realm of the dead; he will surely take me to himself. (Psalm 49:15)

As I read through Psalm 49 this morning, my thoughts go to all of the news we listened to in the weeks following Michael Jackson's death. There were other famous people who also died that same week, but Michael's face was all over the news all day every day for many weeks. I was saddened by his death, and my heart grieves for his family. I have grieved the loss of two brothers and both of my parents. There is nothing at all easy about losing a loved one.

I simply can't imagine having to grieve in front of the whole world! Michael's projected net worth was five hundred million dollars. For all his wealth and fame, he certainly seemed like a lost soul. He had appeared so solemn in recent years. I don't know the state of his heart. Only God knows that. It is clear that his wealth and his fame did not exempt him from problems in this life, and now he is gone. His life in this world is over. It reminds us that we don't really know how long our own life will be. Just because we are here today, does not guarantee that we will be here tomorrow. It is important, then, that we live today deliberately. How are we investing our lives? Are we giving ourselves to things that will last for eternity or to things that are temporal? Is our hope in things or wealth, or is our hope in the living God who gives our life meaning and purpose? Do we know that it is God who redeems us? It is he who rescues us from the grave. He is our life and peace. Only he gives our lives any lasting purpose. Let us live this life for his glory.

Anointed by God

> You love righteousness and hate wickedness; therefore God, your God, has set you above your companions by anointing you with the oil of joy. (Psalm 45:7)

Have you ever struggled with self-esteem issues? If you are like most of the people on this planet you have. There are a few people out there who seem to have all the confidence they need. I was one of those. When I shared the fact that I have a low self esteem, people were always surprised. I did not have confidence. I had a great mask! I rarely let people see the true me, the one who was always afraid and always unsure. I wonder if there really is anyone out there who truly has a healthy self-esteem. Go into any book store, Christian or otherwise, and you will find shelves full of self-help books to address this need. There is a better place to find a cure for the problem of low self-esteem, though. In this Psalm, God is addressing David. God tells him that he is setting him above his friends because David loves righteousness and hates wickedness. In short, David's heart is in the right place. Do you remember when God first anointed David to be king? He was the youngest of Jesse's sons, just a little shepherd boy. There were certainly several of his brothers that were much more qualified for the job of king, weren't there?

It is good to remember that God often calls the most unlikely person to accomplish his will in a situation. When I read this Psalm this morning, I remembered a time years ago when I was reading these words as if for the first time. I could feel in my spirit that God was speaking them to me! Since then, God has indeed turned my sorrow into joy. As I have spent time with him in his Word and in prayer, he has reminded me over and over again that I am his. He confirms his purpose and calling on my life. He encourages me and strengthens me. He reminds me who I am—his. He has taught me how to lay aside my filthy rags and take up a garment of praise. He has anointed me with the oil of joy and gladness. Knowing who we are in Christ is the best cure for low self-esteem.

A Broken and a Wounded Spirit

My sacrifice, O God, is a broken spirit; a broken and contrite heart you, God, will not despise. (Psalm 51:17)

Psalm 51 is a psalm of confession and restoration. The verses just before this one tell us that God doesn't delight in sacrifices. God's people in the Old Testament world made sacrifices in order to receive atonement for their sin. It seems kind of gruesome, doesn't it? According to this verse, God would rather that we didn't need a sacrifice. If his people would only obey him and walk in his ways, there would be no need for the shedding of blood. Because of Jesus' sacrifice for us on the cross, there is no longer any need to sacrifice innocent animals to atone for our sin. Jesus paid it all. Praise God! The verse above is no less true, though. Sometimes we bring our offerings to God thinking we can earn his favor. The truth is: God doesn't need our sacrifices. God doesn't really want our sacrifices. What pleases God is a heart turned toward him. Sadly, we often have stubborn hearts. I should speak for myself, I suppose. Can you remember a time when all you had to give God was a broken heart and a wounded spirit? I can. It was a dark time, but it helped me to understand this verse better. It was only when I reached the place of brokenness that I was ready to admit that I really couldn't figure things out on my own. I tried. I failed. I tried harder. I failed again. No amount of striving on my part could heal my brokenness. Only then, in desperation, did I turn to God ready to listen and learn his ways. I am not talking about when I first accepted Christ. I have to admit that as a Christian of many years I was still trying to do it on my own. I tried so hard to be the kind of person I knew God wanted me to be. Finally, broken-hearted and empty I came to him and laid my life down again. That was when I learned how beautiful God's grace is! He accepted my offering—unimaginable to me! He took my broken heart and wounded spirit and made me new! He helped me to learn to come to him and to trust him to do the work in me that I could never do on my own. There is no better news than that!

A Great Day to Praise the Lord

> Shout for joy to God, all the earth! Sing the glory of his name;
> make his praise glorious. (Psalm 66:1-2)

It is a great day to praise the Lord! I love to sit on my porch and listen to the birds sing. They sing all day long, but I love to listen to their happy chirping especially in the morning. The wind is rustling gently in the trees, a quiet, restful sound. God created everything in such a magnificent way. His glory is all around us. I think all of nature does such a wondrous job of praising the Lord: the mountains in their majesty, the ocean in its immense power, and the flowers in my garden that brighten up the landscape. I think of trees and how they always have their branches reaching upward as though worshiping the Lord who created them, gently swaying in the breeze as though dancing before their maker. The only part of God's creation that doesn't glorify him at all times is people. We can be so full of ourselves that we often neglect to offer praise to the One who created all things. Even God's children who love him with all their hearts can be distracted with life and neglect to glorify him. Of course, we are the only part of creation that has been given a choice. God delights in the praise of his people. Take some time today to just enjoy the Lord and give him praise!

I Cannot Be Shaken

> Those who trust in the Lord are like Mount Zion, which cannot
> be shaken but endures forever. (Psalm 125:1)

What a verse of encouragement for these troubling times! The economy is struggling. Trust in the Lord. The media keeps telling us how awful things are right now. Trust in the Lord. You have a wayward child. Trust in the Lord. You are battling an illness that may consume you. Trust in the Lord. Your marriage is in trouble. Trust in the Lord. You are in need of comfort. Trust in the Lord. I used to think that trust was an emotion. I couldn't help it if I had trouble trusting. I couldn't make myself trust more. I just didn't know how to trust. What an amazing God we serve! He knew that I didn't know how to trust—wasn't able to trust. Some of us have been wounded by those who were supposed to take care of us, and this has left us unable to trust. God is such a wonderful and patient teacher! He tells us to trust him, and then he helps us to do it! How do you learn to trust? First, you recognize that trust is not an emotion; it is a choice. In any situation, I can choose to trust God. Why? Because he is completely trustworthy, I can choose to believe his Word which tells me that I can trust him. He is faithful. I didn't learn this in one moment, but through many difficult experiences I began to choose to trust God and the truth he had given me. Each time he would faithfully bring me through, so the next time it was easier to trust. When I recall first being moved by the words above, I couldn't imagine not being shaken. I was so shaken! As I have grown over the years to trust God, I know the reality of these words in my life. Whenever I choose to trust God, he is faithful, and I can stand firm like Mount Zion!

Fully Known by God

> You have searched me, Lord, and you know me. You know when
> I sit and when I rise; you perceive my thoughts from afar. You
> discern my going out and my lying down; you are familiar with
> all my ways. (Psalm 139:1-3)

Even before we knew him, he knew us. He wasn't just aware of us; he knew the very moment we were conceived. He watched us as we grew. He knows all there is to know about us—and he still loves us! Isn't that amazing? He knows our outward circumstances and our inward thoughts. Does that bring you comfort or make you a little uneasy? I spent a lot of years trying to please people. I would try so hard to be the person that I thought the person I was with wanted me to be that I had no clue who I really was! God knew! God knows. I am comforted by this knowledge. He knows my weaknesses, yet he accepts me as his own. He knows every tear I have ever cried! I am glad that I cannot hide myself from God. It is this very thing that has helped me to accept myself and find courage to be myself with people. To know that I am fully known by God frees me to be myself, not just with him, but with others as well. If God is familiar with all my ways, then he knows how to unravel all my confusion. If he knows when I sit or rise, then he knows when I am stuck alongside the road with a flat tire. He knows more about me than I know about myself! When I struggle with overcoming a particular problem in my life, he can give me the wisdom I need. So often God has helped me to understand myself better, allowing me to grow more and more into the person he has created me to be. What a blessing to be known and loved so completely!

Suffering for Christ

> My soul faints with longing for your salvation, but I have put my hope in your word. My eyes fail, looking for your promise; I say, "When will you comfort me?" Though I am like a wineskin in the smoke, I do not forget your decrees. How long must your servant wait? When will you punish my persecutors? The arrogant dig pits trap me, contrary to your law. All your commands are trustworthy; help me, for I am being persecuted without cause. They almost wiped me from the earth, but I have not forsaken your precepts. In your unfailing love preserve my life, that I may obey the statutes of your mouth. (Psalm 119:81-88)

I recently read Randy Alcorn's book *Safely Home*[12] and was so moved by the fictional account of the persecution of pastors and other Christians in China. Although the book's characters are fictional, this kind of persecution in China is not. This prayer in Psalm 119 could easily be the prayer of thousands of Christians who are being persecuted around the globe today. Let's take a few moments to pray that God would strengthen and encourage those who are facing these kinds of trials today. Pray that these dear people would have the courage to stand for Christ no matter what they face, and that he would allow them to know his wonderful presence and the power of his love in the midst of their tribulation. May God grant his grace to all who suffer in his name.

God Will Rescue You

> In you, Lord, I have taken refuge; let me never be put to shame.
> In your righteousness, rescue and deliver me; turn your ear to
> me and save me. (Psalm 71:1-2)

God is our refuge, a safe place to run to when we need protection. What do we need protection from? Sometimes I need protection from myself! How about you? Sometimes I need protection from other people. I haven't had to worry about physical harm, though some might be in an abusive relationship from which they need protection. I run to God when the words of others wound my spirit. I am sensitive, so that happens a lot. When I am wounded by another's words, I find refuge in God. He speaks truth to my spirit and reminds me that I am completely loved and accepted by him. The most frequent reason I seek God as a refuge, though, is when Satan launches an attack against me. Scripture is clear that our battle is not against flesh and blood, but against spiritual forces of evil (Ephesians 6:12). How do you battle an invisible foe? Run to God! Ask for his help. The words in this Psalm and many others are great models of asking God to come to our rescue. I am thankful that I no longer have to be afraid of demonic attacks. Christ has authority over all. If you are serving Christ, there will be spiritual battles, but when the battle rages, he is able to come to your rescue.

God's Plan for Your Life

> Give praise to the Lord, proclaim his name; make known among
> the nations what He has done. Sing to him, sing praise to him;
> tell of all his wonderful acts. Glory in his holy name; let the
> hearts of those who seek the Lord rejoice. Look to the Lord and
> his strength; seek his face always. (Psalm 105:1-4)

These words take me back to my freshman year in college. Within the first two weeks, I found myself sitting on my bed in the middle of the night, holding my roommate's Bible—because I didn't have one of my own—and crying out to God who seemed to be trying to get my attention. I wanted to know what he wanted and was feeling so desperate to know that I just flipped open the Bible and started reading. "Why do you cry out loudly...?" (Micah 4:9) With those words, I knew that God was with me in that room and that he had something to say to me! Since the first try worked so well, I thought I would try again. I flipped the pages, looked down, and the words above jumped off the page at me. These words were for me. This is what God wanted to do with my life! This is how he wanted me to live. Though there is a lot more to the story than I have space here to tell, that was the beginning of my journey with the Lord. What an adventure it has been and still is! That night I discovered that God loves me and has a plan for my life. I surrendered to his plan, and the rest is history. What is God's plan for your life? Do you have a verse that jumps off the page at you? For what purpose is God calling you? If you are not sure, ask the One who knows and seek his face always.

God's Cheerleading Squad

> May we shout for joy over your victory and lift up our banners in the name of our God. May the Lord grant all your requests. (Psalm 20:5)

V-I-C-T-O-R-Y! Victory! Victory is our cry! All of us remember that cheerleader chant from our High School days. Then, it was usually about football or basketball, but how many of us could use our very own cheerleader to cheer us on to the victories we need in our lives now? I know I could! We can have cheerleaders in our lives if we are willing to share with others the areas of our lives where we need to find victory. That is what the body of Christ is supposed to be, our support and encouragement. All of us should be encouraging one another to be everything that God intended us to be for the sake of the body of Christ. In other words, as we grow, the whole body of Christ benefits. As we encourage others to grow, the whole body of Christ benefits. In order for this to really work, though, we have to be willing to share with others the areas where we need victory. Sadly, we often don't do that because we are too busy trying to protect the image that we are ok. We are afraid to share our struggles because someone might judge us. We don't have to get up and share with the whole church on Sunday morning or even the whole small group on Wednesday night, but we all ought to have at least one or two people who know our stuff, and can support and cheer us on as we seek to be all God created us to be. Without this accountability and encouragement, we often give up and let those unredeemed areas stay unredeemed. Don't have a cheering squad? Ask the Lord to give you one, and may the Lord grant all of your requests!

In God's Hands

> They who want to kill me will be destroyed; they will go down
> to the depths of the earth. They will be given over to the sword
> and become food for jackals. (Psalm 63:9-10)

What can we learn from verses such as these? Like little children should we stick our tongues out and taunt, "Nah, nah, nah, nah, nah!" when we are wronged knowing God will surely judge their acts of hatred one day? I don't think so! The knowledge that God will judge evildoers in the end ought to bring us to our knees. When we understand that God is our advocate when we are wronged, then we can be at peace. We do not need to become defensive and fight back. Jesus words on the cross can become ours, "Father, forgive them, they know not what they do." Those controlled by the powers of darkness do not realize that they are trapped, and they desperately need a Savior. If we pray for those who have wronged us, perhaps we can be a part of their turning to him. God does not take lightly when the wicked come against his children, but he does not need our help in dealing with them! We can trust him to do the right thing in his time. He will make it right in the end. Even if the end is eternity, God will see to it that justice prevails. When we choose to forgive, we release God to work on our behalf. We let go of the situation and rest knowing it is in God's hands. There is no better place for our situation to be!

Don't Miss the Blessing

Your word is a lamp for my feet, a light on my path. (Psalm 119:105)

I love lighthouses. Often our family vacations have been lighthouse visits. I won't forget the time we planned to see a lighthouse in Door County,

Wisconsin. In order to get to see it, we had to wade several hundred feet through knee-deep water. We weren't sure it was worth the trouble, so we asked those who were wading back the other direction if it was worth the extra effort to see it. Having been assured by them that it was, we continued on. Of course, this ended up being one of our favorite lighthouses, and we have wonderful memories of that day. Lighthouses, though often beautiful just standing majestically by the sea, would be worthless if they did not fulfill their true purpose, to light the way for sailors in the dark, foggy, or stormy seas. I think sometimes we forget that God's Word is our light in this dark place. We often forget the spiritual darkness around us and treat God's Word like it is too much trouble to get into. Like a lighthouse whose bulb is broken, God's Word cannot light our path simply by being on our shelf. We need to open it, read it, and reflect on what it says, so that when we face the storms of life, it will light our way to safe shores. Often, like the lighthouse mentioned above, we won't know what we're missing until we see it for ourselves. God's Word is like that too. When we come to God's Word, it does take extra effort and time that we might not feel we have, but the stuff we have to wade through in order to get there will be worth it when God speaks to us from his Word. He longs to speak to us. He longs for us to come and linger in his Word, so he can bless us. Don't miss out on the blessing!

Redeemed

> Israel, put your hope in the Lord, for with the Lord is unfailing love and with him is full redemption. He himself will redeem Israel from all their sins. (Psalm 130:7-8)

When I was just four or five years old, my brothers and sisters and I would take our wagon around the neighborhood and collect empty soda bottles. This was before soda came in cans! When we had a good wagon load, we would take them to the corner store where they would redeem the bottles for five cents apiece. Most considered the bottles worthless because you could only get a few cents for them, but for us they were a great treasure! With the money we earned, we would usually buy a big bag of penny candy, making all of our efforts worthwhile. This story of redeeming the soda bottles helps me to understand the concept of redemption. We brought worthless bottles to the store owner, and he gave us money back. Before we belonged to Christ, Satan had full rights to our lives because of our sin. Christ paid the price for our redemption with his own blood, shed on the cross so that we could again belong to God. Our sin leaves us worthless and dirty, like those bottles, but when the store owner purchases them back, they are cleaned and become usable again. When Christ redeems us, our lives become new again and we are of great value to the King of Kings. We often only think about redemption in terms of salvation, but I am encouraged when I realize that Christ desires to redeem every part of our lives unto the glory of God. Are there parts of your life yet unredeemed by the grace of God? Surrender them to the Maker, who will transform them from worthless baggage to a vessel fit for his service.

A Treasured Vessel

I praise you because I am fearfully and wonderfully made; your works are wonderful, I know that full well. (Psalm 139:14)

This is one of those verses I often struggle to believe. Oh, I believe it with my head, but my heart can't quite agree. I have wrestled with self-esteem my whole life, and if you asked me what I would change about myself, I would be able to shoot off a list a page long. Years ago, a friend who was mentoring me challenged me with this verse. She admonished me to read it and choose to believe it. She said to make it my prayer, giving thanks to God for making me the way he did because I know that he creates only that which is wonderful and good. I just wasn't getting anywhere with the challenge, when one morning I was sitting in the living room having my quiet time with the Lord. I sat there sketching a picture of the vase on my mantle. It was a favorite of mine. In the quietness, the still small voice of the Lord spoke to my heart. *Child, you are like that vase. You do not love it because it is useful to you, but because it is yours. It is beautiful because of the value you place on it, not because of anything it has ever done for you. Even if you decide to use the vase by filling it with water and refreshing your guests, it is not the vase that is working it is the owner of the vase. The vase is merely a container. You are as that vase to me. You are beautiful. You are of value to me because you are mine, and I love you. When I use you to pour out my grace to others, child, you are the vessel I use, but the living water comes from me. You are my precious vessel, child.* I understood the verse! My body is just a vessel, and it may have flaws that come from living in a sinful world, but I belong to the Maker, and he loves me. If he can love me, I can love me.

Thirst for the Living God

As the deer pants for streams of water, so my soul pants for you, my God. My soul thirsts for God, for the living God. (Psalm 42:1-2a)

Can you say with the psalmist that your soul is thirsty for the living God? I wonder if we here in America, who are so used to having whatever we want whenever we want it, don't really understand being thirsty. When we are not spending adequate time in the presence of God, though, we become spiritually hungry and thirsty for living water, even if we are unaware of it. I have discovered that the mocha mint cappuccino at Barnes & Noble is amazing! It is a real treat, since I don't live close to Barnes & Noble. If I get anywhere in the vicinity, I will go out of my way for this treat. That is the kind of thirst this verse is talking about, a longing for, a willingness to go out of your way for. Now, do I long for God the way I might long for a tall cup of mint mocha cappuccino? I remember when I didn't have that kind of thirst for God. The truth is: I didn't even know what I was missing until in desperation I sought God in a deeper way. When God met me there, I learned that he wanted to pour himself into me, if I would only come. Once you've had a taste of God in this way, you can never go back! Like that cup of mint mocha cappuccino, I now know what I had been missing and want more and more! Unlike cappuccino, we can never have too much of God! Enjoy!

Delight in the Lord

Take delight in the Lord, and he will give you the desires of your heart. (Psalm 37:4)

Let's take time to meditate on this promise today. *Delight*...what do you delight in? I have seen delight in the eyes of many grandparents! They just love their grandchildren and seem to enjoy watching and participating in all they do. There is no greater delight on earth than can be seen in the eyes of parents at the birth of a child. There is such wonder in the miracle of birth! *Delight yourself…*In that phrase, the imperative is used. It is a command, not a suggestion. It is for you—and me. Whenever I hear people quote this verse, it is often because of the promise at the end. What a great promise! In fact, I quoted this promise many, many times as a young single woman hoping for a husband and a family. However, I have realized that the promise comes with a condition. As much as I wanted God to fulfill his promise, I know now that I really had no idea what it meant to delight myself in him. God was gracious to me and did bless me with a wonderful husband and a beautiful family, and then he taught me what means to delight in him. It is a lot like that grandparent described above. I love to watch and participate in what God is doing. He is amazing, and the things he does are so wondrous. It is not difficult to delight in such a God! It is also amazing that as I delight in him, the desires of my heart have become the desires of his heart. If we want what he wants, then we can have confidence that he will grant those desires in his perfect time.

Delight in the Word

> Blessed is the one…whose delight is in the law of the Lord, and who meditates on his law day and night. That person is like a tree planted by streams of water, which yields its fruit in season and whose leaf does not wither—whatever they do prospers. (Psalm 1:1-3)

Psalm 1 is one of my favorite Psalms. It begins by making a statement about those with whom we spend our time, and then it tells us that those who meditate on God's law day and night will prosper in all they do. Well, who can do *that*? It is not as difficult as you might think. First, we need to understand what this word *meditate* means. It does not mean to sit in the lotus position and chant "Ohmmm." It simply means to consider, to think about, to ponder. I learned this skill at a time in my life when I was not free to just sit and study the Bible for hours at a time. With three children younger than five years of age, personal time was at a premium! I loved to study and read God's Word, but I had one child that was an early riser, and by bedtime I was too exhausted. I would start reading and fall asleep. Naps? I tried, but my children didn't usually cooperate and all take a nap at the same time. Tired and frustrated, I shared my dilemma with a friend. She told me to try to read a Psalm a day—or even a part of one. I began to do that, and even on days when I only managed a verse or two, I found there were many minutes while I was caring for my children, or making lunch, or while hanging out wash that I could talk to the Lord about what I read. I would ask him to help me find truth in those verses that would nourish my spirit, and I would think about them throughout the day. I was amazed at how God used those verses to encourage and strengthen my faith. Now that I have more time, the process is still the same. I start the day with a passage or a verse or whatever I have time for, and then throughout the day, I percolate on the truth, asking the Holy Spirit to teach me. The result is growth, and when the season is right, there is fruit. It is not hard, but it never happens by accident. I have to choose to spend those free moments letting God speak to my heart. It is worth every moment!

For God's Glory

Not to us, Lord, not to us but to your name be the glory, because of your love and faithfulness. (Psalm 115:1)

This verse surely helps us keep all of life in perspective. If we can really grab hold of the knowledge that everything we do ought to be done with the motive to bring glory to the name of Jesus, then we will always be balanced in our thinking of our own accomplishments. Whatever we do, it is not to be noticed, not to be appreciated, and not to be complimented. It is only to glorify the Lord. This is not to say that we don't sometimes appreciate a compliment or a kind word about our efforts, but these should not be our goal. Our goal is to glorify God. If that is our goal, not only are we not working for our own glory, but we ought to do all things well, so that we do indeed bring glory to the name of the Lord. Today, if you are cleaning the bathroom or doing the dishes, or finishing a task you don't really want to do, do it as though you are doing it for the Lord. If you are singing a solo, teaching a Sunday school class, making a presentation, or whatever you have to do, do it for the glory of God.

The Fear of the Lord

> The fear of the Lord is the beginning of wisdom; all who follow
> his precepts have good understanding. To him belongs eternal
> praise. (Psalm 111: 10)

What do you fear? I have struggled with all kinds of fears that have kept me
from being all that God wants me to be. Fear that has a stranglehold on us
is not from God. Perfect love casts out fear (1 John 4:18). Does this verse
mean that we should be afraid of God? Imagine if you were a member of
Gideon's army facing a strong enemy. Those who oppose God and those
who don't have a personal relationship with him ought to fear him. Sadly,
often they do not. Their pride and arrogance cause them to believe they
have nothing to fear. The truth is that God could destroy any or all of us in a
heartbeat because he is all powerful, but his wrath is reserved for those who
have chosen to ignore his gift of salvation and disobey his commands. God's
children ought to fear God in the sense that we respect that he is sovereign
over all. Think of a child who fears his dad's discipline. As a child, I would
usually choose to do what was right because I was afraid of letting my dad
down. This kind of fear is a healthy respect for, an understanding of who
God is. He is all powerful. He is also loving and kind. He is perfectly just.
If we, as his children, truly grasp a sense of who God is in all of his glory,
and we know that we belong to him, then there is nothing to be afraid of.
This is the beginning of wisdom: to understand who we are in light of who
God is. Those who are his children can rejoice. If the One who is over all is
caring for us, then there is absolutely nothing to fear!

My Help Comes from the Lord

> I lift up my eyes to the mountains—where does my help come
> from? My help comes from the Lord, the Maker of heaven and
> earth. (Psalm 121:1-2)

I think this is one of those truths that we know with our heads, but we don't
always live it out. My kids taught me this lesson one dark, foggy night as
we were coming home from church. We took the shortcut onto some back,

A Blameless Heart

> I will be careful to lead a blameless life—when will you come to me? I will conduct the affairs of my house with a blameless heart. I will not look with approval on anything that is vile. (Psalm 101:2-3a)

Psalms is so full of treasures, isn't it? There are so many promises, there is encouragement, and there are challenges. Can you say these words along with the psalmist? Are you being careful to lead a blameless life? Are you walking in your house with a blameless heart? I sometimes find that I am more successful appearing blameless when I am out of my house, in church for instance. I am careful to appear blameless when I am with other believers. Often, though, I do not try very hard to be blameless at home. At home, I am who I am. As a young married woman, I knew my husband didn't approve of watching soap operas, but I had watched a couple of stories for as long as I could remember. Instead of honoring his wishes, I frequently would turn on my favorite soaps with one eye watching out the front window, so I could quickly flip the channel if he came home. It embarrasses me now to say so, but I was not even trying to honor God in that situation. Do you think God cares what I watch on TV? I think so. God cares about everything I do and say. Though I am declared blameless before the Lord because of the blood of Christ, I think he wants me to work at being more like him each day. For me, the litmus test of how I am doing is often how I am at home. Do I honor God when I am the most comfortable to be myself?

A Glimpse of His Glory

> I will praise you, Lord, among the nations; I will sing of you among the peoples. For great is your love, higher than the heavens; your faithfulness reaches to the skies. Be exalted, O God, above the heavens; let your glory be over all the earth. (Psalm 108:3-5)

God is so good! His love is higher than the heavens. Wow! Not one of his children ever needs to feel unloved. We do sometimes, though. Perhaps that is because we know how unlovable we can be at times. God doesn't love us just when we deserve it; he loves us every day—always—just because we are his. His faithfulness reaches the skies. What he says he will do, he will. He is *for* us. His promises are true, every one. How amazing! His glory is over all the earth. Everything around us declares God's glory. We often miss it because we are busy or distracted, or not looking, or too focused on ourselves. There is no greater joy on earth than to behold the glory of God. It blesses and strengthens. It encourages and brings joy. Today, ask God to let you glimpse his glory in a fresh way and let's praise him together!

Immeasurable Love

> For as high as the heavens are above the earth, so great his love for those who fear him; as far as the east is from the west, so far has he removed our transgressions from us. As a father has compassion on his children, so the Lord has compassion on those who fear him. (Psalm 103:11-13)

His love for us is as high as the heavens. Wow! That phrase is written in a number of Psalms. Have you ever stopped to meditate on that thought? From down here looking up, it is hard to get a sense of how high that really is. When I started flying with my husband in our little plane, I began to get a better appreciation for how high is up. He talks about where the ceiling is when it is cloudy in thousands of feet. When the ceiling is unlimited, we would often fly up at around 5,000 or 6,000 feet. Jet airliners fly up around 20,000 feet or 30,000 feet. The space shuttle has travelled thousands of miles into space, and still there is more beyond that than our minds can imagine. God's love for us is like that. It is so great that it is immeasurable. That is amazing! That love has brought us salvation. When we seek his forgiveness, he removes our sin as far as the east is from the west. He doesn't just forget about our sins, he removes them from us like they were never there. Sin is like a stain on our lives, and the blood of the Lamb is the stain remover. Thank the Lord today for his great love and forgiveness.

Rescue from the Slimy Pit of Despair

> I waited patiently for the Lord; he turned to me and heard my cry. He lifted me out of the slimy pit, out of the mud and the mire; he set my feet on a rock and gave me a firm place to stand. He put a new song in my mouth, a hymn of praise to our God. Many will see and fear and put their trust in him. (Psalm 40:1-3)

The other day my husband called to tell me that the bulldozer he was driving sunk into the mud of a pond that he was working to fill in. Talk about a slimy pit! It was no easy task to get that machine out of the pit. If you've ever been in pit of depression, you know that it is not easy to get out. It feels downright impossible while you are there. You feel stuck and alone. Tears keep the soil of your heart so muddy that you cannot seem to get on solid footing. David was in such a place when he wrote this Psalm. His solution: Wait patiently for the Lord. This is not like waiting for a bus or a doctor's appointment. It is not doing nothing and waiting for God to change the situation. To wait for the Lord in a time like this means to come to a quiet place and sit before him. Talk to him. Tell him how you are feeling. Cry out to him, and when you have cried it out and talked it out, there is nothing more to do except wait. Wait in his presence. Be still there and listen. Expect him to meet you there, because he will. He will bring peace to your spirit and restore your joy. Be prepared to wait for some time. He will set your feet back on solid ground, but you may have to wait patiently as David did. Have you ever noticed that you only need patience when you don't seem to have any? God rescued me out of a pit years ago. For weeks I came, sat at his feet in the quiet of my room, cried out to him, and waited. It took me that long to learn to be still enough to hear him speak to my heart. I was so glad that I had learned to wait, because he lifted me out of that pit of despair and put a new song on my lips!

Release from the Snare

> My eyes are ever on the Lord, for only he will release my feet from the snare. Turn to me and be gracious to me, for I am lonely and afflicted. Relieve the troubles of my heart and free me from my anguish. (Psalm 25:15-17)

As I was preparing the devotion for this morning, those first few words jumped off the page at me, "…my eyes are ever on the Lord." "Yes, that is what I need to write about," I thought. I put my Bible down and went to get my coffee, thinking it is a good day to remind all of us to keep our eyes fixed on Jesus. Then I got myself settled again and read the rest of the verse and the next several verses as well. I wanted to write about something positive today, not about being afflicted or in a snare or in anguish. I reread those first few words and knew this is today's passage. The truth is, so often when our eyes are fixed on the Lord it is because there is a problem or difficulty. I wonder what our lives would be like if our eyes were indeed always on the Lord. Perhaps we could avoid some of the snares we get caught in. Perhaps these verses are indeed something positive. When our hearts are in trouble or we are in anguish, when we are lonely, afflicted or caught in a snare, if we fix our eyes on Jesus and call out to him, he will hear our cries and rescue us. That is good news!

Magnificent Creations

> Great are the works of the Lord; they are pondered by all who delight in them. Glorious and majestic are his deeds, and his righteousness endures forever. (Psalm 111:2-3)

God's glory can be seen in the majesty of his creation everywhere, in great things and small. Each year some of us teachers collect a few monarch butterfly caterpillars just before school starts, so our students can watch their transformation into butterflies. These caterpillars are found on the milkweed plant. Last year, I noticed a few milkweed plants at the very end of the road leading up to our house. I decided to harvest some seed pods from those plants to plant on our property, so I would have no trouble finding those caterpillars next year. Of course, I had forgotten about it until one day a month ago I was weeding in my garden and noticed three milkweed plants growing! Two weeks ago, I was checking those plants and found two caterpillars that were already about two inches long—just about the size they get before they make their chrysalis. I was so excited that my little plan worked! The more I thought about it, though, I became more and more amazed. First, there's the whole seed thing. What a miracle! It was God's idea that plants would make seeds so they could reproduce themselves. All that life in one little seed! But the more amazing thing to me was how the butterfly that laid the eggs on that plant knew where to find it. In all of my eight acre property I had never had milkweed. The first year I grew some, a butterfly found it. Wow! I also marvel that the little hummingbirds know that there is a little feeder on my porch. What a marvel of creation those little creatures are! They are tiny masterpieces. I love their sparkly red throats. How could anyone believe those things could happen without a genius Designer?

Dealing with Pride

Though the Lord is exalted, he looks kindly on the lowly; though lofty, he sees from afar. (Psalm 138:6)

Pride is not easily dealt with in our lives, is it? It is often difficult to see in ourselves, though surely others see it. It can be very subtle, and sometimes not so subtle, but is surely something we can see in the lives of others even if we have trouble seeing it in ourselves. It is easy to pretend that we don't struggle with the sin of pride, until God, in his own gentle way, reveals it to us. Some of us are sure we are always right, and others are always wrong. That is pride. Some of us need to have our voices heard, but do not listen to others. That is pride. Some of us might look on some poor soul and think, "I am glad I am not like that." That is pride. Humility looks at another through the eyes of Christ, seeing their value and worth. Humility means I look at myself also through the eyes of Christ, a sinner saved by grace. Without Christ I am nothing. With Christ I am made perfect and righteous. This is really the key. When we are not afraid to see ourselves in our sinfulness and admit it to God, ourselves, and those around us, we experience humility. We no longer need to pretend we are something we are not, and we are free to be the person we have been created to be. I have struggled with low self-esteem. This is also a form of pride, because it keeps me always focused on myself and what others may think of me. Those with the healthiest self-esteem should be those who have been redeemed by Christ. He makes us new. We are free to be all we were meant to be, and we can extend others the same freedom. Draw near to God. In his presence, pride melts away in the light of his glory.

The Way of Faithfulness and Truth

> I have chosen the way of faithfulness; I have set my heart on your laws. I hold fast to your statutes, Lord; do not let me be put to shame. I run in the path of your commands, for you have broadened my understanding. (Psalm 119:30-32)

There are many today who believe the lie that truth is relative. Whatever is true for you may not be true for me. How sad! Satan surely knows the lies that will lead to the downfall of mankind. He knows that if we know the truth, the truth will set us free. What better way to prevent us from knowing the truth than to convince people that there is no truth! If you test out that idea, though, you quickly find that it holds no water. Two plus two is always four. That is the truth. It doesn't change because you may not believe it. Gravity is invisible, so you may not believe in it; but drop an apple, and it will fall to the ground. This is a truth you cannot deny. God's truth is the same way. People may choose not to believe it because they cannot see it or understand it, but it is nonetheless true. If someone asks you how you know God's Word is true, how would you answer them? I have actually encouraged people to test it out—like dropping an apple tells you that gravity is still an active force in the world today, applying God's Word to your life will soon reveal to you how true it is. I have dared people who have come to my door with a "different truth" to ask God to show them his truth. I know God's Word is the truth because I have seen its effectiveness in my life. When I live by the truth, I have peace, joy, and blessing. When I live counter to the truth of God, those things are missing. God is not afraid of our questions. If you doubt God's truth, ask him to show it to you. He is always glad to reveal his truth to those who want to find it.

The Plans of the Lord Stand Forever

> The Lord foils the plans of the nations; he thwarts the purposes of the peoples. But the plans of the Lord stand firm forever, the purposes of his heart through all generations. Blessed is the nation whose God is the Lord, the people he chose for his inheritance. (Psalm 33:10-12)

We live in troubling times, don't we? World leaders are making decisions that affect our lives every day. National leaders try to solve global issues with the wisdom of man and often do more harm than good. It is good to remember that God is not surprised or intimidated by world leaders. He has a plan for the earth, and his purposes will prevail. Though this passage is referring to the nation of Israel, the people he chose for his inheritance, we are a nation founded on the faith of our fathers who trusted in God for the leadership of our country. All those who trust in him will receive his inheritance. He isn't afraid that swine flu is going to close our schools. He is not worried about the economy and how to solve the problem of climate change. He cares about his children. He knows our needs. He understands every predicament we get ourselves into, and the Bible is clear that those who seek his help will find it. That is good news! Ultimately, the story of this life will come to an end just as God told us it would, and we will spend eternity worshiping our amazing Creator.

A Few Moments in the Morning

> In the morning, Lord, you hear my voice; in the morning I lay
> my requests before you and wait expectantly. (Psalm 5:3)

I love the quiet of the morning before anyone else in the house is awake. I have a favorite chair where I like to sit and watch out the window. We have a raised ranch, so looking out the back windows reminds me of a treehouse. I can see right into the tops of the trees. It is peaceful and quiet. It is a wonderful spot to talk with the Lord in the morning. For the first few moments of the day, I can quietly come to the Lord and lay my requests at his feet. Isn't it wonderful that he cares for us? How amazing that he would actually delight in my coming to him with my praises! He already knows everything, so why does he want me to tell him? It is because the God who created the universe wants to have a relationship with me! He wants his children to know him and to enjoy being in his presence. I can wait expectantly, because I know he is good, and he will answer my prayers. He wants to bless his children. It is not much, just a few moments in the morning, but it is a wonderful way to start the day.

How Long Will This Last?

> How long, Lord? Will you forget me forever? How long will
> you hide your face from me? How long must I wrestle with my
> thoughts and day after day have sorrow in my heart? How long
> will my enemy triumph over me? (Psalm 13:1-2)

What I love about Psalms is the honesty we see as the psalmist pours out his
heart to the living God. He doesn't pretend he is alright when he is not. He
understands that God already knows his heart. He knows our every thought,
so we can be completely honest with him. Have you ever felt abandoned by
God? Has there ever been a time when your prayers seemed to fall on deaf
ears, and you could not sense the presence of God in your life? It is more
than frightening to feel as though you have slipped from God's hand. There
is no more alone feeling in the whole world! Sometimes it can seem to go
on forever, and it is hard to wait on God. I don't know about you, but I am
comforted by the fact that even those God used to write his Word struggled
with self-pity from time to time. Self-pity can destroy you. It never produces
anything good in your life. What is the psalmist's answer to feelings of self-
pity and abandonment? Verse six tells it all. "But I will trust in your unfailing
love; my heart rejoices in your salvation. I will sing to the Lord, for he has
been good to me" Wow! That is amazing! When you feel alone and forgotten
by God, praise him anyway, because you know the truth. He is faithful and his
love is unfailing; even if you cannot sense him with you, he is. He is with you,
and he will rescue you from this time of trouble. He will show you the way
through, so don't give up. Don't let self-pity win; trust in the Lord and rejoice.

The Creativity of God

> How many are your works, Lord! In wisdom you made them
> all; the earth is full of your creatures. There is the sea, vast and
> spacious, teeming with creatures beyond number—living things
> both large and small. (Psalm 104:24-25)

How truly amazing is all of God's creation! The most amazing place I
have ever been is to Hawaii. My husband and I went snorkeling while we

were there. It was so awesome to swim among all the different varieties of beautiful fish. There were fish of all shapes and sizes swimming among the coral reef. We learned that the coral reef is a fragile ecosystem, one that can easily be destroyed by man. I was fascinated by the large sea turtles and the bright orange and white angel fish. Upon seeing such beauty and creativity, how could anyone doubt that it was our Creator who put them there? How could anyone presume to think that all those many amazing varieties of creatures in the sea just happened by chance or mutation? We also visited a rain forest while we were there. God is such a genius! The immensity of the flora and fauna of the rain forest is stunning. I remember taking a picture of my husband next to a gigantic tree. He looked like a dwarf next to it. The rain forest is an amazing ecosystem. God designed it perfectly to sustain the life of every creature there. If you change it, though, the ecosystem can be destroyed. God created it to be balanced. Left alone it would stay balanced. It is man who often comes into the picture and messes up God's amazing creation. Take some time today to marvel at the works of God's hands and praise him for his amazing creativity and genius!

Learning to Be Still

> He says, "Be still and know that I am God; I will be exalted among the nations, I will be exalted in the earth" The Lord Almighty is with us; the God of Jacob is our fortress. (Psalm 46:10-11)

We live in a noisy, busy culture. Being still does not seem to come naturally to most, but it is a skill that can be learned. God tells us to be still so that we can know him. I am embarrassed to say that it took desperation to bring me to the place where I was willing to learn to be still. I had exhausted every means of helping myself and could not. My last hope was to fall at the feet of God and beg for his help. When I turned off the radio and TV and made the house quiet, I was disturbed by many accusing thoughts. I was afraid of being still, because when I was still the voices in my head would assault me, telling me what a lousy person I was. In desperation, I came into my bedroom and closed the door. I knelt down and poured out my heart to

God, and then I simply sat quiet for as long as I could bear, waiting to hear from God. At first, I could only sit there for thirty seconds or so, but slowly I learned to be still before the Lord for longer periods. Finally, after many weeks, I began to hear the small voice of the Lord speaking to my heart in that quiet place. I knew those thoughts were from him because they brought peace and not agitation. They brought comfort and encouragement instead of condemnation. When I was willing to risk being still, God met me there and helped me to learn healthier ways of thinking. He brought peace to my life and taught me how to walk in his ways. I won't ever forget the struggle it was for me to learn to be still. Even now, it is easy to become distracted with all the noise in my life, but in order to draw near to God we need to find the stillness. It is definitely worth the effort!

Amazing Love

> Your love, Lord, reaches to the heavens, your faithfulness to the skies. Your righteousness is like the highest mountains, your justice like the great deep. You, Lord, preserve both people and animals. How priceless is your unfailing love, O God! People take refuge in the shadow of your wings. They feast on the abundance of your house; you give them drink from your river of delights. For with you is the fountain of life; in your light we see light. (Psalm 36:5-9)

These verses bring me into the presence of God with songs of his unfailing love on my lips. Who can measure how great God's love is for his children? God loves you with more love than there is water in the ocean or sand on the seashore! I marvel at how God loves me with such a personal love. He knows my every need and every tear I have cried. He knows the longings of my heart. He knows every flaw I have, too, yet he loves me. How amazing is that! The recent deaths of several celebrities have saddened our nation. When we see such tragedy in a life, it is easy to see that every person on this planet has a God-sized hole in their heart. Unless they turn to God and let him fill that hole with his love, there is great emptiness. Wealth, fame, power, people, or things cannot fill that hole. Only God's love can fill it. It is very sad to see a life end that has not found the Savior's love nor experienced a life lit by the Light of life. Rejoice today if you have experienced the wondrous love of Christ! Take a few moments to pray for those around you who still walk in the darkness looking for something to fill their God-sized hole, and pray that they would come to know the height, depth, and breadth of the Savior's love.

Every Corner of the Heart

> Search me, God, and know my heart; test me and know my anxious thoughts. See if there is any offensive way in me, and lead me in the way everlasting. (Psalm 139:23-24)

Psalm 139 begins with "Lord, you have searched me and known me…" It is interesting that the Psalmist ends this psalm with the words above. God already knows our thoughts and our hearts, so why would we ask him to search us and know us? It is a matter of cooperating with God. Are you in a place in your relationship with God that you would feel comfortable asking him to be your accountability partner? Would you be willing to have God examine your heart and your thoughts to see if they measure up? This request, asking God to test what is in your heart and in your thoughts, is also an act of submission to the Lord. When we express to God that we want him to complete the work he has begun in us, we acknowledge that he is Lord of our lives. It is an act of humility when we recognize that God knows us even better than we know ourselves. We can be pretty good at fooling ourselves into believing that we are doing pretty well in our walk with the Lord when buried deep in our hearts is a root of bitterness or an unwillingness to forgive someone. I wonder how many of us are afraid to ask God to check our hearts and our thoughts. I have been at times. It is silly really. He already knows every thought and every motive of our hearts. Why do we still think that we can hide from him? It is rather that we hide from ourselves the impurity that still resides in us. If we don't look at it, maybe it isn't there. God is not usually in a rush with us, though. When we are ready to yield to his touch, he will come and redeem every corner of our hearts and every thought in our heads. Let's yield to his loving touch today and let him complete the work he has begun in us. May we let go of our way of doing things and let God teach us to do things his way.

The Cost of Unity

> How good and pleasant it is when God's people live together in
> unity! It is like precious oil poured on the head, running down
> on the beard, running down on Aaron's beard, down on the
> collar of his robe. It is as if the dew of Hermon were falling on
> Mount Zion. For there the Lord bestows his blessing, even life
> forevermore. (Psalm 133)

There were nine children in my family, and let me tell you that my mother would definitely agree that it was wonderful when all of us were doing something together. It didn't happen often, but that is likely true of any home where a lot of people live together. Why is that? Consider what is needed to have unity. I am convinced that unity doesn't happen by accident. In fact, when people are together, the natural result is strife. That is because our sin nature causes us to be selfish and want our own way. You can see this whenever they televise what is going on in government—not a lot of unity there! Watch Judge Judy for an afternoon, and you will see that unity is not an accidental thing. On the contrary, strife comes pretty naturally, doesn't it? How do we get to the place of unity in our families, our workplaces, our communities, and in our churches? The only way that I know of to attain true unity is to put on the mind of Christ. When each person is seeking to have Christ rule in his own heart, then as we are led by the Spirit, we will have oneness of heart and mind. The solution is simple but not easy. Simply put, if we all follow Christ, unity will result. Why, then, even in our Christian families and churches do we see so little unity? Sadly, it is because we are Christ followers who still haven't let go of selfishness. We will follow Christ as long as it doesn't interfere with what we want and when we want it. We all struggle with this because it is what comes naturally. It isn't until, with God's help, we crucify our own self-centeredness, dying to our own will, and choose to follow Christ in all things that unity can truly happen. When we each begin to live as Christ saying, "Not my will, but yours, Father," then he can enable us to be of one mind. The result of unity is blessing upon blessing. Let's pursue unity today by seeking the Lord's will in all things.

He Is My Shield

All you Israelites, trust in the Lord—he is their help and shield.
House of Aaron, trust in the Lord—he is their help and shield.
You who fear him, trust in the Lord—he is their help and shield.
The Lord remembers us and will bless us: He will bless his people
Israel, He will bless the house of Aaron, he will bless those who
fear the Lord—small and great alike. (Psalm 115:9-13)

In the psalmist's day, Israel encountered many battles. When they trusted God, he protected them and they found victory. Most of us will not experience such physical battles, but it is good to know that God is with the men and women serving our country who trust in him. All of us endure many battles with an unseen enemy. We may not even be aware of him, but he is at work around us nonetheless. When I was struggling to find my way through deep depression and despair, I didn't want to hear when God tried to teach me about spiritual warfare. I was afraid to think about demons and the powers of darkness, because from a young girl I had been taught that they were real and very powerful. I will never forget a day long ago when my husband had left on a business trip, leaving me home with three children under the age of five. I began to sob uncontrollably. It was frightening to me because it felt like I was out of control and couldn't stop. With children napping, I went back into the bedroom, closed the door and cried out to God for help. Immediately, I felt peace envelop my whole being. "What happened, Lord?" I asked

"I sent them away," he said.

"Who?" I asked.

"Depression, Despair, and Grief." I was stunned. I could no longer pretend that my problem wasn't a spiritual one. I had to learn to deal with those demons that had been tormenting me, like it or not. God was amazing to me during those days, weeks, and months! In his Word, he very clearly showed me that I didn't need to be afraid, because he himself is my shield. He would protect me from the powers of darkness and help me to be free of their torment forever. As I learned, my fear was replaced with confidence that comes only when one has experienced God's amazing protection. I am thankful now that he allowed me to see the true problem, so that I could know the truth that he is my shield in battle. Without knowing and understanding the true problem, I might never have been set free. How thankful I am for my freedom in Christ!

The Heavens Declare

> The heavens declare the glory of God; the skies proclaim the work of his hands. Day after day they pour forth speech; night after night they display knowledge. They have no speech, they use no words; no sound is heard from them. Yet their voice goes out into all the earth, their words to the ends of the world. (Psalm 19:1-3)

Last night there was a bright spot in the sky a little to the right of the moon. I had heard on the news that you would be able to see Jupiter, so I knew that is what I was seeing. With a telescope, they said you would even be able to see Jupiter's moons. How cool! My husband and I enjoy sky watching together. We always look forward to seeing the Perseid meteor showers and are disappointed when it is too cloudy to get a good view. Our most amazing view of the night sky was in Hawaii. We were driving around the Big Island on our way back to the hotel, and it was quite late. The road was deserted, and it was the darkest place I have ever been. I have never seen so many stars! There is a conservatory there where scientists view the skies. I understand why. These verses tell us that God put those lights in the sky to proclaim his glory. Everywhere in the world people have clear evidence that there is a creator. Sadly, though many are fascinated by what they see in the sky, they don't listen to the voice proclaiming God's handiwork. For some it is easier to believe that all of this is an accident or a result of a big explosion. I have never seen an accident that brought about such majesty! Neither have I seen an explosion that has ever created such perfection. Praise God today for putting the heavens together in such a magnificent display of his glory!

God Is With You

> But you, Lord, are a shield around me, my glory, the One who lifts my head high. I call out to the Lord, and he answers me from his holy mountain. I lie down and sleep; I wake again because the

Lord sustains me. I will not fear though tens of thousands assail me on every side. Arise, Lord! Deliver me, my God! Strike all my enemies on the jaw; break the teeth of the wicked. From the Lord comes deliverance. May your blessing be on your people. (Psalm 3:3-8)

The other day, I wrote a devotional about God being our shield. Since then, I can't tell you how many times I have seen that phrase throughout the Psalms I have been reading. As you read through Psalms, you will see that it is a phrase used again and again. Considering David's life, we understand that he probably needed reminding often that God would shield him from the danger he faced because he had a plan for David's life. Do you ever wonder, though, why God let him get into so much trouble in the first place? I mean, God could have spared him from having any trouble at all, so why didn't he? I believe there is no other writer in Scripture who shows us what it is like to know God so intimately as David. Such a vibrant relationship David exemplifies! That is the kind of relationship I want with the Lord, so that I can also say if tens of thousands assail me, "I will trust the Lord because he sustains me." I can say this confidently: God never allowed a battle in my life that he did not use to draw me closer to himself. With each battle comes a victory—not my victory, but God's victory—that gives me greater confidence every day. Although it used to be true that I had difficulty trusting God, now I do trust him to be with me in all of my circumstances. He strengthens me and encourages me, and yes, there are times when he even lifts my head because I become so discouraged and weary that I cannot lift it myself. If you are presently in the midst of a battle, know that your God is with you and will deliver you in due time. Seek his face, and he will restore your joy!

Dare to Listen

The Lord confides in those who fear him; he makes his covenant known to them. My eyes are ever on the Lord, for only he will release my feet from the snare. (Psalm 25:14-15)

What an amazing idea to think that God confides in his people! What does it mean that God confides in those who fear him? When we confide in someone, we tell them something that we have not told to many people. It is a display of trust on our part. We confide in someone when we need support. When we have a deep issue we don't want to share with the world, but we cannot carry the burden alone, we confide in someone else. To think that God might confide in us is amazing! I am sure it is not because he has a burden too great to bear alone. Why do you suppose God would choose to trust us with information that he has not made known to many others? The radical idea here is that God still speaks to his people. He does. Those who will listen can learn the secret things of God. If God still speaks to his people, is anyone listening? Knowing God is about having a relationship with him. How can we have a relationship without learning to listen to the One with whom we have the relationship? God doesn't shout or send email. He doesn't text or send a letter through snail mail. He speaks in a still small voice to those who will listen. He longs to confide in us, because that is the level of intimacy he desires with his children. Dare to listen. Dare to ask God if there is something he would like to confide in you.

Flourishing

> But I am like an olive tree flourishing in the house of God; I trust in God's unfailing love for ever and ever. For what you have done I will always praise you in the presence of your faithful people. And I will hope in your name, for your name is good. (Psalm 52:8-9)

Most of Psalm 52 speaks of the judgment that comes to those who trust in their own abilities, those who love evil and boast in their participation. In contrast, the psalmist declares that he will be fruitful because he trusts in God alone. He knows that God is good and that all he does is good. He doesn't waste his time or energy boasting of his own merits; instead, his boasting is in the Lord. What do you boast about? When you are with other believers, do you find yourself sharing the wonderful things that God is doing in your life? We talk about the things that matter to us, don't we? How often do you find yourself talking about the Lord? Does your conversation reflect what God is doing in your life? What better way to encourage someone else today than to share a story about something God is teaching you or some way that God has revealed himself to you lately. Declare his praise.

God Gives Strength to His People

> Sing to God, you kingdoms of the earth, sing praise to the Lord, to him who rides the highest heavens, the ancient heavens, who thunders with mighty voice. Proclaim the power of God, whose majesty is over Israel, whose power is in the heavens. You, God, are awesome in your sanctuary; the God of Israel gives power and strength to his people. Praise be to God! (Psalm 68:32-35)

Where better to learn the words of praise than from the psalmist! Take the psalmist's words and lift them to God in praise. Let the psalmist help you as you learn to delight in giving praise to God. Amid the praise, we find the most glorious nuggets of truth for daily living! "The God of Israel gives power and strength to his people." Are you weary and laden down with burdens today? God will give you power and strength. Are you facing powerful enemies? God will give you power and strength. Wow! How amazing! I don't need to depend on my own limited source of strength, because God is my strength. He empowers me to accomplish all that he has given me to do. Jesus said, "... my yoke is easy and my burden is light." (Mathew 11:30) Oh, if we could only learn to live in that truth. How can our burden be too heavy if the Lord of the universe carries it with us? We are sometimes so foolish, though, aren't we? We often try so hard to carry our heavy burden in our own strength. We know if we just try a little harder, we can do it! Why is it sometimes easier for us to struggle to the edge of our own ability than to let God help? I think our culture of self-sufficiency holds us back from letting God have the role in our lives he wants to have. Let this truth sink deeply into your heart today: He gives strength to his people and power to his saints!

If My People

> If my people would only listen to me, if Israel would only follow my ways, how quickly I would subdue their enemies and turn my hand against their foes! Those who hate the Lord would cringe before him, and their punishment would last forever. But you would be fed with the finest of wheat; with honey from the rock would I satisfy you. (Psalm 81:13-16)

As I read these words this morning, I sense God's sadness that his people do not listen to him. How he longs to bless but cannot because his children's hearts are divided. What wondrous love God has for his children! He wants to bless, but he disciplines because he knows that is what will ultimately lead his children home. I am teaching my class about early American history. Our founding fathers listened to God's plan when they established our nation. Early Americans trusted in the Lord our God, and though life was difficult, he blessed those who followed him. I get so discouraged sometimes when I see how far our nation has come away from God. The people who lead our nation and those who have influence over the national media call things good which are not good. Each one has ideas they are trying to convince us will lead to an improvement in our economic situation, but those answers don't include God. We have been blessed in so many ways, and God has certainly been merciful to this nation. I wonder what our nation could be if we were a nation who yet listened to the Lord. Those who love him know what is possible with God and long for heaven where Christ will reign, but do we dare hope that God can lead this nation back to himself? Could there be another Great Awakening in our future? Is there some man or woman in our day who, empowered by the Lord, could speak to the hearts of his people and lead them back to God? Let's pray today for God to do a mighty work in this land. Nothing is impossible with him!

Morning Is Coming

Let the morning bring me word of your unfailing love, for I have put my trust in you. Show me the way I should go, for to you I entrust my life. (Psalm 143:8)

Have you ever had to endure a long trial that felt like it would never end? You cry out to God for help, but he seems to be on vacation or something. You seek his help and counsel, but he doesn't seem to be listening or you can't hear him for some reason. You wait through a long, dark night of the soul thinking morning may never come. Such is the state of David's life as he pours his heart out to God in this Psalm. I remember such a time in my life. I sought the counsel of my pastor, and I will never forget his words, "It's always darkest before the dawn." Honestly, I could have slapped him! He meant well, but I wasn't really encouraged by that. Much later, I realized how true his words were. It really *is* darkest just before dawn. He was trying to tell me that morning was coming. There was hope, so I shouldn't give up. It was a situation completely out of my own control, so I could do nothing but wait for the morning, so to speak. David's solution is a good one. "I have put my trust in you." During such a time, we can make it through more easily if we choose to put our trust in God's unfailing love. We remind ourselves of every time that he has been faithful to bring us through difficult times in the past. We read Scripture that reminds us that God is always with us and will never leave us, so that even though we cannot sense his presence, we know he is there. When all we can do is lift our soul up to the Lord, it is enough, because he is faithful and will not allow our trial to go on one second longer than is necessary to accomplish whatever must be accomplished. Sometimes what needs to be accomplished is not even in our life, but in the life of someone close to us. Another person may need to see how we handle difficulty. Have courage, my friend, morning is coming.

Eternal Perspective

Precious in the sight of the Lord is the death of his faithful servants. (Psalm 116:15)

As I write this, it is Patriot Day, a day to remember those whose lives were lost in the terrorist attacks of 9/11. I led our school in a chapel to commemorate the day. We watched a video that explained how the Star Spangled Banner was written by Francis Scott Key on September 11, 1814[*] after a fateful battle, when he saw the American flag still flying. We followed the video with a discussion of why bad things happen. The number one reason is sin, maybe not ours, but someone's. In the case of 9/11, it was the sin of a group of terrorists. We also asked some other questions: "Was God surprised by 9/11?" "Could he have prevented it?" "Why didn't he?" "Is there any possible good that could come from this" These are not easy questions to answer. No, God was not surprised. Yes, he could have stopped it. Why didn't he? We will have to wait for heaven to know that, but this we do know:

_____

[*] some sources say that this was September 14th

God cares about the death of those who love him. I believe he cares about the death of those who don't as well. He knows what eternity holds—for every soul. When death happens, it is not easy for any of us. We miss and long for those who are gone, but God knows that now is such a short time compared to eternity. I believe that every experience in this life, both good and bad, is designed to draw us into the hands of a loving God. If there were any good that might come out of 9/11, it would be to see this nation return to God. The sacrifice of those lives would have some meaning if it meant souls might be saved for all eternity. Grief is never easy, but God understands our grief, and he will walk with us through it if we let him. We who are his children do not grieve without hope, for we know that eternity is waiting.

That None Should Perish

> Lord, do good to those who are good, to those who are upright in heart. But those who turn to crooked ways the Lord will banish with evildoers... (Psalm 125:4-5)

God is good. He is good to those who love him, but God is also just. He will judge all of us in the end. Not one of us could stand before a holy God. All of us struggle with a sin nature. All of us sin. How can there be anyone whose heart is upright? There is only one way. When we accept the sacrifice Christ paid for us on the cross and seek his forgiveness, we are forgiven. We are redeemed. We are declared righteous, not because of anything we have done or ever could do, but because of Christ alone. When we consider those in our world who do evil and inflict harm on others, it is easy to want revenge and let anger and hatred rule in our hearts. It is not ours to judge. God alone will judge the terrorists who were responsible for the deaths of over 3,000 people. Jesus told us to bless those who persecute us and pray for those who despitefully use us. He told us to love our enemy. It goes against all human reason to do so, and without God's help we cannot do so. Why should we forgive and pray for such evil men? They don't deserve it. It's true. They don't, but then again neither do we. Not one of us deserves forgiveness. It is given freely to those who ask. We must obey the Lord and forgive those who do us harm. In fact, we should pray for them. Who on this planet needs God more? We must leave the judgment to God, because he will judge. One day, all of those who have chosen to live a life apart from God will receive their just reward. That is true, but it should not bring us joy. The judgment that God brings will be eternal, and there will be no turning back. Those who have refused God—the terrorist, the dictator, or your neighbor down the street—will regret for eternity the choice they have made. This life is so short. Take time today to pray for those who still need to find the Savior. He is longing for them. He loves them and wants to redeem their lives, even as he has redeemed yours. He would rather that none should perish.

In the Shadow of His Wings

Keep me as the apple of your eye; hide me in the shadow of your wings. (Psalm 17:8)

There is so much to learn about our God as we read Psalms! David has learned to call out to God in good times and bad. He knows it is always God who saves. It is God who protects. It is God who brings victory. Consider the request David makes that God keep him as the apple of his eye. This expression means that David wants God to keep him as his favorite person, the one that is most special to him. We know from Scripture that David was special to God—a man after his own heart. Isn't it amazing to think that David understood how precious he was to God? He didn't just hope he was. Time after time in Psalms we see that David knew beyond a doubt how precious he was to God. What difference did it make in his life? Because he understood how precious he was to God, he always seemed to know that everything would work out. He just knew God would help him and lead him on the right path. Friend, David is not God's only favorite! A parent knows that you shouldn't have favorites. Each child is favored. Each child is loved. Each child is special in his or her own way. So it is with God. What is different about David is that he understood how special he was to God, and that made all the difference in his life. How can you get a deeper understanding of how special you are to God? Ask him to show you. Ask him to help you to know how special you are to him. Because it never occurred to me that I was special to him, I never would have dared to ask. God loves me so much that he demonstrated to me time after time the depth of his love for me until I finally accepted this truth. You see, the fact that I felt unlovable, didn't make me unlovable to God! He longs for us to understand who we are to him. He doesn't just lump us all in with the rest. He knows each one of us by name, and all who would follow after him are the apple of his eye. Dare to believe that you are God's favorite! It will change your life!

You Are Loved

> For you have been my hope, Sovereign Lord, my confidence since my youth. From birth I have relied on you; you brought me forth from my mother's womb. I will ever praise you. (Psalm 71:5-6)

After writing yesterday's devotional, I couldn't stop thinking about what a difference it can make when a person really has an understanding of the depth of God's great love God. People who know they are loved are so much healthier of heart. As a teacher, I see that in my students. All of my students are loved, but not all of them believe it. You can tell by observing them. Those who know how greatly they are loved are confident and sure of themselves. Those who aren't always seem to need reassurance, and lack confidence. That shows in their work, in their friendships, everything. As a parent, you can also see this. All of us love our children, but not all of our children feel loved. Those that really understand how deeply their parents love them are free to be themselves. They have confidence in themselves and in their parents, so that if they need something, they will come and ask. The child who is unsure will hold back. Why do some children know how deeply they are loved and some do not? Gary Chapman and Ross Campbell[15] teach that children receive love in particular ways, and when you as the parent do not love them in their love language, they can feel unloved. Parents, on the other hand tend to love according to their own love language, so unless they understand this principle, their child may feel unloved if they each have different love languages. In any case, the point I want to make is that all of us need to feel loved, and all of us *are* deeply loved by God, but some of us have a hard time accepting that we are loved. God knows your love language! He wants to help you understand how deeply he loves you. He wants to break down the barriers that keep you from accepting this truth.

He knows a deeper understanding of his love for you will set you free to be the person you were created to be. If you struggle in this area, ask God to show you his amazing love today.

Declare His Praise

> The righteous will flourish like a palm tree, they will grow like a cedar of Lebanon; planted in the house of the Lord, they will flourish in the courts of our God. They will still bear fruit in old age, they will stay fresh and green, proclaiming, "The Lord is upright; he is my Rock, and there is no wickedness in him."
> (Psalm 92:12-15)

When you read these words, do you desire this for yourself? To flourish is not only to grow but Webster[16] says it is to thrive or to grow luxuriously! Can it be possible that even in our old age, those who seek the Lord will continue to grow and bear fruit? I can think of one dear lady of whom this is true. She absolutely has a glow about her, and when she speaks about the Lord, her passion and zeal can be seen in the gleam of her eyes. This dear saint never grows tired of telling about the things the Lord has done for her. She has a passion to see young people (anyone younger than herself) drawing near to God. Her story is amazing. She told our ladies group of how she had watched the Nazis burst into their home and kill her father. She told us how God had shown her the way of forgiveness and grace since then. She loves to worship and even produced a CD of music which she composed herself. She is certainly the poster child for this verse! How do we flourish? These verses talk about being planted and bearing fruit. If we remain rooted and grounded in the Lord Jesus Christ, we will continue to grow. Isn't it true that the more you learn about God, the more you know there is to learn? The more we know God, the more we long to know him. When we abide in him, he will lead us, teach us, and enable us to continue to grow. All of this growth, this life, seems to be for one purpose: to declare his praise to the next generation. I have noticed that there is an exuberance that comes when sharing what God has done in your life. Joy bubbles up within you and never stops flowing when you declare his praises to others. What is the Lord doing in your life? Tell someone today!

How Great Is Our God!

> Praise the Lord, my soul. Lord my God, you are very great; you are clothed with splendor and majesty. The Lord wraps himself in light as with a garment; he lays the beams of his upper chambers on their waters. He makes the clouds his chariot and rides on the wings of the wind. He makes winds his messengers, flames of fire his servants. He set the earth on its foundations; it can never be moved. (Psalm 104:1-5)

As I was reading this Psalm today, it reminded me of the song "How Great is Our God"[17] and I began to sing. Psalm 104 is filled with images that remind us just how great our God is. There are days that we need such a reminder, aren't there? Want to take your walk with the Lord up a notch? Read Psalm 104 and then follow the psalmist's example and just begin to think about all that God has done, all that God is doing, and all that he is going to do. Praise him. Every time you take a break from your work today, praise him for who he is. While you are doing your chores today, praise him. Just tell God how awesome he is. Don't ask for anything. Don't talk to him about you today. Just praise his wonderful name. Consider his majesty and praise him. Imagine you are standing before him and let your praises flow. Your praises will bring delight to the Lord, and I am sure you will be blessed as well.

I Will Not Be Shaken

> I will praise the Lord, who counsels me; even at night my heart instructs me. I keep my eyes always on the Lord. With him at my right hand I, will not be shaken. (Psalm 16:7-8)

Consider the words of the psalmist who tells us that God gives him counsel. He instructs him. Because he knows God is right there with him, he won't be shaken. What amazing truth is found in those few words! I have heard some say they wish God would just send them a letter and tell them what to do. Friends, he has! The Word of God is a love letter from the Almighty! Unlike other letters, it is living and active and sharper than a two-edged sword! God still speaks through his Word every day to those who listen. When you read his Word with the knowledge that it is for *you*, it can transform your life. I remember in my younger days being told that I needed to have a daily quiet time in order to grow. I needed to spend time daily in God's Word, so I did. I learned to love God's Word. I will say that it was not easy to be disciplined, though. Sometimes I would read in God's Word, and other times I would feel guilty because I hadn't read in God's Word. I also enjoyed studying the Bible for long periods of time, dissecting the Word and digging for truth. I want to tell you, though, that when I began to understand that God wanted to speak to me from his Word, my life was dramatically changed! For me, reading the Bible is no longer just a discipline; it is a conversation with God. When I began asking God to teach me his truth through the Word, the Holy Spirit began to show me things I had never seen. Though I could not see God or physically hear him, I knew he was with me, and indeed he began to counsel me through many issues. I no longer had to fight with myself about getting in God's Word, because I was not just doing an activity. I was meeting with God. Although I still love the Bible, I have fallen in love with the God of the Bible who counsels me daily on how to grow, how to love, how to forgive, and how to find peace. At one time I was shaken by the slightest upset, but because I know now that he is with me, I will not be shaken.

Pray the Word

> How can a young person stay on the path of purity? By living according to your word. I seek you with all my heart; do not let me stray from your commands. I have hidden your word in my heart that I might not sin against you. Praise be to you, Lord; teach me your decrees. With my lips I recount all the laws that come from your mouth. I rejoice in following your statutes as one rejoices in great riches. I meditate on your precepts and consider your ways. I delight in your decrees; I will not neglect your word. (Psalm 119:9-16)

What a great prayer! Want to revitalize your prayer life? Look at the examples given in Scripture and especially Psalms. Begin by praying these very prayers back to the Lord. Let them be from your heart to his. There is also wisdom in this prayer to help us know greater victory in our lives. Look at all those verbs! Seek him with all your heart. Hide his word in your heart. Recount all God's laws. Rejoice in following God's decrees. Rejoice in following his ways. Meditate on his word. Consider his ways. Delight in his word. Do not neglect his word. Wow! Notice they are all actions. This is not a passive faith! Yesterday I was thinking how easy it is to sometimes fall into the habit of going through the motions. A person who takes these things to heart is not going to be in danger of simply going through the motions. Are you seeking him with all your heart? Do you enjoy learning and following his Word? Do you talk about what you're learning in his Word? Do you consider and meditate on the Word you have read? When going into the Word becomes like a treasure hunt looking for new truth to encourage and uplift you, then it is simply a delight to spend time with the Lord there. Try it. You'll be amazed what a difference it can make!

Pass It On

> May the Lord answer you when you are in distress; may the name of the God of Jacob protect you. May he send you help from the sanctuary and grand you support from Zion. May he remember all your sacrifices and accept your burnt offerings. May he give you the desire of your heart and make all your plans succeed. (Psalm 20:1-4)

This is my prayer for you today. If you are in distress, may the God of the universe comfort you and bring you help. If you are in need of protection from the enemy of your soul, may God hide you in the shelter of his wings. If you need help and support, may God who gives generously give you all that you need. As you worship the Lord, may he teach you by his Spirit to worship him in spirit and in truth. May all that you offer him be acceptable in his eyes. God sees and knows every longing and desire in your heart. May he pour out his love to you by granting those desires that are hidden so deeply in your heart that only he knows they are there. As you make your plans, may the God of all wisdom and knowledge guide you in your planning and cause your plans to succeed. These verses are a great model for us to use when praying for others too. Pass it on.

With All Your Heart

> Praise the Lord. Praise the Lord from the heavens; praise him in the heights above. Praise him, all his angels; praise him all his heavenly hosts. Praise him, sun and moon; praise him, all you shining stars. Praise him, you highest heavens and you waters above the skies. Let them praise the name of the Lord, for at his command they were created, and he established them for ever and ever—he issued a decree that will never pass away. (Psalm 148:1-6)

Let everything that has breath praise the Lord! All creation declares the glory of God. How glorious it will be when we can join the angels in worshiping our God! The closest I have come to understanding what that might be like was when I attended a Christian music festival. There were about 60,000 believers there all praising God together. As we sang "Lift High the Lord Our Banner"[18] several women walked down each aisle waving banners. It was the most wonderful worship experience I have ever had! Everyone was enthusiastically declaring God's praise. It was awesome! Now imagine that same scene with millions, maybe billions from every tribe, nation, and tongue. Wow! God is more than worthy of all our praise. As you worship today, worship him with all your heart, soul, mind, and strength. He delights in your praise!

In Light of Eternity

> Lord, what are human beings that you care for them, mere mortals that you think of them? They are like a breath; their days are like a fleeting shadow. (Psalm 144:3-4)

Do you ever wonder why God cares so much about the human race? He has all those angels to worship him. Why is it that God chose to create people, knowing how foolishly we would reject him? God has gone to a lot of trouble to have a relationship with the people he created, and yet we live in a time when few follow him. Could it be that God looks at us with a different perspective? We think in terms of here and now, but God thinks in terms of eternity. He knows that today is just a blink in light of eternity. I discovered a more eternal perspective after one of my brothers died suddenly without warning. It helped me to see that life on this earth is short, and we really have no guarantee of tomorrow. Even the precious woman who died this week at the age of one hundred fifteen was young compared to Methuselah! Even Methuselah's life of over nine hundred years was short compared to the length of eternity. God is not limited to time and space. He thinks in terms of eternity. When he sees us suffering, he knows that this time will pale in comparison to the eternal days we will spend with him in glory. It doesn't mean that our days on earth are not important. They are, and if we could learn to view each day in light of eternity, I believe it would transform our lives. I miss my family members who have gone to be with the Lord, but I know that they are with the Lord, and when my life on this earth is complete, I will get to spend eternity with them and all those who have gone before me. It is amazing to me that God should want to have a relationship with such limited people, but he does! He longs for us to trust him and to follow his plans for our lives so we can enjoy an unhindered relationship with him. It matters to him how we spend our days. Are we making them count for eternity?

He Will Watch over You

> The Lord watches over you—the Lord is your shade at your right hand; the sun will not harm you by day, nor the moon by night. The Lord will keep you from all harm—he will watch over your life; the Lord will watch over your coming and going both now and forevermore. (Psalm121:5-8)

I had the opportunity to visit my sister at the beach this summer. It was a wonderful visit. I love to sit by the ocean and watch the waves or walk along the shore and walk in the surf, but I can't go to the beach without my arsenal of protection! My skin is very fair and I have encountered several bad burns throughout my life, so I know that I need the highest sunscreen I can buy. Even that is not enough! I would be the one sitting under the big umbrella, so I could be shielded from the sun's dangerous rays. From my comfortable beach chair in the shade, I could sit and enjoy the ocean all day long. The psalmist reminds us in these verses that God is our protection.

He is our shade from the sun. It says he will protect us from all harm. I sometimes struggle with this verse because I have suffered harm from time to time. Does that mean God was on a break or something? I don't think so. I believe God does watch over us wherever we go, but he has a different perspective on our lives. There are things he allows in our lives for reasons we may not know until we see him face to face. If we know he is watching over us, and he has, for some reason, allowed us to be in the middle of a painful situation, then we know that he will help us through it. How difficult it must be for God to see us suffer! His love is even greater than the parent who must watch a child struggle through a hard time. I wonder, though, if we could stand back and see throughout our lives how often God has kept us safe from trouble or protected us from danger, if we might have a different perspective. Know that God is watching over you today and trust in his unfailing love.

The Work of His Hands

> In the beginning you laid the foundations of the earth, and the heavens are the work of your hands. They will perish, but you remain; they will all wear out like a garment. Like clothing you will change them and they will be discarded. But you remain the same, and your years will never end. (Psalm 102:25-27)

Our God is simply amazing! When we stop to consider all he has made, our only response can be awe! From the tiniest cell to the distant solar systems, our God created them all. I have been teaching my class about cells. What a work of genius! I heard a scientist explain once the miracle of cells and the amazing truth that each part of a cell is vital to its existence. My God designed those cells! It seems silly to me to think that such a marvelous design could have occurred accidentally as some think. Sometimes it just leaves me speechless to consider how big our God is that he created the heavens and the earth! Every detail about our planet that allows it to sustain life is fascinating! If Earth were just a little closer to the sun, it would be too hot here for life. If Earth were just a little farther away from the sun, it would be too cold here for life. If the mixture of gasses in our atmosphere were just a slightly different composition, we could not breathe, and there would be no life. Almost everyday I see advertising about climate change, and the fact that our earth will not exist forever. Is that a mistake—an accident? No, God had a plan from the beginning! Like you and I change our clothes, God will one day change this planet for a new earth and a new heaven. Lift up your hands and sing praise to our Creator today. He is truly amazing!

King of Kings

> For God is the King of all the earth; sing to him a psalm of praise. God reigns over the nations; God is seated on his holy throne. The nobles of the nations assemble as the people of the God of Abraham, for the kings of the earth belong to God; he is greatly exalted. (Psalm 47:7-9)

I was watching the news last evening, and they were discussing all of the world's dignitaries coming into the city of Pittsburgh for the G-20 summit today and tomorrow. I wanted to tell you a different story today, but as I was reading this morning, these verses caught my attention. The world seems so far removed from following our God as King that we might easily forget the truth of these words. Our God is King over all the earth. He is indeed the King of Kings, whether the world acknowledges this or not. I am greatly encouraged to be reminded of this truth. The politics of world government is so volatile and forever changing. The influences of the decisions being made is far reaching, but I am encouraged to remember that God is not sleeping or on vacation. Though the people of Earth may be unaware of his presence, he is present here. He is active here. He has a plan for our world and its peoples. Of course, we know that God allows rulers to make decisions that can be harmful to themselves and others. This is freewill. Though it may seem that God is not involved in world politics, it is clear from Scripture that one day every knee will bow and every tongue will confess Jesus Christ is Lord. The eyes of the blind will be opened to the truth that our God reigns, and we will finally celebrate the reign of our King. Pray for the leaders of the world today. May they be led by the Spirit of God as they make decisions that impact all of us. May their eyes be opened to the truth that he is Lord. Our God reigns!

Worship While You Work

> I will give thanks to you, Lord, with all my heart; I will tell of all your wonderful deeds. I will be glad and rejoice in you; I will sing the praises of your name, O Most High. (Psalm 9:1-2)

As a mom of three preschoolers, I had a lot of difficulty finding time to meet with the Lord every day. I wanted to, and I knew that I needed to, but I couldn't find any extra moments in my day. I sought the Lord's help with the problem. It still amazes me that God put creative ideas in my head, so that I could meet with Him! God said, "You have that ironing to do every week. Why not let that be a time when you come to me? Talk to me while you work." I obeyed. I would set up my ironing board and begin to iron. Instead of turning on a television program to watch, I would pray, sing, and praise the Lord. It was really wonderful how that dreadful chore became one of my favorite times of the week! I don't have to do that chore on a regular basis any longer, but for that season in my life, God helped me to find ways to meet with him. Enjoy some time with the Lord today.

A More Excellent Way

> It is God who arms me with strength and keeps my way secure.
> He makes my feet like the feet of a deer; he causes me to stand
> on the heights. He trains my hands for battle; my arms can bend
> a bow of bronze. You make your saving help my shield, and
> your right hand sustains me; your help has made me great. You
> provide a broad path for my feet, so that my ankles do not give
> way. (Psalm 18:32-36)

If you have never read the book *Hinds' Feet on High Places* by Hannah Hurnard[19], it is a book worth reading. It is an allegorical tale of a girl named Much Afraid who is called by the Shepherd to come to meet him in the High Places. Much Afraid is pursued by her relatives, the Fearlings, and struggles to follow the Shepherds directions. As the story unfolds, Much Afraid learns to let Truth help her win over fear. It is a wonderful picture of the Savior's love and protection in the spiritual battles of life. We see in this story how the Shepherd transforms Much Afraid through the journey. He makes her deformed feet like the feet of a deer and enables her to reach the heights to which he is drawing her. Spiritual battles can leave us broken, afraid and unable to move forward, much less upward, but God has a plan for our victory. As we learn to follow him in the midst of a battle, he is able to broaden our path and help us understand that our own ways of doing battle are often counter-productive. Unless we learn to let him lead us into a victory won by him alone, we can never know the victory that is ours through Christ. Yes, there is a battle. Yes, victory can be ours. No, we cannot do it our own way. Often we need to leave behind all that we know to follow a more excellent way. This can be frightening, but it is a journey worth taking!

He Sends the Rain

> I know that the Lord is great, that our Lord is greater than all gods. The Lord does whatever pleases him, in the heavens and on the earth, in the seas and all their depths. He makes clouds rise from the ends of the earth; he sends lightning with the rain and brings out the wind from his storehouses. (Psalm 135:5-7)

Those who don't know God will say that Mother Nature is in charge of the weather. Consider how dependent mankind is on the weather. We take rain for granted until there is too much or not enough of it. We are wise to remember that our God is the One who still sends the rain upon the earth. He is the One who establishes weather patterns. There is no storm that is too great for him to still. There are no weather surprises for God! With all of today's technology, those who track and forecast the weather are still often wrong. Even when they are right, there is absolutely nothing about the weather that people can control. We can plan for it, run from it or enjoy it, but we cannot change it. Our God brings the rain upon the earth. We can study it, but God invented it! All of life is so dependent on water. With all of the world's oceans, without rain, we would still be thirsty. Praise God for this blessing! May the Lord pour out his Spirit like a soaking rain to quench our spiritual thirst.

Wait for the Lord

> I wait for the Lord, my whole being waits, and in his word I put my hope. I wait for the Lord more than the watchmen wait for the morning, more than the watchmen wait for morning. (Psalm 130:5-6)

Waiting for the Lord does not come naturally for most of us. Rather than wait for the Lord, some of us try to solve problems our own way, and the end result is usually failure. Some of us won't even begin to wait upon the Lord until we have exhausted ourselves with our own attempts. I was like that! When I reached the point of tired desperation, I was ready to learn to wait for the Lord. I would go into my bedroom, close the door and kneel down at the end of my bed. I lay my head on the end of the bed and imagined I was laying my head in Jesus' lap. There I waited to meet with the Lord. I needed him and knew that he would help me. Waiting for God is not like waiting for a bus. The bus is on a schedule. It will show up pretty much when you expect it, but waiting for God can be unpredictable. Sometimes we fail to remember that he is with us already, and we wait for him as though he hasn't shown up yet. He has promised to never leave us nor forsake us, so he is already with us, though we may be unaware of his presence. The watchmen wait for the morning when their shift will be over. They know that the morning will come. There is no doubt at all that morning will come. It always does. So it is with God. We may long for his presence through what seems like an endless night. We need to remember that he is already with us. We may not perceive him there, so we wait. We wait for him to speak to our hearts. We wait for him to minister to our need. We wait for him to lead us in the direction we need to go. We wait. With a humble heart we wait, because we know that God is faithful. Those who wait for the Lord will never be disappointed! He so delights in the heart of one who longs for him enough to wait. Great are the blessings for those who learn to wait.

God Shows Himself

> To the faithful you show yourself faithful, to the blameless you show yourself blameless, to the pure you show yourself pure, but to the devious you show yourself shrewd. (Psalm 18:25-26)

How does God show himself to you? I used to read these verses and be glad that I fit into the faithful, pure and blameless category! As I have continued to grow in Christ, I realize how arrogant it is to think that way. If I am at all faithful, blameless and pure, it is only because of the work of Jesus Christ on the cross! He purchased my redemption and freedom from sin, so that I am blameless in the sight of the Father. If I am faithful, it is only because of his faithfulness at work in me. If I am pure, it is because he has cleansed me from my sin until I am white as snow. Because he has made—is making—me all of these things, God is able to show himself to me, and he does. Years ago our Bible study group studied Henry Blackaby's book *Created to Be God's Friend*[20]. He does an excellent job of teaching believers how to learn to see God in our day to day lives. He calls them God sightings. God is indeed at work all around us—and in us—everyday. We fail to notice sometimes, because we are not looking. May God show himself to you today in an amazing way!

I Will Wait

Be still before the Lord and wait patiently for him… (Psalm 37:7)

There is a song by Twila Paris called "I Will Wait"[21] which I have not been able to get out of my head since the other morning when I wrote about waiting for the Lord. The most powerful part of the song is this: "…before I move, before I speak, perfect wisdom I will seek. I will wait for his holy Word. I will wait. I will wait…And I will wait as long as it takes…" Some of us have spent a great deal of time in God's waiting room. You may be there now. You may be waiting for God to move in your situation or waiting for God to give you the wisdom you need to move forward. You may be in the middle of a long struggle and have been waiting for God to finally bring it to an end. You may be waiting for healing, physical or emotional. You may be waiting on God to bring healing to a broken or strained relationship, or you may be waiting for God to just help you know that he is there because you haven't sensed his presence in a long while. Friend, I am confident of this: Wait for the Lord. He will not disappoint you. Wait for the Lord. Be strong, take heart, and wait for the Lord. He is faithful and will meet your need.

Teach Me Your Ways

Show me your ways, Lord, teach me your paths. Guide me in your truth and teach me, for you are God my Savior, and my hope is in you all day long. (Psalm 25:4-5)

The book of Psalms has so much to teach us about how to talk to God, what to ask of him, and how to have a deeper, more intimate relationship with him. I was reading verses similar to Psalm 25 one day when, as a teacher, I realized that if I had a pupil who came to me and asked me to teach him, I would never turn him away! The only way I can teach my students is if I talk to them! Oh, my! An epiphany happened in that moment. Then, if I ask God to teach *me*, I'll bet he will. How can he teach me unless he talks to me somehow? Well, I went straight to prayer. In childlike wonder I told the Lord that if it was possible for me to hear his voice, I wanted to, so that he could teach me his ways. I had never really considered the possibility that God would speak to *me* before! I am not Moses or Isaiah or anybody. I wanted to learn from my Savior, so I asked him to show me his ways. The doorbell didn't ring with a telegram from heaven. There was no hand writing on the wall. I heard no audible voices, but I went to the Word of God with a fresh hunger, and God was more than faithful. I began to get thoughts in my head that I knew were not mine. How? If I could have figured my own way out of the mess I was in, I would have done so long ago! How did I know Satan wasn't trying to deceive me? He wasn't going to be giving me ideas that originate in the Word of God and bring me wholeness and peace! I accepted the Word as I read the Bible. I tested every thought against Scripture, and I learned that God was willing to always confirm his Word to me. I had no confidence in my ability to hear correctly and made many mistakes! I learned that God is able to speak to me, or anyone, in a way that they can understand. He may speak to you differently than he speaks to me, but always, always, always it will align with Scripture, and it will always lead to peace, not confusion or chaos. God is a very good teacher! Dare to ask him to instruct you in his ways.

Hunger and Thirst for God

> You, God, are my God, earnestly I seek you; I thirst for you, my
> whole being longs for you, in a dry and parched land where there
> is no water. I have seen you in the sanctuary and beheld your
> power and glory. Because your love is better than life, my lips will
> glorify you. I will praise you as long as I live, and in your name I
> will lift up my hands. I will be fully satisfied as with the richest of
> foods; with singing lips my mouth will praise you. (Psalm 63:1-5)

Have you ever noticed how often the psalmist says he is hungry or thirsty
for more of God? Just as our body hungers and thirsts for food and drink,
our spirit hungers and thirsts for God. We would never think of not feeding
our body for long periods of time, yet we often let our spirit go unsatisfied
for days, weeks, or even months. I believe it is because we may not realize
how important it is to feed our spiritual hunger and thirst. We may not even
know that it is there at all. One of the things you can learn by fasting is how
strong our physical drive for food and drink is. It isn't until you refrain from
food and drink that you even notice the spirit's desire for spiritual food and
drink. We easily sense physical hunger and thirst, but spiritual hunger can
be undetected. When our spirit or soul is deprived of spiritual food, we
become complacent, hopeless and discouraged among other things. Perhaps
you have never given it much thought. How do you keep your soul fed? We
feed our souls by spending time with God in his Word and in prayer. Jesus is
the bread of life and the Word is the water that will never let us thirst again.
How hungry is your spirit? How thirsty is your soul? Let them be satisfied
with the banquet God provides!

Confess Your Sins

> Create in me a pure heart, O God, and renew a steadfast spirit
> within me. Do not cast me away from your presence or take your
> Holy Spirit from me. Restore to me the joy of your salvation and
> grant me a willing spirit, to sustain me. (Psalm 51:10-12)

David loved God from the time he was a boy, the shepherd of his father's sheep.
He was a man after God's own heart, because he trusted God and served him

faithfully. Even so, he fell to temptation and sinned. This prayer of restoration reminds us that we still need a Savior. If David, who knew God so intimately, could fall to temptation, then surely we can too. We know that David hid his sin at first. We do that too. We forget that is impossible to hide anything from God. God sent Nathan to David, so that David would know that God was ready to forgive him. He needed to acknowledge his sin, and there would be consequences, but God wanted to restore him to fellowship and help David move past his wrongdoing. I am greatly encouraged that the Bible contains examples like this one of God followers who sinned, if for no other reason than to let the rest of us know that God is faithful to forgive. He will forgive us, and he wants to restore us to fellowship with himself. Only God is able to give us a pure heart. Only God can restore our joy when we have failed him. He is willing. May we be willing to allow him to examine our hearts and expose any unrighteousness that is still harbored there, and when we fall short of the mark, may we be quick to find our Savior, so that we can be restored. Thank God for his forgiveness and his patience with our shortcomings.

Praise the Lord

> Praise the Lord. Praise, you his servants; praise the name of the Lord. Let the name of the Lord be praised both now and forevermore. From the rising of the sun to the place where it sets, the name of the Lord is to be praised. (Psalm 113:1-3)

In these few verses, the word *praise* is used five times! The psalmist knows how important it is to praise the Lord. Praise comes more naturally to some than others, they say. I think it doesn't come naturally at all! In our natural man, we are too full of thoughts of ourselves to be filled with praise. Praising God together can be a wonderful and uplifting experience. When we come to worship together, we come for a variety of reasons. Some come because someone else makes them come. Some come because it is expected of them. Some come because they have always come. Some come because they want to see their friends. Some come to hear a good sermon. Some come just for something to do on Sunday morning. Those reasons are not necessarily wrong, but the primary reason we come to worship is to worship the Lord our God. What does God enjoy about our worship? *Does* God enjoy our worship? I know the Lord enjoys our worship when we worship him with all of our heart, soul, mind and strength. He wants us to worship him in spirit and in truth. He loves when we worship him from our hearts and praise him with our lips. May the Lord enjoy our worship as we join together to give him praise this week.

No Condemnation

> The Lord will rescue his servants; no one who takes refuge in him will be condemned. (Psalm 34:22)

When you live under condemnation, it is a heavy weight. You know everything you have ever done that does not please God, and it consumes your life. I lived like that for too long, even as a Christian. I did not understand that there is no condemnation for those who are in Christ (Romans 8:1), and so when the devil's accusing thoughts attacked me, I believed them. In fact, there were so many accusing thoughts that I think I accepted them as truth and joined in with my own accusing thoughts. "You're fat. You're ugly. You'll never have victory in that area." "You're not good enough." I cannot describe the freedom I experienced when God showed me in his Word that he does not condemn; he redeems. He does not imprison; he sets free! My thought patterns were such a habit, however, that I had to consciously pay attention to every thought. I had to take every thought captive unto Christ. I learned to reject every thought of condemnation as not from God. Instead, I began to speak words of life. "I am forgiven." "I am fearfully and wonderfully made." I belong to Christ who does not condemn." Unlearning wrong ways of thinking can take time and effort, but by God's grace I no longer live in condemnation.

Choose Peace

> Even though I walk through the darkest valley, I will fear no evil, for you are with me; your rod and your staff, they comfort me. (Psalm 23:4)

Years ago when our children were small, my husband traveled often. I hated it. I dreaded being alone especially at night. I would hear every noise in the house and imagine all sorts of things. I couldn't run any appliances at night, because the sounds would make me so afraid. However, as God began to transform my life in many areas, he showed me that this kind of fear was not from him. He offered peace and rest. He offered protection. I could choose to accept his peace or continue to live in fear. It wasn't just one choice. Every time my husband would go away, I had to go through the same process. I armed myself with every Scripture I could find on peace and posted them all over the house. When evening would come, I would put the children to bed and then get out my Bible or my guitar and spend time with the Lord. He was so wonderful! I sensed his presence in a new way as I turned to him. I didn't pretend I wasn't afraid, but I brought my fear to him, and he gave me peace and rest. I once dreaded those business trips, but I learned to look forward to them as an opportunity to spend extra time alone with the Lord. He never disappointed me! Today, he is still the mighty rock I run to when I am afraid. There is no way to counterfeit the peace of God. You can't talk yourself into it. It comes from him alone, and it is a great blessing to know his peace in the midst of the darkest night or the wildest storm. Choose peace.

In the Shelter of His Wings

On my bed I remember you, I think of you through the watches of the night. Because you are my help, I sing in the shadow of your wings. I cling to you; your right hand upholds me. (Psalm 63:6-8)

As much as we don't like the hard times in our life, they often bring us closer to the Lord. When it is difficult, we just naturally come and cling to our Savior. We can be comforted that even at night as we lie awake unable to sleep, God is with us. We draw near to him and he draws us close. He pulls us under his wing, and there we can find voice to sing. Even during our hard times when we are close to him, there is always a song. The song soothes and brings comfort, for the Lord is singing too! He sings over us, and it is like the healing balm of Gilead! We cling to him, and he holds us up. When we cannot stand on our own, his right arm keeps us standing. Let the Lord be your strength today. As he sings over you, may you know the hope that is yours in Christ!

Let the Son Shine Through

> The heavens proclaim his righteousness, and all peoples see his
> glory. (Psalm 97:6)

The sunrise was beautiful this morning, painting colors all across the sky!
Do you ever notice what it takes to make the best sunrises or the best
sunsets? Clouds. When there are clouds in the sky, they reflect the different
colors that we see, and it is beautiful. When the sky is completely clear, the
light show is not nearly as spectacular. This is a wonderful illustration of the
light of Christ in our lives as well. When everything is going well, we do
not reflect the glory of God nearly as well as when there is some reason to
depend on him. When we are brought to the throne of grace needing the
Savior's love and help, he pours his love into us, and it is reflected to the
world. We appreciate God's blessing most when we know we don't really
deserve it. We are an independent people, and we are most comfortable
when we can do things on our own and things are going well, but when we
need to depend on the Lord, then the light of Christ can shine through. Let
the Son shine through your life today!

Healing Rain

> You care for the land and water it; you enrich it abundantly. The
> streams of God are filled with water to provide the people with
> grain, for so you ordained it. You drench its furrows and level
> its ridges; you soften it with showers and bless its crops. You
> crown the year with you bounty, and your carts overflow with
> abundance. (Psalm 65:9-11)

I awoke this morning to the sound of pouring rain. It made me think of
Michael W. Smith's song *Healing Rain*[22]. As rain cleanses and nourishes the
earth, so the Word of God nourishes and cleanses our spirit. *God, your love is
so amazing. You care for the earth you created. You cleanse our hearts with the blood
of the Lamb, and we are refreshed by your Spirit, O Lord. Remind us today of your love
and grace, Lord. As the rain falls upon the earth, may your Spirit rain new life into
our hearts. Cleanse our hearts, Lord, as the rain cleanses the air of all its pollutants.*

May we be refreshed in your presence and walk in the fullness of joy as though every drop that falls from heaven has filled us again with the joy of our salvation. We love you, Lord. Thank you for your blessing. Amen

Walking in the Light

> Righteousness and justice are the foundation of your throne; love and faithfulness go before you. Blessed are those who have learned to acclaim you, who walk in the light of your presence, Lord. They rejoice in your name all day long; they celebrate your righteousness. For you are their glory and strength, and by your favor you exalt our horn. Indeed, our shield belongs to the Lord, our king to the Holy One of Israel.
> (Psalm 89:14-18)

We can learn so much from the psalmist about the character of God. We can learn about God's attributes as the writer of this Psalm praises him. We can also learn how to praise God more wonderfully. We could study the attributes found in these few verses for the next month—righteous, justice, love, faithfulness, the light of his presence, glory, strength, and shield—a lot can be learned by taking one word and finding the definition for it or looking up other verses with the same word. In my study of Psalms, that is exactly what I did. I looked up every verse in Psalms with the word *righteousness* in it; then I looked up *faithfulness* and *strength* and so on. I was so blessed by what I discovered! I learned to acclaim him with each new truth I discovered, and I am still uncovering truth in the book of Psalms whenever I spend time there. I am not just learning *about* God. I am getting to know him better. As I discover more, and delve more deeply into the Word, I worship more freely as the psalmist did, and I am drawn into the light of his presence where I have learned to walk with great joy. To walk in the light of his presence isn't a quick five minute devotional before you start your day. It is spending the day mindful of his presence, speaking freely with him as you go through your day. It is being quiet of heart, so that you can hear his still small voice speaking to you in the quiet moments. Oh, the joy that can be found as we learn to acclaim him and walk in the light of his presence!

Recounting God's Blessing

> The Lord is gracious and righteous; our God is full of compassion.
> The Lord protects the unwary; when I was brought low, he saved
> me. Return to your rest, my soul, for the Lord has been good to
> you. (Psalm 116:5-7)

Do you need some encouragement today? Take a few moments and jot down
all the ways God has been good to you. Throughout Psalms, David recounts
all the wonderful things God has done for him and for the Israelites. Often
just after he has poured out his heart to the Lord about how desperate he
is, you will find a list of the ways God has blessed him in the past. This is
one reason I keep a journal. I often write my prayers to the Lord and keep a
record of the ways he answers. Over the years, I have been amazed at all the
Lord has done in me and through me. Things I have forgotten are brought to
mind, and I am blessed all over again. God is gracious and compassionate. He
has protected me and been my help in time of trouble. He has led me in paths
of righteousness and restored my soul. He has given me hope in desperate
situations and filled my mouth with songs. He has redeemed me and made
my life brand new. I am so grateful for his blessing and encouragement. How
has the Lord been good to you?

Laboring in Vain

> Unless the Lord builds the house, the builders build in vain.
> Unless the Lord watches over the city, the guards stand watch
> in vain. In vain you rise early and stay up late, toiling for food
> to eat—for he grants sleep to those he loves. (Psalm 127:1-2)

Are you laboring in vain? Most of us work very hard, and many of us are
also involved in work at church. Our schedules are full of activities and
obligations. We are busy, always busy. The words of Psalm 127 remind
us that unless the Lord is in it, we're doing what we're doing for nothing.
I had to face this truth at the brink of exhaustion. My schedule was full
of all kinds of ministries at the church. Being involved in ministry is
good, and we should be involved, but I was involved in more things than

I could handle—so busy that I didn't have time to be nourished in the Word or spend time with God in prayer. I became so discouraged and empty that I finally stopped and asked the Lord what to do. He lovingly told me I had to stop trying to do everything! When I filled roles in the church that someone else was meant to fill, I robbed them of the opportunity to serve. It is true that God will enable you to do all that he calls you to do, but what about those things you're doing because you couldn't say no? Friends, God will never call us to be so busy in ministry that we don't have time to be with him. We need to let God direct us in our activities and only say yes to those things that God has specifically led us to do. Follow Christ. Do only what he gives you to do. Don't labor in vain.

Overflowing with Praise

May my lips overflow with praise, for you teach me your decrees.
(Psalm 119:171)

How do you pray for yourself? *Do* you pray for yourself? The psalmist demonstrates a wonderful variety of prayers. He worships the Lord in prayer. He prays for others. He pours out his heart to God about his situation, and here we see a magnificent prayer for his own life. He asks God to hear him. He asks God to help him understand his circumstances in light of Scripture. He asks for deliverance, and reminds God of a promise. He asks God to fill his lips with praise and songs of his Word. When was the last time you asked God for such things? These are prayers God is sure to answer! Imagine if God would fill our lips with songs of praise. We wouldn't have to worry about grumbling and complaining! I had a friend a few years back who was the art teacher at my school. She had the most joyous spirit I have ever seen. As she hung art in the hallways or cut out letters at the die cut machine, she always had a song of praise on her lips. What a testimony of God's work in her life! Joy filled her whole being and spilled over into the rest of our lives. Dare to ask God today to fill your heart with songs of praise, to deliver you from every vain thing in your life, and to help you take delight in his Word.

He Bears Our Burdens

> Praise be to the Lord, to God our Savior, who daily bears our
> burdens. Our God is a God who saves; from the sovereign Lord
> comes escape from death. (Psalm 68:19-20)

What burdens do you carry? Is your heart broken for a loved one who has
gone astray? Are you or someone you love fighting an illness that only God
can cure? Is there a relationship in your life that is in trouble and you don't
know how to fix it? Do you have a problem you don't know how to solve?
Praise to the Lord our God who daily bears our burdens! Most of my life I
have carried the weight of the world on my shoulders. It took me a long time
and coming to the point of complete emotional exhaustion before I finally
let God have my burdens. He will carry them. He will lift them from our
shoulders. Why, then, do we still cling to our burdens and let the weight
of them crush us? I think it is because we are having trouble trusting our
Savior. If our burden is weighing down our back, at least we know where it
is in case we think up a solution. My problem was that I wanted others to see
what a great burden I had. How sad is that! I made myself a martyr as though
that somehow gave me an excuse for my struggle, but I am grateful that God
showed me a better way. He let me carry that burden as long as I wanted to,
but when I was ready to give it up, he was ready to lift it from my shoulders.
He even showed me that I am very prone to taking back that burden time
and time again because it gives me a feeling of being in control. Of course,
I am not in control of the burden when it is weighing me down. In fact, the
burden is controlling me! It is God's desire that we walk in freedom. He
would carry our heavy burden as we walk the path he has chosen for us, if
only we will trust him with it! Whatever your burden today, God is faithful.
He will lift it from your shoulders. Will you let him?

Spectacular Display of Glory

> Lord our God, you answered them; you were to Israel a forgiving
> God, though you punished their misdeeds. Exalt the Lord our
> God and worship at his holy mountain, for the Lord our God is
> holy. (Psalm 99:8-9)

I am so glad that I live in a place where I get to see the changing of the seasons. Each season holds its own place in my heart, but I think fall displays the glory of God the very best. Our God is such an amazing creator! He didn't have to make trees that lose their leaves when the weather turns cold, and he certainly didn't need to make it be such a beautiful event! You don't realize what an awesome thing it is until you don't have it anymore. When my family moved to Wisconsin, I missed the colors of fall the most, because we lived in an area that had mostly evergreens. In the fall, people would take the weekend off and travel north several hours just to see the leaves changing color. I love to see the mountains where we live now in Pennsylvania when they are vibrant with full color. It is the most awesome display of God's glory to me! Worship the Lord on his holy mountain for our God is holy!

To Him Be the Glory

> Ascribe to the Lord, you heavenly beings, ascribe to the Lord
> glory and strength. Ascribe to the Lord the glory due his name;
> worship the Lord in the splendor of his holiness. (Psalm 115:1)

Do you ever stop and ask yourself why you do things? What is your motivation? I was a very insecure person for most of my life and still struggle with this at times. Most of my life I found myself doing things so that others would accept me. I wanted to be liked, so I tried to always be the person I thought the person I was with wanted me to be. If you think that sentence was confusing, it was even more confusing to be me! I am a singer and have sung many solo performances. It was always so wonderful to have people tell me what a beautiful voice I have, until one day I couldn't talk. I had a vocal nodule and had to receive vocal therapy for six weeks. For a singer to not be able to sing is the worst kind of torture! As a result, I no longer take my voice for granted. As I have learned who I am in Christ, I have been able to let go of most of my insecurities. It is wonderfully freeing to know that he is the only one I really need to please. Now I don't need to steal the Lord's glory. When I receive accolades, I know it is only because of the work that he has done—and is doing—in me that I am able to accomplish anything at all. I love the freedom to do things for his glory alone. He deserves all the praise for everything good in my life. How about yours?

Longing for God's Word

> Your statutes are wonderful; therefore I obey them. The unfolding of your words gives light; it gives understanding to the simple. I open my mouth and pant, longing for your commands. Turn to me and have mercy on me, as you always do to those who love your name. (Psalm 119:129-132)

How important is God's Word to you? Would God agree with your answer? In America, where we can find Bibles everywhere and in any translation that we want, I think we take it for granted. The psalmist knows how vital God's Word is to survival. He is relying on the Word of God for understanding and wisdom. Years ago, I had a friend who invited me to join her in her weekly running. She was patient as we started running only once or twice around the block, but she kept stretching me until we were running six miles three times a week! I still can't believe I could do that. On the last leg of our run, she would have us sprint with all our might. We would end up panting like crazy to catch our breath, like our lungs just couldn't take in all the oxygen we needed. That is the picture I get here of the psalmist's need for the Word of God. He says he pants in longing for God's commands like the very air he needs to breathe. I wonder how many of us share that kind of passion for the Word. It is like the very air we need to breathe. To keep our spirit alive, we need to take in the Word of God. We would never think that we have enough air if we just take a few breaths in the morning, at meals, and at bedtime. We know we need to breathe all day long. So it is with the Word of God. I don't mean we need to stop everything in our lives and read the Bible all day long; but when we read God's Word, if we learn to meditate on it all day long, God can use it to nourish our spirit. We wonder why we feel so depleted spiritually. Maybe we need to breathe in more of his Word.

God Is Within Me

> God is within her, she will not fall; God will help her at break of day. (Psalm 46:5)

When you read God's Word, are there ever times when the words seem to just jump up off the page at you? The words of this Psalm were like that in my life. At a time when I was hurting and down and didn't think I would ever get up again, God spoke these words to me as I read his Word: "God is within her, she will not fall; God will help her at break of day." I know this is referring to Jerusalem, the city of God, but could it refer to me too? Yes, I am the holy place where the Most High dwells. He lives in me! If he is in me, then I will not fall. If he is in me, then I can believe he will help me when the new day dawns. Yes, there is hope for me, because my God lives within me! I am not God, but his Spirit lives within me, and he promises to help me. Perhaps the river in this verse is the River of Life that flows through me! One word from God and everything can change. His voice can melt the earth. Have you ever seen the molten rock coming out of a volcano? I have, and it is simply awesome to see. God made it. He is more powerful than that hot molten rock! So what could be too difficult for him? Nothing! Absolutely nothing. If you are hurting, look to God for help. He is our refuge in time of need.

We Need a Shepherd

> The Lord is the strength of his people, a fortress of salvation for his anointed one. Save your people and bless your inheritance; be their shepherd and carry them forever. (Psalm 28:8-9)

I don't know much about sheep, except that they need a shepherd. I have heard they are pretty stupid and will walk right into trouble. We have all seen the picture of Jesus carrying the lost sheep around his neck. That was the one sheep that wandered off and got lost. Jesus still rescues lost sheep! And though we don't like to think of ourselves as stupid, we certainly are compared to God! If you put yourself in the place of that lost sheep, wrapped around Jesus' neck, you're feeling pretty secure. Jesus not only saved you, he's carrying you and protecting you from further harm. God's people, his inheritance, need a lot of rescuing. They need the voice of their Shepherd telling them where to go. They depend on the protection of the gentle Shepherd to guide them and keep them safe. I always find hope in the knowledge that Jesus is still the Good Shepherd. When I wander, he will gather me in and carry me upon his shoulders. Even more, I know a lot of lost sheep out there. I rejoice that God knows how to rescue them. *Thank you, Lord, for being our Shepherd, for protecting us against dangers we can't even see, and for seeking after the lost ones we love.*

God Gives the Victory

> You are my King and my God, who decrees victories for Jacob. Through you we push back our enemies; through your name we trample our foes. I put no trust in my bow, my sword does not bring me victory; but you give us victory over our enemies, you put our adversaries to shame. In God we make our boast all day long, and we will praise your name forever. (Psalm 44:4-8)

What battles do you face? Victory comes from God alone. David was a skillful soldier, but he had learned that every victory he had won came only from God. Though God used David to fight the battle, he alone brought the victory. David knew that if God did not ordain victory for him, there would be no victory. Whatever battles we face, this is still true. Sadly, many of us are so busy fighting the battle that we have forgotten God is greater than any battle we encounter. God will not let us win any battle when we are still busy trusting in ourselves alone—I know this from experience. My willpower alone is not going to win any battle. My strength alone is not going to bring victory. It doesn't matter how many people, how many weapons or how many anything. Without God, I can do nothing! With God, though, I can trample every enemy as though it were nothing. God brings hope to those who fight a losing battle. He is never on the losing side, but we must put our trust in him. We must not give up the fight. We must give up fighting in our own strength. Whatever battles you face today, trust God to bring you victory.

Victory over Darkness

> Give us aid against the enemy, for human help is worthless. With God we will gain the victory, and he will trample down our enemies. (Psalm 108:12-13)

I grew up in an area where witchcraft was prevalent. There were at least two secret societies that held strongholds over our town. We also had at least one palm reader. When I return home after being away for awhile, I can sense the powers of darkness as I drive into town. Ephesians 6:12 tells us our battle is not against flesh and blood, but against rulers, authorities and the spiritual forces of evil in heavenly realms. Missionaries tell us of accounts with the forces of evil when they return from foreign fields, but we do not like to think about demons and darkness and evil here in our country, unless it is in a thriller we know is fiction. Too often we think that if we don't believe in evil, it doesn't exist, but this is not true. Just like God exists whether or not we believe in him, so Satan and all his demons exist whether we believe that or not. All of this can be kind of scary to think about, but we need not fear because our God has dominion over all. There is nothing that is not under his authority. Satan is happy when Christians choose to ignore him, because then he is free to do what he wants, but when we put on the full armor of God and take our stand against the enemy of our souls, God will bring victory. We can ask God to give us wisdom to know how to pray against the forces of darkness at work in our area, in our lives, or in the lives of our family members. If we choose to ignore Satan, he wins. If we are too afraid of him to get involved, he wins. If we seek God on this matter, and learn to use the weapons of spiritual warfare he has given us, we can know victory over the forces of darkness as he leads us.

Free From Anguish

> When hard pressed, I cried to the Lord; he brought me into a spacious place. The Lord is with me; I will not be afraid. What can mere mortals do to me? The Lord is with me; he is my helper. I will look in triumph on my enemies. (Psalm 118:5-7)

If you have never been in anguish, you may not relate to these verses at all. If you have experienced anguish, either yourself or in someone you love, you know it is like a torturous prison. It is impossible to free yourself from anguish. Anguish goes deeply into the heart and becomes firmly rooted there. It takes over every thought and holds you captive. You want to break free but cannot. Some of us have become so used to anguish, that we wouldn't know how to act without it. We feel safe in our anguish and getting free does not even occur to us. Have you been there? Do you know someone who has or is? The psalmist has the only solution for anguish—he cried out to the Lord. Only God can set a soul free that is held captive by anguish. There may be many reasons for anguish, but only one way to victory—through Christ. A soul in anguish becomes so consumed with whatever has caused it, that he cannot find the way through to peace. When we are imprisoned by anguish, there is no hope. We don't have the strength to believe that it will get better. It is like a strong rope that binds us up so we cannot move, but there comes a moment when we are so sick of the anguish that we cry out to God. He alone can save us. He alone can rescue us from the darkness. He alone can loosen the ropes that imprison our souls. He alone can replace our anguish with peace, perfect peace. Are you in anguish? Call out to him today. Is someone you love in anguish? Bring them to Jesus in prayer, pleading for their freedom. He will help them and bring them triumph over this enemy.

Darkness Must Flee

The Lord is God and he has made his light shine on us. With boughs in hand, join in the festal procession up to the horns of the altar. You are my God, and I will praise you; you are my God, and I will exalt you. (Psalm 118:27-2)

The last few devotionals have been about the powers of darkness. It is a topic that makes many uncomfortable. Others become so fascinated by it that it veers them off course. This verse speaks of the hope we have in Christ. Though the world around us is dark and the powers of darkness prevail, Christ shines his light upon us and darkness must flee. Where Christ is, evil must bow its knee. Our hope and victory, then, come only in the very presence of God. When the powers of darkness threaten our peace, or the peace of our homes, our communities, and even our work places, we have only to invite Christ to be present there with us. As we worship the Lord today, let us give thanks for the Light of the world, who dispels all darkness in our lives. *Lord, we worship you today, for you are a mighty God. Thank you for your light within us, your very presence within us that causes darkness to flee. We praise you, God, for you are good, and your love and faithfulness are eternal. We need you, Lord, to teach us how to have victory over darkness in our lives and in our communities. We love you, Lord. Amen*

The Lord Is My Strength and My Song

> All the nations surrounded me, but in the name of the Lord I cut them down. They surrounded me on every side, but in the name of the Lord I cut them down. They swarmed around me like bees, but they were consumed as quickly as burning thorns; in the name of the Lord I cut them down. I was pushed back and about to fall, but the Lord helped me. The Lord is my strength and my defense; he has become my salvation. (Psalm 118:10-14)

Can you imagine this scene with David in battle? His army is surrounded and it looks like they are going to lose. He is weary and discouraged, but he remembers every time that God has faithfully protected him in the past. His courage swells and he goes forward declaring victory in the name of the Lord. Somehow, miraculously he has cut off the enemy and gained a victory he knew he could not win. Praise God! I have never been in a physical battle, but I have battled a number of demons in my life, and at one point truly did feel surrounded and helpless. I knew their strength was way greater than mine, and I was sure I didn't have enough faith to win the battle. I didn't ever doubt God's ability to win, but I was pretty confident that I had absolutely no skills to win a battle with demons I had only recently had the courage to admit were tormenting me. Like the psalmist, I was pushed back and about to fall, but the Lord helped me. He gave me the right words and strengthened my faith. Like the sixth chapter Ephesians, I was able to take my stand against the devil's schemes. God was indeed my strength and my defense. He was my salvation in time of need. This is not referring to the salvation that comes when we accept him as Lord, but even as believers our God will rescue his children from trouble. He is yet our Savior! Hallelujah! Whatever demons may be tormenting you, whatever the battle you face, whatever the trouble in which you find yourself, God will be your champion.

Christ Is the Capstone

> The stone the builders rejected has become the cornerstone; the Lord has done this, and it is marvelous in our eyes. The Lord has done it this very day; let us rejoice and be glad. (Psalm 118:22-24)

I have struggled with rejection my whole life. Rejection tells you that you are not loved and not wanted. Rejection tells you that you are not good enough. Rejection tells you that you are worthless. I am comforted to know the Jesus understands my struggle with rejection, for he was rejected by the very people he came to save, like a stone that is rejected because it is not good enough. Praise God that Jesus did not let rejection stop him! He knew that humans are often blind to the truth and foolish in their understanding. He loved us enough to endure rejection and to become the cornerstone. The cornerstone is the very most important stone in a building project! I no longer let rejection convince me that I am not good enough. Christ paid his very life for mine. That means I am valuable to him. I am wanted. I belong. I am loved. With that in mind, this is the day the Lord has made; let us rejoice and be glad in it!

Courage to Go Forward

> He will cover you with his feathers, and under his wings you will find refuge; his faithfulness will be your shield and rampart. You will not fear the terror of night, nor the arrow that flies by day, nor the pestilence that stalks in the darkness, nor the plague that destroys at midday. A thousand may fall at your side, ten thousand at your right hand, but it will not come near you. You will only observe with your eyes and see the punishment of the wicked. (Psalm 91:4-8)

When God opened my eyes and my heart to understand that my problems with depression were because of spiritual forces of evil at work around me, I could have been terrified. My dad had spoken often of the very real powers of evil. He had also told me that I need not fear evil, but I didn't comprehend that part and was too afraid to even think about demonic things. That is until the Lord showed me how much influence it was having in my life. One of the first Scriptures I read at that time was Psalm 91, and it was as though God himself was speaking to me. As I read these words, I was comforted and knew that although God was taking me on a journey I wasn't all that thrilled to be taking, he was going with me and would keep me safe. I felt the presence of God with me, and knew that I was safe and protected by his covering. As he taught me how to face the enemy and not to shrink back, I learned that I could only do that because he was my shield. During the most frightening time of my life, I had peace because of the presence of God and his promise of protection. In this day when evil abounds, let us not shrink back. Neither let us rush forward trying to defeat the enemy in our own strength and wisdom, for we will surely fail. Let us wait upon the Lord, and as he leads us into battle against the forces of darkness, let us have courage to go forward in the strong name of the Lord!

From the Sheep Pen to a Palace

He chose David his servant and took him from the sheep pens; from tending the sheep he brought him to be the shepherd of his people Jacob, of Israel his inheritance. And David shepherded them with integrity of heart; with skillful hands he led them. (Psalm 78:70-72)

It is pretty amazing to think about the story of how David became king of Israel. When God sent Samuel to anoint a new king, he sent him to the house of Jesse. None of the other brothers were even considered by God, and Jesse didn't consider his youngest son David to even be a candidate. He was out watching the sheep. From the sheep pens to a palace—only God would think of that! God often thinks like that, though. Where was the Savior born? In a lowly manger stall. God sees things differently than we do, doesn't he? He sees with the eyes of eternity. He sees with the eyes of potential. He sees not just what a person is but what he created that person to be! Oh, if we could have eyes to see like that! Like Jesse, sometimes as parents we only see what is and not what can be when God is in the mix. I wonder what Samuel thought of God's choice? I see two applications for us here in these verses. We might be nothing special. We may doubt our worth in the eyes of God, but what might be possible for our lives as we let God work in us the fullness of his plan? We may see no potential in the brother or sister or child next to us, but what does God see? Let us pray today that God would give us eyes to see the potential in others—and in ourselves— that he sees. What might God want to do with us? Will we serve him with integrity as David did? Will we let him take us to our fullest potential? I hope so!

Saved From Darkness

Some sat in darkness, in utter darkness, prisoners suffering in iron chains, because they rebelled against God's commands and despised the plans of the Most High. So he subjected them to bitter labor; they stumbled, and there was no one to help. Then they cried to the Lord in their trouble, and he saved them from their distress. He brought them out of darkness, the utter darkness, and broke away their chains. (Psalm 107:10-14)

One of the most difficult experiences in life is to have a child turn away from the Lord. It is even worse if in their rebellion against you and against the Lord they turn to drugs and become imprisoned in that lifestyle. Take that sorrow and consider how God must feel about the rebellion of all his wayward children! This Psalm tells us that those in rebellion will have consequences. He will leave them in a dark prison, suffering until they turn back to him. He doesn't take any joy in their sorrow. He grieves, as we would, because he knows what they could do with their lives if he were guiding them. The moment a rebellious soul calls out to God, he is there ready to bring release. He is ready to bring freedom. We do not know as humans what it may take to turn a rebellious loved one back to the Lord, but he does. We do not know which moment may be the one that brings them to the point of calling out to the Lord for help. Let us not grow weary in praying for those we love who have turned from the Lord. Let us be reminded that he is able to set them free, and he is willing to set them free if they will turn to him. Pray for hard hearts to be softened and to hear his loving call!

Let Everything That Has Breath Praise the Lord

Praise the Lord. Praise God in his sanctuary; praise him in his mighty heavens. Praise him for his acts of power; praise him for his surpassing greatness. Praise him with the sounding of the trumpet, praise him with the harp and the lyre, praise him with timbrel and dancing, praise him with the strings and pipe, praise him with the clash of cymbals, praise him with resounding cymbals. Let everything that has breath praise the Lord. Praise the Lord. (Psalm 150)

How do *you* praise the Lord? Do you play an instrument? Praise him with your instrument. Do you sing? Praise him with your singing. Do you love to talk? Praise him with your words. Do you love to work with tools? Praise him as you hammer and saw. Do you love to clean? Praise him while you clean. Whatever you love to do, you can do it for the praise and glory of the Almighty God. When it is a beautiful day, praise the Lord! When it is storming, praise him for his protection and his power that is greater than the storm. When things are going well, praise him. When things are not going well, praise him for his help, comfort and control of the situation. When you are happy, praise the Lord! When you are filled with sorrow, praise the Lord that he understands your sorrow and will walk with you through it. Let everything that has breath praise the Lord!

His Love Never Fails

> Some wandered in desert wastelands, finding no way to a city where they could settle. They were hungry and thirsty, and their lives ebbed away. Then they cried out to the Lord in their trouble, and he delivered them from their distress. He led them by a straight way to a city where they could settle. (Psalm 107:4-7)

There are times when God brings us to a difficult place and leaves us there to wander because of our own unfaithfulness. He loves us so much that he is willing to watch us suffer in order to make our hearts ready to be restored to him. As parents, we sometimes ground our kids for the things they do wrong, but then when the punishment is too difficult for us to bear, we give in, and the hard lesson goes unlearned. God is patient with us. It grieves his heart when we wander. When we wander, it is because we have set out on our own, so he leaves us alone for awhile and what happens? We get lost, lonely, hungry and thirsty. The part of this story I love the most, though, is that when the Israelites cry out to the Lord, he brings them straight home and feeds them! He is longing for the moment of turning! He does not delight in our suffering, but is ready to restore us the moment we cry out to him! Let us give thanks to the Lord today that he is still ready to restore those who will turn. Thank him for his unfailing love. Though our love may fail him often, his love will never fail.

Blessed Are Those Who Mourn

By the rivers of Babylon we sat and wept when we remembered Zion. There on the poplars we hung our harps, for there our captors asked us for songs, our tormentors demanded songs of joy; they said, "Sing us one of the songs of Zion!" How can we sing the songs of the Lord while in a foreign land? If I forget you, Jerusalem, may my right hand forget its skill, may my tongue cling to the roof of my mouth if I do not remember you... (Psalm 137:1-6)

Today is my dad's birthday, and I miss him. He has been gone a long time, but missing my dad makes me feel the loss of my mother a few short months ago even more. It is difficult to sing when your heart is heavy with grief. Music has a way of touching deep into your soul and revealing your true heart. You know what I mean. Sometimes when we gather together for worship, we pretend everything is ok and when someone asks how we are doing we tell them, "Fine." For the moment we may indeed be fine, but then the singing starts and tears begin to roll down our cheeks as our sadness comes up to the surface. Grieving can be very difficult work, and for a person who likes to feel in control, sometimes all that crying can make one feel out of control. Over the years and several losses I have learned that you cannot bury grief, you must express it. It must be released in order for us to be healthy. There is no time table. Though there are some predictable stages that a person goes through, no two people go through them in exactly the same way or time. The sorrow of grief goes on in our lives long after the people around us remember that we are hurting. We can feel as though grief is taking too long. Others expect a song, but there is none. Take heart. There will be soon, for the Singer has planted a song within all of us that needs to be sung. Singing can soothe the heart of those who mourn. Blessed are those who mourn, for they shall be comforted.

Give Thanks

Give thanks to the Lord, for he is good. His love endures forever. Give thanks to the God of gods. His love endures forever. Give thanks to the Lord of lords: His love endures forever. (Psalm 136:1-3)

It is good to give thanks to the Lord. It is good to stop and remember who God is and all that he has done. He is the God of all gods and Lord of all lords whether people recognize him as that or not. Which of us can turn back the waters of the Red Sea or the Jordan River or make water gush out of a rock? Which of us could create an entire universe filled with stars, planets, and solar systems? How often do we take a few moments and just thank God for his wonderful creation? Do we tell him often how great we think he is because of his many wonders or his great love? Our God is an awesome God! Let's take a few moments today to thank him for the amazing wonders that tell of his greatness and thank him for his love which knows no end.

His Kingdom Come

> Gird your sword upon your side, you mighty one; clothe yourself with splendor and majesty. In your majesty ride forth victoriously in the cause of truth, humility and justice; let your right hand achieve awesome deeds. Let your sharp arrows pierce the hearts of the king's enemies; let the nations fall beneath your feet. Your throne, O God, will last for ever and ever; a scepter of justice will be the scepter of your kingdom. (Psalm 45:3-6)

I was reading this Psalm yesterday, and it brought to mind the coming election. Who could forget the election? About this time, I get very tired of the negative campaigning, the lies disguised as truth, and the rhetoric that will mean nothing following inauguration day. I look forward to the coming Kingdom where God will rule supremely. I look back to a day when truth meant something and politicians really did want to serve their country instead of their own self interests. I wonder if perhaps we romanticize days gone by. Do you suppose that those who ran for political office years ago were any less ambitious than today? The human heart is desperately wicked. Unless God rules in a heart, how can anyone's motives be pure? Unless God replaces our greed and lust for power and control with his righteousness what hope is there? We must pray for God's will to be done in every election, and we must vote our conscience. We must believe that God is sovereign and whatever happens, he is in control. We must do all that we can to prepare for the coming Kingdom, even while we are active citizens in this one.

Nothing Is Impossible With God

> I pursued my enemies and overtook them; I did not turn back till they were destroyed. I crushed them so that they could not rise; they fell beneath my feet. You armed me with strength for battle; you humbled my adversaries before me. You made my enemies turn their backs in flight, and I destroyed me foes. (Psalm 18:37-40)

This past week or so I have found myself reading and rereading Psalm 18. I always find great encouragement there. I find hope there that one day I will finally win my battle with obesity and depression. They seem to go hand in hand in my life. It is like a never ending cycle—when my weight is up I feel depressed, so I eat and that makes my weight increase all the more, which makes me more depressed and frustrated with myself until I reach the point of giving up. When I moved seven years ago, I thought I had finally won my battle with obesity. I remember sharing a testimony in church that God had finally given me victory. It was a wonderful place! Soon after that, though, something happened to trigger an old self-protection mechanism in me and I lost focus on my eating. I started down that old road of "I can never be good enough" and stopped caring what I weighed. I ate because I was depressed, and now I am back to that same old place where the enemy seems too big to conquer. These verses have reminded me that obesity is an enemy that only God can help me conquer, but he has promised to help me defeat my enemies. I cannot resign myself to let obesity be an unwelcome guest in my house. I have to pursue this enemy until he flees forever. With God nothing is impossible!

His Eternal Word

> Your word, Lord, is eternal; it stands firm in the heavens. Your faithfulness continues through all generations; you establish the earth, and it endures. Your laws endure to this day, for all things serve you. (Psalm 119:89-91)

I am so very thankful for God's Word! His Word is eternal. That means it is just as true and powerful now as when it was first spoken by God through the hand of each writer. God's Word is personal too. Have you ever noticed how after a moving sermon on a particular Scripture each person has been challenged or encouraged in a different way from the same text? The Holy Spirit speaks God's word to our spirit, or inner being, and we know that it is a word from God to us. I am always amazed and blessed when I have a particular spiritual need and God addresses it in the pastor's sermon. I am not alone. Others will say the same thing on the same day. That is the power of the Word of God. Or should I say, that is the power of God through his Word. Our God is a faithful God. His Word has the power to create the largest solar system or the tiniest atom. His Word remains true. We can count on it. All of the laws he has given us through his Word are still in effect, whether we choose to abide by them or not. When we don't, our lives suffer for it. Though sometimes our world does not seem like it, all things were made to serve God. What an awesome God we serve!

His Magnificent Dwelling Place

> Great is the Lord, and most worthy of praise, in the city of our God, his holy mountain. Beautiful in its loftiness, the joy of the whole earth, like the heights of Zaphon is Mount Zion, the city of the Great King. God is in her citadels; he has shown himself to be her fortress. (Psalm 48:1-3)

What a glorious picture of our Lord! He is certainly most worthy of praise! God's holy city is where he dwells. Nothing on earth compares to the dwelling of God! I don't think we can even imagine accurately the glorious presence of our awesome God in his dwelling place! Some days I get so homesick for heaven! As I read these words this morning, I am so encouraged. Although these verses refer to Jerusalem, the Holy City of the God, I know that he has made me his dwelling place. He is within me and has made himself to be my fortress. His presence in me changes everything! It makes beauty out of ashes. It makes streams flow in the desert. It makes water come from a rock. It takes a barren land and turns it into a lush garden. Yes, the presence of the Lord changes everything! Great is the Lord and most worthy of praise! Let's offer him praise from deep within our hearts as we recall who he is and all he has done for us. He is such a magnificent Savior! *Lord, we praise you with all of our hearts. You are magnificent, and there is none like you, O God, our mighty King!*

Attitude of Gratitude

> I will give thanks to the Lord because of his righteousness; I will
> sing the praises of the name of the Lord Most High. (Psalm 7:17)

Do you have an attitude of gratitude? Our God is so great. He gave himself so that we could know righteousness that we had lost forever because of sin. He himself is completely righteous. We are declared completely righteous because of the blood of Christ upon the cross. Too often, though, we are content to know that we are forgiven, so we do not allow the Holy Spirit to do the work of sanctification in our hearts. We are declared righteous, but we walk in unrighteousness. We are satisfied with just being ok, rather than letting God complete the work of righteousness in us. I wonder why that is. Is it too hard to go through the process of refining? Perhaps we just don't really believe that he can fix us. Unbelief keeps us bound to old patterns and sinful choices. We have the very righteousness of the Almighty God within us. We have the empowerment of his Holy Spirit to help us walk in that righteousness. Thank the Lord today for his righteousness, and then thank him for yours—the righteousness purchased for you at the cross of Calvary. May his righteousness be evident in you today.

Enter His Gates with Thanksgiving

> Enter his gates with thanksgiving and his courts with praise; give
> thanks to him and praise his name. (Psalm 100:4)

My sister and I spent all of last week sitting by my mother's bedside in the intensive care unit. She was confused and didn't know who we were for some of that time, and we thought she was not going to pull through. As I sat by her bed, I sang Psalm 100, one of her favorites. As I sang, her lips mouthed the words. She wasn't sure who we were, but she remembered the words to this Psalm because it is so much a part of her! How do you come into the Lord's presence? Do you come with a thankful heart, full of praise for all he has done for you? Do you take time to thank God for giving you another day upon this earth? Do you celebrate your life with him by singing? Oh, how God loves to hear the praises of his people! It is right and good that we bring our needs to the throne of grace, but we should always bring our praises and our thankful hearts first. I am thankful for my mother's life. She was a strong woman who taught me so much. What do you have to be thankful for today?

He Heals the Broken-hearted

> I will praise you, Lord, with all my heart; before the "gods" I will sing your praise. I will bow down toward your holy temple and will praise your name for your unfailing love and faithfulness, for you have so exalted above your solemn decree that it surpasses your fame. When I called, you answered me; you greatly emboldened me. (Psalm 138:1-3)

Give thanks to the Lord for his love and faithfulness. If you have ever felt unloved or unlovable, then you know how wonderful it is to finally come to know the love of the Most High God whose love never fails. We can love because he first loved us. For me, these are not just words. I have spent much of my life feeling unloved, unlovable actually. I believed Satan's lie that I was unwanted and worthless, and it kept me unable to accept the love that others wanted to give. I praise God that he unraveled those lies that kept me from accepting his love and then poured his love out to me in so many amazing ways! I am thankful that God accepted me as I was, but then loved me enough to help me become the woman he created me to be. I give praise to God because, though I have not always been faithful to him, he is always faithful to me. I have not forgotten the days when I did not praise God with all my heart because my heart was broken and shattered in many pieces. He gathered me up in his arms and led me on a road to wholeness and healing. He gave me wisdom to know how to let go of old thought patterns and how to walk in his wonderful ways. He bound up my broken heart and made me new. My heart belongs to Jesus, and I worship the Lord with all my heart because he lifted me up and helped me to stand when I was beaten down and weary. He brought me hope and restored my life. I am so grateful for the love of God! When I called to him, he answered me. He took every fear and filled me with confident boldness in his name. Praise the Lord who has done great things!

He Restores My Soul

Give thanks to the Lord, for he is good; his love endures forever.
(Psalm 118:29)

I am curious how often in Scripture we are commanded to give thanks. Ok, my curiosity got the best of me, so I went to biblegateway.com and looked it up. There were fifty-one references for "give thanks" in the New International Version. This reinforces for us the importance of having an attitude of gratitude. I have kept a journal since my tenth grade English teacher gave me my first journal and assigned us to write a daily entry. I keep a record of verses that God has helped me to understand, thoughts about those verses, and prayers and thoughts I want to share with the Lord. Over the years, it has been a wonderful tool for me. When I am down or discouraged, I pull out one of these journals and just begin reading. I am always amazed and encouraged by the things God has done in my life, things I might have forgotten had I not written them down. I am constantly surprised how God seems to keep speaking to me about certain topics, helping me to grow in the truth. There are times when I write in my journal every day. Sometimes it is more sporadic. It is easy to find ways to thank God when I read how often he has rescued me from trouble, or how many times he has answered my prayers, or how wondrously he has encouraged me with his Word. Take a few moments today to write down a list of all the ways God has blessed your life, and then thank him for everything on that list.

A Fully Devoted Heart

I will praise God's name in song and glorify him with thanksgiving. This will please the Lord more than an ox, more than a bull with its horns and hooves. The poor will see and be glad—you who seek God, may your hearts live! The Lord hears the needy and does not despise his captive people. Let heaven and earth praise him, the seas and all that move in them, for God will save Zion and rebuild the cities of Judah...
(Psalm 69:30-3)

Before the cross, God had given his people a way to know redemption through the sacrifice of animals. There were many different sacrifices depending on the need. God is more pleased with a heart that praises him and a soul filled with thanksgiving than any sacrifice, though. Christ was the final sacrifice for us. He paid every debt we will ever owe God. All that is left to give God is us, our own lives laid down for him. God asked Abraham to sacrifice Isaac. Of course, we know that he was not going to let Abraham harm Isaac on that altar. Why, then, did God instruct Abraham to do this? He was testing Abraham's heart. Would Abraham be willing to give up the one thing he had desired his whole life—a son? Who was that test for anyway? God already knew Abraham's heart, because God knows everything, right? Perhaps the test was ultimately for Abraham, so he could know that God had to be first in all things. Perhaps Abraham needed to know that as much as he treasured Isaac, Isaac still belonged to God. Abraham passed the test, and God provided the ram needed for the sacrifice. I'll bet Isaac never forgot that lesson either! The point is, for God it was never about the sacrifice, it was about the heart. He wants to know that our hearts are fully devoted to him. When we offer him our praise and thanksgiving, he is blessed. He values our praise more than any sacrifice when it comes from the heart. May your heart be filled with songs of praise and thanksgiving today, and may your praises bless the Lord your God!

Clothed With Joy

> You turned my wailing into dancing; you removed my sackcloth and clothed me with joy, that my heart may sing your praises and not be silent. Lord my God, I will praise you forever. (Psalm 30:11-12)

In some translations of the Bible the word *wailing* is translated as mourning. In the Jewish culture, wailing and sackcloth are signs of mourning. The psalmist is thankful that God has brought him from the place of grieving to a place of joy. If you have ever grieved the loss of someone you have loved, you know this place, the place of deep sadness and loss. Someone is missing and life is never going to be the same on this earth. It can be very difficult to move through the process of grief, and some never make it through. They continue to grieve the rest of their lives. The psalmist offers us this hope for those who grieve; God is able to move us through grief to know joy once again. It will not be a quick journey, but joy awaits those who mourn. God will comfort those who mourn and walk with them in the valley of this shadow.

A Prayer of Thanksgiving

"Come, let us sing for joy to the Lord; let us shout aloud to the Rock of our salvation. Let us come before him with thanksgiving and extol him with music and song. For the Lord is the great God, the great King above all gods. In his hand are the depths of the earth, and the mountain peaks belong to him. The sea is his, for he made it, and his hands formed the dry land." (Psalm 95:1-5)

Father, at a time when much of our nation does not know who to give thanks to, we give you thanks, because you have created us. You formed every mountain peak and filled every ocean with water. Lord, you are greater than our greatest imagination! We give you thanks because you have remained faithful to us, though we have often been unfaithful to you. Lord, we praise you because of your great love and mercy which demonstrated itself on the cross of Calvary. Fill us, Lord, that we might be a channel of your love and grace to others. Thank you, Lord, for your forgiveness, which allows us to begin again. We are a weak and needy people, Lord, and we often lose our way. Forgive us and help us to long for you as a person longs for water in the desert. Thank you, dear God, for the outpouring of so many blessings upon our lives. We are grateful for all that you have done for us. May we serve you this day with glad and joyful hearts, knowing that you are with us and you will keep every promise. Amen

When the Daily Struggle Is Too Much

For in the day of trouble he will keep me safe in his dwelling;
he will hide me in the shelter of his sacred tent and set me high
upon a rock. (Psalm 27:5)

Psalm 27 is one of those Psalms I go to frequently and am always encouraged by the truth I find there. The psalmist is not in a great place. He has endured hardship and trouble for a long time. Have you been there? Have you ever felt like the trouble was never going to end? Have you ever wondered if God has forgotten you because it seems so long that you have heard from him, and the daily struggle just seems too much? It is from such a place the psalmist pens these words. He focuses on the truth he knows about God and declares with confidence that God will deliver him from trouble. One day soon, he will see God's blessing again. He may not understand why he is going through the difficulty, but he knows that it won't go on forever. I am always most encouraged by the psalmist's confidence that he expects God to come to his aid in this life. He does not have to wait until he dies to see God's goodness. He declares with confidence that he will wait for God. He will be strong and keep his eyes focused on the Lord, and he will remind himself that God is coming. God will be faithful. God will help him, of this he is sure. There are times when we all have to remind ourselves that our trouble is not forever. We can be strong and trust that God is with us today. He will lead us through to higher ground. Let us fix our eyes on the author and finisher of our faith. Be strong and take heart and wait for the Lord.

The Voice of the Lord

The voice of the Lord strikes with flashes of lightning. The voice of the Lord shakes the desert; the Lord shakes the Desert of Kadesh. The voice of the Lord twists the oaks and strips the forests bare... (Psalm 29:7-9)

Dear Father, we long to hear your voice today. One word spoken by you can change everything. One word spoken by you can bring peace and hope. Lord, we long to hear your voice above every other voice clamoring for our attention today. We know your voice is powerful, and yet we have been told that you speak to your children in a still small voice. Your voice, Lord, can tear down strongholds and set the captive free. Your voice can heal the sick and make the lame to walk. Your voice, Lord, encourages like no other. You speak and all of nature listens. The wind and the waves obey your voice. Lord, help us to tune our ears to hear your voice and your voice alone. Speak to our hearts today. Help us to be still that we might hear you speaking to us. As we listen for your voice, may we be willing to obey. Amen

A Prayer for Peace

> The Lord gives strength to his people; the Lord blesses his
> people with peace. (Psalm 29:11)

It is my prayer that God will bless you with peace today. May he fill your
life with joy and peace, for even amid turmoil there is a peace which passes
all understanding. Only God can give that peace. Satan cannot counterfeit
God's peace, even if he wanted to. May the peace of God fill up every fiber
of your being today, and may you go wherever you go filled with the joy of
knowing that Jesus loves you. He loves you so much that he was willing to
leave all of the glory of heaven to come to this earth knowing that his work
would not be completed until he was crucified. He did this for you and me.
What great love he has for us! Rest in that knowledge today.

Awaiting Our Savior's Return

> Show us your unfailing love, Lord, and grant us your salvation.
> I will listen to what God the Lord says; he promises peace to
> his people—his faithful servants--but let them not turn to folly.
> Surely his salvation is near those who fear him, that his glory may
> dwell in our land. (Psalm 85:7-9)

What we know about the time of Christ's birth in Bethlehem reminds
me a lot of today. The Prophets of old had said Messiah would be born in
Bethlehem. The people of Israel were awaiting a Savior, but it had been
hundreds of years since anyone had really heard from God. The people were
waiting. Why is it, then, that when he came, most of them missed it? Most
of God's people couldn't believe that Jesus was really the Messiah. Why?
For one thing, Jesus came as the son of Mary. They expected a king. Jesus
was born in a stable. Oh, there were a few who believed—God sent angels
to declare the coming of the Messiah to the shepherds in the fields, and the
wise men from the East noticed the star in the sky and came to worship him.
Mary's cousin Elizabeth knew the baby Mary carried would be the Messiah.
The Holy Spirit confirmed it when John the Baptist, yet in Elizabeth's
womb, jumped as Mary approached. God does things his way, doesn't he?

I believe God's people, though they were waiting, did not recognize Jesus because they were expecting something different. How eagerly the people of England waited to hear if Princess Kate was expecting a baby. All eyes were watching her tiny tummy to see when it would begin to bloom with new life. No one would miss it! Jesus told us just before he ascended into heaven that he would come again. We have been waiting a long time, but are we ready? I want to be like the shepherds and the wise men. I want to be like Elizabeth, Simeon and Anna who knew as soon as they came close that the child was the Messiah. Come, thou long expected Jesus!

Choose to Trust God

> But I trust in your unfailing love; my heart rejoices in your salvation. I will sing the Lord's praise, for he has been good to me. (Psalm 13:5-6)

If you read all of Psalm 13, you will find that verses five and six follow verses that express the psalmist's feelings of being forgotten by God. He is wondering when God is going to help him with the trouble he is in and asks God for an answer. The first three letters of verse five say a lot—*but*. Even though he is in trouble, and he has not yet heard from God, the psalmist chooses to trust God. What is happening here in the heart of the writer of this Psalm is a change of focus. He begins by telling God what is on his heart, but then he turns his eyes on the truth of God. He tells God—and reminds himself—I am going to trust you because your love is unfailing. I am going to wait on you, Lord. I am so sure of your salvation that I will rejoice and sing. I remember all the good that you have done previously, and so I know you will come through again. Lord, you are faithful, so I will rejoice. It is not always easy to take a heart that is discouraged and feeling abandoned by God and bring it around to rejoicing, but the psalmist shows us how. Remember all the good God has done before. Think about the truth you know of God. Express confidence in God and praise him for his faithfulness and unfailing love. Nothing can lift a downcast heart like singing praise in the presence of the Most High.

A Beautiful Bride

> Listen, daughter, and pay careful attention: Forget your people and your father's house. Let the king be enthralled by your beauty; honor him for he is your lord…All glorious is the princess within her chamber; her gown is interwoven with gold. (Psalm 45:10-11, 13)

Psalm 45 is a wedding song for the king and his bride. What does that have to do with us? We are the bride of Christ. The church is the bride of Christ. One day he will return for his bride and we will celebrate the wedding supper with the Lord our God! What a glorious day that will be! Even now, as I read this Psalm, I am reminded of how the Lord has spoken these words to my own heart. Woman of God, do you know that you are indeed a princess, a child of the King of Kings! Often we don't think of ourselves that way. We see a frumpy old hag, but God sees beauty! Could there really be beauty in there that God sees? Why do we struggle to see ourselves as beautiful? Perhaps it is because we have a tendency to look at and dwell on all of our flaws. God sees all that is good in us, all that he intends for us to be, all that we will be as we allow him to complete his work in us. Even a princess can struggle with self-image. We saw that in Princess Diana's life. Sadly, her groom did not cherish her, and though she was beautiful, she did not see herself that way. When we can see ourselves through the eyes of an adoring Bridegroom, we will see the beauty he sees. When we spend time with our adoring Lord, his beauty begins to radiate through us. Ladies, making yourselves more beautiful doesn't take hours in a beauty salon. That kind of beauty does not last. True beauty comes from the inside out and grows as we spend time with our adoring Lord. Give yourself a beauty treatment today as you sit in the presence of the King!

God's Fingerprint

> All your works praise you, Lord; your faithful people extol you. They tell of the glory of your kingdom and speak of your might, so that all people may know of your mighty acts and the glorious splendor of your kingdom. (Psalm 145:10-12)

Last evening I was preparing Christmas ornaments which I am making out of sand dollars for each student in my class. I had purchased them this summer while vacationing in North Carolina. To go along with each ornament, I made a bookmark with "The Legend of the Sand Dollar" poem[23]. The poem declares the good news which is found on this small creature from the sea. God has left his fingerprint everywhere for those who are looking for it! I marvel at this wonder of nature and the details so intricately etched on this amazing creature. Through his creation, God tells his wondrous story. It is also true of us. Each one of us is an amazing creation of the Lord God. Upon our lives is etched the fingerprint of God which declares the Good News to all who are seeking. We may not believe it. We may not see it, but it is true nonetheless. God declares his glory through his creation. Though sin has marred creation and our ability to see God's handiwork, it is there. When we least expect it, God may use his fingerprint on our lives to draw another to himself. There is no greater joy than to be there when God chooses to use your life to touch another with the good news that he loves them! Each sand dollar, though similar, is unique. Each snowflake, though similar is unique. Each persontoo, is unique, bearing the very fingerprint of God. May we each see God's fingerprint today in the life of another, and may others see God's fingerprint in us.

White as Snow

> Have mercy on me, O God, according to your unfailing love; according to your great compassion blot out my transgressions. Wash away all my iniquity and cleanse me from my sin…Cleanse me with hyssop, and I will be clean; wash me, and I will be whiter than snow. (Psalm 51:1-2,7)

I love to wake up to a snow-covered world! It always reminds me of this passage. Though our sins are as scarlet, they shall be as white as snow. How grateful I am that God covers our sin, like the snow covers the earth. It is so very beautiful to see snow covering the branches of all the trees, and everything that looked gray and dull yesterday is breathtakingly beautiful this morning. Not only does he cleanse us from our sin, so that we are pure as the new fallen snow, he takes a life that is disfigured with the effects of sin and transforms it by his grace into a breathtakingly beautiful testimony of his love. Praise God today that he has freed you from sin. Praise him today that he is making your life more beautiful every day even as the falling snow transforms a dull and dirty world into work of art!

He Spreads the Snow like Wool

> He sends his command to the earth; his word runs swiftly. He spreads the snow like wool and scatters the frost like ashes. He hurls down his hail like pebbles. Who can withstand his icy blast? He sends his word and melts them; he stirs up his breezes, and the waters flow. (Psalm 147:15-18)

When the weather surprises the people of earth, they blame Mother Nature. I find myself wondering this morning why that is. It is God who created all things, and it is God who controls the weather. It is God who sends a blanket of snow to places that never have snow! The same God who calms the storm unleashes the hurricane with one word from his mouth. The voice of God is powerful, and he speaks on behalf of his children. The rain falls on the righteous and the unrighteous, doesn't it? So does the snow! There are cultures that believe there are gods that control the forces of nature, and they are afraid. Those who trust in God do not need to be afraid. Even when the weather seems out of control, God remains in control. He cares for his children, so we need not fear. I rejoice this morning as I consider the wonder of weather. Meteorologists watch the weather and try to predict it, but they cannot control it. God does.

Who Is This King of Glory?

> Lift up your heads, you gates; be lifted up, you ancient doors, that the King of glory may come in. Who is this King of glory? The Lord strong and mighty, the Lord mighty in battle. Lift up your heads, you gates, lift them up, you ancient doors, that the King of glory may come in. Who is he, this King of glory? The Lord Almighty—he is the King of glory. (Psalm 24:7-10)

God's people had gone hundreds of years without hearing from him, yet they awaited a Messiah. They had been waiting so long! Why, then, did most of God's people not recognize him when he came? They knew the Scriptures and they believed he would come. Indeed, they were waiting, but who were they waiting for? They were waiting for a king, a mighty warrior, a powerful leader. They knew what they wanted. They knew what they needed, but God, when he sent his Son to this earth, sent a tiny baby to a lowly manger. Even family members did not recognize the Messiah when he came! Mary and Joseph knew, although God had to convince Joseph. The wise men knew. The shepherds knew. God revealed the truth to a few humble people. They were invited to come and worship the King of glory! There in a cold and lonely stable, the King of Kings came to earth! Most of God's people missed the blessed event because they were looking in the wrong place. They were looking for the wrong things. They knew the prophecies, but missed their fulfillment! Imagine yourself there when Christ was born. Would you have missed it? So many still miss out on knowing the King of glory. We get all psyched up for Christmas and enjoy the festivities. It certainly is a time for celebration, but in all the celebration, may we not miss the opportunity to worship Christ, the Lord Almighty; he is the King of glory!

Sing a New Song

> Sing joyfully to the Lord, you righteous; it is fitting for the upright to praise him. Praise the Lord with the harp; make music to him on the ten-stringed lyre. Sing to him a new song; play skillfully, and shout for joy. (Psalm 33:1-3)

There are so many special Christmas carols that we enjoy at Christmastime as we worship the Lord. I love them all! Christmas carols can be heard on nearly every radio station wherever you go. People sing and hum these carols all through the season. I also enjoy that many of today's musical artists have written more modern songs of praise for the Christmas seasontoo. It is great fun to take a group of people caroling. What fun to see the light come into the eyes of those elderly folks who may not have sung for a long time! I have my Heavenly Father's love of music. I love to sing and play the guitar. I love to write new songs and sing along to almost every song I hear. Music is in my heart and yearns to get out! It is not just that I enjoy music. I love to worship my Savior! I know that he delights in my praise, so it fills me with great joy to offer him my songs of worship. He is listening to my songs of praise! I love the song about the little drummer boy. It reminds me that whatever my talent, God delights that I bring it to him and use it for his glory. Make a song of praise as a gift to the Lord. Can't sing? Then shout for joy! Imagine if we learned to worship God with all the enthusiasm we demonstrate at a football game! All the shouting and celebrating! Wow! What joy!

His Mighty Angels

> Praise the Lord, you his angels, you mighty ones who do his bidding, who obey his word. Praise the Lord, all his heavenly hosts, you his servants who do his will. Praise the Lord, all his works everywhere in his dominion. Praise the Lord, my soul. (Psalm 103:20-22)

Last year our Christmas musical had a song we all enjoyed. One of the shepherds sang, "Angels, angels everywhere. Angel wings and angel hair..." It was a great number. We are all familiar with angels as part of the Christmas story. Do you ever stop and wonder what angels are doing these days? Are they like Clarence in "It's a Wonderful Life" trying to earn their wings by helping some poor soul? Or do they work in teams like on "Touched by an Angel?" Are they nearby and we don't know it? A friend of mine once told me that she saw three angels bowed in prayer as we prayed together during a very difficult time in her life. According to this passage, angels are his servants who do his will—whatever that is. From Scripture, we know that angels have been seen by humans from time to time. What do we need to know about angels? They are God's servants—like us. They worship him—like us. God has sent his angels to help humans in need or to announce his plans. Some people believe we each have our own angel to watch over us. I am not sure if the Bible is clear about that, but one day we will know. One day we will stand beside the angels and praise the Lord together. Hey! Why wait? Let's praise the Lord with his angels today!

A Silent Prayer

> But let all who take refuge in you be glad; let them ever sing for joy. Spread your protection over them, that those who love your name may rejoice in you. Surely, Lord, you bless the righteous; you surround them with your favor as with a shield. (Psalm 5:11-12)

This Psalm offers a wonderful way to pray for the people who touch your life. As you go though the next few days, weeks, or even the whole next year, write these words on a note card, and keep it handy. Each time your life touches another life, stop and pray this prayer for them. You don't need to tell them, just take a few quiet moments to talk to God on their behalf. *Father, I pray for each of my readers that you would fill their hearts with gladness as they take refuge in you. Let your joy fill them to overflowing and a song fill their hearts. Spread your protection over them, Lord, and may they rejoice as they see you working in their lives. Father, bless these friends of mine and surround them with your favor as with a shield. Thank you, for the blessing of these friends and family. Amen*

Endnotes

1   http://dictionary.reference.com/browse/steadfast?s=t, January 2015
2   Corrie ten Boom, *The Hiding Place* (Boston, G. K. Hall, © 1973)
3   http://earthquake.usgs.gov/earthquakes/eqarchives/year/graphs.php, January 2015
4   Ted Sandquist, "All That I Can Do" (Brentwood-Benson Music Publishing, Inc., Franklin, TN, ©1974)
5   Rick Warren, *The Purpose Driven Life* (Grand Rapids, Michigan, Zondervan, © 2002)
6   John Bunyan, *Pilgrim's Progress* (Wheaton, Ill. : Tyndale House Publishers, © 1989)
7   Ibid.
8   Randy, Alcorn, *Edge of Eternity* (WaterBrook Press, © 1998)
9   Clinton Utterbach, "The Name of the Lord" (Universal-Polygram International Publishing and Utterbach Music, Inc., © 1989)
10 Kay Arthur, *Living with Discernment in the End Times* (Eugene, Oregon: Harvest House Publishers, © 2002
11 http://dictionary.reference.com/browse/seek?s=t, January 2015
12 Randy Alcorn, *Safely Home* (Carol Stream, IL : Tyndale House Publishers, © 2011)
13 Ibid.
14 Gracia Burnham, *To Fly Again* (Wheaton, Illinois: Tyndale House, © 2005)
15 Gary Chapman and Ross Campbell, *The 5 Love Languages of Children* (Chicago, Illinois, Northfield Publishing, ©1997
16 http://www.webster-dictionary.org/definition/flourish, January 2015
17 Chris Tomlin, "How Great Is Our God" (worshiptogether.com Songs (ASCAP/Six Steps Music, © 2004)
18 Macon Delevan, "Lift High the Lord Our Banner" (Integrity's Hosanna! Music, © 1984)
19 Hannah Hurnard, *Hinds' Feet on High Places* (Floyd, Virginia: Wilder Publications, © 2013)
20 Henry Blackaby, *Created to Be God's Friend: How God Shapes Those He Loves* (Nashville, Tennessee: Thomas Nelson, Inc, © 1999)
21 Twila Paris, "I Will Wait" (Ariose Music; Mountain Spring Music, © 1990)
22 Michael W. Smith, "Healing Rain" (Songs From The Farm Publishing, © 2014)
23 http://www.allfreecrafts.com/images/christmas/sand-dollar-legend.gif, April 2010

CPSIA information can be obtained at www.ICGtesting.com
Printed in the USA
BVOW02s1154120615

404252BV00002B/2/P